God's Words, Women's Voices

The Discernment of Spirits in the Writing of Late-Medieval Women Visionaries

YORK MEDIEVAL PRESS

York Medieval Press is published by the University of York's Centre for Medieval Studies in association with Boydell & Brewer Ltd. Our objective is the promotion of innovative scholarship and fresh criticism on medieval culture. We have a special commitment to interdisciplinary study, in line with the Centre's belief that the future of Medieval Studies lies in those areas in which its major constituent disciplines at once inform and challenge each other.

All inquiries of an editorial kind, including suggestions for monographs and essay collections, should be addressed to: The Secretary, University of York, Centre for Medieval Studies, The King's Manor, York YO1 2EP (E-mail: LAH1@unix.york.ac.uk).

Previous publications in *York Studies in Medieval Theology*:

Medieval Theology and the Natural Body, ed. Peter Biller and A. J. Minnis (1997)

Handling Sin: Confession in the Middle Ages, ed. Peter Biller and A. J. Minnis (1998)

Previous publications of The Centre for Medieval Studies:

Latin and Vernacular: Studies in Late-Medieval Texts and Manuscripts, ed. A. J. Minnis (1989) [Proceedings of the 1987 York Manuscripts Conference]

Regionalism in Late-Medieval Manuscripts and Texts: Essays celebrating the publication of 'A Linguistic Atlas of Late Mediaeval English', ed. Felicity Riddy (1991) [Proceedings of the 1989 York Manuscripts Conference]

Late-Medieval Religious Texts and their Transmission: Essays in Honour of A. I. Doyle, ed. A. J. Minnis (1994) [Proceedings of the 1991 York Manuscripts Conference]

God's Words, Women's Voices

The Discernment of Spirits in the Writing of Late-Medieval Women Visionaries

ROSALYNN VOADEN

THE UNIVERSITY *of York*

YORK MEDIEVAL PRESS

First published 1999

A York Medieval Press publication
in association with The Boydell Press
an imprint of Boydell & Brewer Ltd
PO Box 9   Woodbridge   Suffolk IP12 3DF   UK
and of Boydell & Brewer Inc.
PO Box 41026   Rochester   NY 14604–4126   USA
and with the
Centre for Medieval Studies, University of York

ISBN 0 9529734 2 1

A catalogue record for this book is available
from the British Library

Library of Congress Cataloging-in-Publication Data
Voaden, Rosalynn, 1949–
    God's words, women's voices : the discernment of spirits in the
writing of late-medieval women visionaries / Rosalynn Voaden.
        p.   cm.
    'A York Medieval Press publication in association with the
Boydell Press . . . and with the Centre for Medieval Studies,
University of York' – T.p. verso.
    Includes bibliographical references and index.
    1. Women mystics – Europe – History.   2. Private revelations –
History of doctrines – Middle Ages, 600–1500.   3. Discernment of
spirits – History of doctrines – Middle Ages, 600–1500.   4. Kempe,
Margery, b. ca. 1373. Book of Margery Kempe.   5. Bridget, of Sweden,
Saint, ca. 1303–1373. Revelations.   6. Pecha, Alfonso, 1329 or 30–1389.
I. University of York. Centre for Medieval Studies.   II. Title.
    BV5091.R4 V62 1999
    248.2'9 – dc21   98–40430

This publication is printed on acid-free paper

Printed in Great Britain by
St Edmundsbury Press Ltd, Bury St Edmunds, Suffolk

CONTENTS

For Martin

ACKNOWLEDGEMENT

Writing an Acknowledgement is, I imagine, like making a speech at the Academy Awards. One either expresses appreciation to everyone, from the cats to the cleaners, or one offers a brief and general thanks. The audience is usually more appreciative of the latter. However, since I am reluctant to relinquish this opportunity to express my gratitude to those people who have helped bring this book to fruition, I intend to strike a middle course, and leave out the cats.

A number of colleagues have shared their time, energy and knowledge with me. In particular, Alastair Minnis and Felicity Riddy have stimulated my mind, challenged my assumptions and read innumerable drafts of this work. Discussions with Kathryn Kerby-Fulton first interested me in this topic, and succeeding discussions have sustained my interest and expanded my awareness. Roger Ellis has been generosity itself in making available to me his vast knowledge of St Bridget.

My parents and family have been supportive in all ways, and have never wavered in their faith in me.

I would like to recognize the financial assistance provided by the Association of Commonwealth Universities and the Social Sciences and Humanities Research Council of Canada. Without their awards, I would not be in the happy position of writing this Acknowledgement. I would also like to thank the Camargo Foundation, in whose remarkably beautiful premises I was able to revise the manuscript.

At this point, gratitude is generally expressed to one's partner, as last but, naturally, not least. So, to Martin, my first and foremost, all my thanks.

My words, my voice – but words, as medieval women visionaries knew, are never enough.

NOTE ON STYLE

My practice with Latin source material is as follows: where I have used a published translation, I have quoted it in the text, giving references to the Latin source in the notes.

In referring to St Bridget's *Revelaciones*, I have used this spelling. However, when the title is cited by another author as *Revelationes*, I have reproduced that spelling. In Chapter Three, quotations from the *Epistola solitarii ad reges* are from the Middle English translation which forms an Appendix to this study. In order to be consistent, quotations from the *Revelaciones* of Bridget of Sweden are also from the Middle English translation, in R. Ellis, ed., *The Liber Celestis of St Bridget of Sweden* (Oxford, 1987). In both cases, references to Latin sources have been given in the notes.

Biblical quotations are from the Douai Bible.

ABBREVIATIONS

A&P	I. Collijn, ed., *Acta et Processus Canonizacionis Beate Birgitte*, SSFS, ser. 2, Lat.skrifter 1 (Uppsala, 1924–31).
BMK	S. B. Meech and H. E. Allen, ed., *The Book of Margery Kempe*, EETS (Oxford, 1940).
CC	*Corpus Christianorum, series Latina.*
EETS	Early English Text Society.
OS	Original Series.
Lat.	A. Jönsson, ed., *Epistola solitarii ad reges*, in *Alfonso of Jaén: His Life and Works with Critical Editions of the Epistola solitarii, the Informaciones and the Epistola serui Christi* (Lund, 1989), pp. 115–71.
LC	R. Ellis, ed., *The Liber Celestis of Bridget of Sweden: The Middle English Version in British Library MS Claudius Bi*, EETS (Oxford, 1987).
LMG	Augustine, *The Literal Meaning of Genesis: Books 7–12*, trans. J. H. Taylor, Ancient Christian Writers: The Works of the Fathers in Translation XLII (New York, 1982).
PL	*Patrologia Latina*, ed. J.-P. Migne (Paris, 1844–64).
RE	Bridget of Sweden, *Reuelaciones Extrauagantes*, ed. L. Hollman, SSFS, ser. 2, Lat.skrifter 5 (Uppsala, 1956).
Revs.	Bridget of Sweden, *Revelaciones.*
SSFS	Samlingar Utgivna av Svenska Fornskrift-Sällskapet.
ST 2a2ae	Thomas Aquinas, *Summa theologiae, 2a2ae, qu. 171–8* XLV, ed. and trans. R. Potter OP (London, 1970).
Undhagen	*Sancta Birgitta Revelaciones*, Book I, ed. C. Undhagen, SSFS (Uppsala, 1978).

INTRODUCTION

Representations of transcendental experiences have a universal, timeless lure. The human desire to know what – if anything – lies beyond the sensible world guarantees an audience for those who claim to have knowledge or experience of this realm. And apart from the content of these reports, their structure is equally fascinating. How do you speak, or write, about the ineffable? How much does culture, gender, economic or social status, religious orientation, psychological or physical constitution or education influence the articulation of a transcendental experience? Indeed, to what extent do these factors affect the experience itself?

The urge to examine such questions has attracted to medieval religious literature a wide range of scholars, from the devout to the dissident, and an equally wide range of critical approaches, from the exegetical to the post-structuralist. My study has benefited particularly from the explosion of interest in the spirituality of medieval women which has occurred over the last twenty years or so, as well as from the development of feminist and gender criticism. Carolyn Bynum's stimulating and encyclopedic study, *Holy Feast and Holy Fast: The Religious Significance of Food to Medieval Women*, broke new ground in its delineation of specifically feminine modes of devotion which co-existed with, and at times subverted, the masculine ecclesiastical establishment.[1] Marxist approaches, such as David Aers' study of Margery Kempe, 'The Making of Margery Kempe',[2] or Sarah Beckwith's cultural materialist analysis, *Christ's Body: Identity, Culture and Society in Late Medieval Writings*,[3] have been invaluable in representing medieval women's spirituality as products of an entire culture, of which the Church was just a part. Feminist scholars such as Karma Lochrie have highlighted the importance of the female body in medieval women's religious praxis, and have also examined the blurring of gender boundaries and subsequent negotiation of authority which can occur in the writing of women visionaries.[4]

In my desire to open the texts of medieval women visionaries to new insights, I have tried to reap judiciously from this rich harvest. My critical attitude is similar to that of Aviad Kleinberg. In his challenging study of medieval hagiography, *Prophets in their Own Country: Living Saints and the*

---

[1] Berkeley, 1987.

[2] *Community, Gender, and Individual Identity: English Writing 1360–1430* (London, 1988), pp. 73–116.

[3] London, 1993.

[4] *Margery Kempe and Translations of the Flesh* (Philadelphia, 1991).

1

Making of Sainthood in the Later Middle Ages, he writes: 'I found many theoretical "systems" useful, and have used them in my work, without becoming a devotee of any of them.'[5] I too have found a variety of approaches useful, and evidence of this variety will be found throughout my study.

I do not, of course, believe that there is any one reading of a text. Nevertheless, taking a leaf out of Alfonso of Jaén's book, I will now attempt to influence the reception of my own text. To that end I will outline the method and explain the terminology which I employ in my interpretation of the texts discussed in this study.

One of the major problems in studying the writings of medieval women visionaries is the question of agency in their construction. Generally, this question manifests itself as a concern with distinguishing the relative contribution to the text of the visionary and her associates – spiritual director, scribe, translator and/or editor. In medieval Christian culture, the voice of the woman was rarely heard in the land. May it be heard in the text? My belief is that it may, but in a way which is ambivalent and deeply problematic; this question is inextricably entwined with questions relating to the ways in which that culture shaped the medieval woman visionary's articulation of her experience, and indeed her experience itself. My reasons for this belief are, inevitably, based on the evidence of the texts as I read them. And I have chosen to work with women visionaries who are represented as being involved in the creation, writing and editing of the texts which record their experiences, rather than with women who are the passive subjects of texts written about them, often posthumously, entirely by men.

All of the former texts incorporate statements about their composition which affirm the agency of the visionary. They testify to the collaboration of the woman with her male spiritual advisors and/or scribes – as well as with her God – and to her ultimate approval of the text in its present form.[6] The reason given is always that the words and incidents recorded in the text are divinely inspired, and must be transmitted unchanged.

> The texts always define themselves as being entirely a product of inspiration,
> though that inspiration may operate in very different modes. In every case,

---

5 Chicago, 1992, p. x.

6 Bridget of Sweden, for example, is described as dictating to her scribes as soon as she emerged from ecstasy, and then checking the accuracy of their recording (*A&P*, p. 84). Margery Kempe's scribe chronicles her active involvement in the writing (*BMK*, pp. 5, 216–20). Angela of Foligno's confessor describes his frustration with the accounts of her visions that he had written down (Angela of Foligno, *Complete Works*, trans. and ed. P. Lachance OFM (New York, 1993), pp. 137–8). Often the scribe or editor's role is represented as divinely ordained; see, for example, Alfonso of Jaén's celestial selection (*RE*, pp. 165–6), and that of Fra Arnoldo, Angela of Foligno's scribe (pp. 217–18).

though, divine utterance is both what founds the text, and what it must make manifest.[7]

Although, of course, this is part of the authorizing discourse through which the credentials of the text are established, it would be a very cynical – and dehistoricizing – reading which would discount entirely the validity of this statement. In the first place, such a reading would completely privilege the male voice over the female. As Carolyn Bynum points out:

> It is . . . crucial not to take as women's own self-image the sentimentalizing or the castigating of the female in which medieval men indulged. . . . we must pay particular attention to what women said or did, avoiding the assumption that they simply internalized the rhetoric of theologians, confessors or husbands.[8]

Such a reading would also deny to women the respect, authority and power which we know, from a wide variety of sources, some of them achieved as visionaries and prophets. I find in my chosen texts little evidence that these women were merely puppets of a patriarchal society. The testimony of the texts is rather that these women visionaries were agents in their own composition. They co-operated with the prevailing ideology in general, and with certain representatives thereof, in the persons of spiritual directors and scribes, in particular, thus participating in their own empowerment.

In order to acknowledge both this participation, and the consistent testimony of the texts to the agency of the women visionaries, I assume, throughout this book, that the composition of the works of certain women visionaries was a collaborative affair involving the visionary, her scribe, her editor and/or her translator. Untangling the intricacies of that collaboration – determining who wrote or composed exactly what – is often impossible, rarely definitive, and certainly beyond the scope of this study.

When I write of the visionary both constructing herself and being constructed, I fully recognize that I am not using these terms in the strict post-structuralist sense in which 'subjects' are said to be constructed, where they are termed as 'sites' at which things happen rather than agents who make things happen. I have found these concepts of formation useful, up to a point, and have borrowed some of the relevant terminology. I do, of course, as already stated, concede the array of cultural and social constraints which act upon and shape an individual. My own use of the terms 'fashioning' and 'constructing' is a convenient shorthand to convey the idea of the forces at work in the creation of the text. Visionary and amanuensis were a construction team, working according to a number of culturally determined blueprints – read discourses –

---

7 M. de Certeau, 'Mystic Speech', in *Heterologies: Discourse on the Other*, trans. Brian Massumi (Manchester, 1986), p. 92.

8 Bynum, *Holy Feast*, p. 29.

to build, to the best of their abilities, the edifice which was the text testifying to the immanence of the divine. As Stephen Greenblatt observes:

> . . . self-fashioning derives its interest precisely from the fact that it functions without regard for a sharp distinction between literature and social life. It invariably crosses the boundary between the creation of literary characters, the shaping of one's own identity, the experience of being molded by forces outside one's control, the attempt to fashion other selves.[9]

Although Greenblatt is writing of the early modern period, his statement is equally relevant to the writings of women visionaries of a slightly earlier period.

The construction blueprint with which this study is principally concerned is the ecclesiastical doctrine of *discretio spirituum*, the discerning of spirits. Although scholars of medieval visionaries, particularly of women visionaries, have sometimes briefly acknowledged this doctrine as a factor in the lives and texts of their subjects, its importance as a mechanism whereby visionaries were controlled, authorized, and empowered has not hitherto been fully recognized.[10] *Discretio spirituum* defined the visionary experience, decreed the virtue and deportment of the visionary, established forms of expression and laid down criteria for assessment. And it facilitated – or restricted – dissemination of the writing of visionaries, under an implicit *imprimatur*.

This book examines the influence of *discretio spirituum* on the visionary experiences of medieval women, and on the written representations of those experiences. It argues that the doctrine was, in effect, a discourse, developed and elaborated by ecclesiastical authorities, a discourse which provided both a vocabulary to articulate visionary experience and a set of criteria to evaluate the vision and the visionary. In addition, *discretio spirituum* supplied a pattern for self-fashioning which extended to behaviour, demeanour and modes of expression. Familiarity with, and skill in, the discourse was a vital factor in the textual – and physical – survival of the visionary. Facility with *discretio spirituum* empowered medieval women visionaries and enabled them to fulfil their divine mandate to communicate revelation.

Although I maintain that *discretio spirituum* was a cardinal influence on all medieval women visionaries, my principal focus is on the writings of Bridget

---

[9] *Renaissance Self-Fashioning: From More to Shakespeare* (Chicago, 1980), p. 3.

[10] Mention of the importance of *discretio spirituum* to medieval women visionaries is found in, for example: H. E. Allen's 'Prefatory Note', *BMK*, pp. lvii–lviii; C. W. Atkinson, *Mystic and Pilgrim: The Book and the World of Margery Kempe* (Ithaca, 1983), pp. 121–8; W. A. Christian Jr, *Apparitions in Late Medieval and Renaissance Spain* (Princeton, 1981), pp. 188–203; K. Kerby-Fulton, *Reformist Apocalypticism and Piers Plowman* (Cambridge, 1990), pp. 124–5; Beckwith, *Christ's Body*, pp. 80, 157 n. 8. However, none of these scholars assess its function in the experience and writings of the visionaries concerned.

of Sweden and Margery Kempe. Alfonso of Jaén, spiritual director and editor to Bridget of Sweden wrote the *Epistola solitarii ad reges*, a treatise on *discretio spirituum* which was attached to her *Revelaciones*.[11] She was therefore an obvious candidate for my study; her scrupulous construction in the *Revelaciones* according to the dictates of the doctrine results in her presentation as an exemplary visionary. My study of *The Book of Margery Kempe*, on the other hand, demonstrates that the power of *discretio spirituum* and the penalties incumbent upon failure to conform are evident in both the ambivalent reception of Margery by her contemporaries and of her *Book* by modern critics.

In Chapter One I offer a survey of two areas which are crucial to the understanding of the construction of late-medieval women visionaries. First is an examination of medieval perceptions of the nature of vision. The second area I consider is medieval perceptions of, and attitudes towards, women. Chapter Two explores the development of the doctrine of *discretio spirituum*, examines the discourse which it produced, and considers its specific application to women visionaries. Chapter Three looks at the textual construction of Bridget of Sweden, and the role which the *Epistola solitarii ad reges* of Alfonso of Jaén played in that construction. Chapter Four examines *The Book of Margery Kempe* and assesses the influence of *discretio spirituum* on the text. The Conclusion evaluates the implications of my study of the role of *discretio spirituum* in the lives and works of medieval women visionaries.

---

[11] My edition of the Middle English translation of this treatise from London, British Library, MS Cotton Julius Fii forms an appendix to this study.

CHAPTER ONE

Women and Vision: The Devil's Gateway

First, every teaching of women, especially that expressed in solemn word or writing, is to be held suspect, unless it has first been diligently examined by another . . . and much more than the teaching of men. Why? The reason is clear; because not only ordinary but divine law forbids such things. Why? Because women are too easily seduced, because they are too obstinately seducers, because it is not fitting that they should be knowers of divine wisdom.[1]

Introduction

The statement above, by Jean Gerson, fifteenth-century French theologian, mystic and influential churchman, neatly encapsulates centuries of belief about the nature of women, its effect on their spiritual capacity, and the consequent restrictions which should be placed on their participation in the life of the Church. Theological attitudes towards women derived from two main convictions: first, that women are by nature corporeal, sensual, and carnal, and second, that all women bear the taint of Eve. The first conviction arose from the primary identification of women with their reproductive function; the second from the belief that all women are prone to being deceived, incapable of distinguishing God's truth from the devil's blandishments, willing to deceive in their turn and a source of spiritual contamination. Medieval Christian thought held that women are subordinate to men in the order of creation, although they are equal in the order of salvation: souls are equal, bodies are not. The Church's mission was to enable the salvation of each and every one of its members. Theoretically, this should mean that a woman actively pursuing her own salvation could follow the same kind of pious life as a man engaged in the same quest. However, beliefs about female corporeality and intellectual weakness restricted women's access to a spiritual life. The conception of women as intellectually and morally defective led to proscriptions against their teaching in public, and against their learning more of religion than was strictly needed for salvation.

---

1 Jean Gerson, *Oeuvres complètes*, ed. P. Glorieux, 10 vols. (Paris: Desclée, 1960–73), IX, 468. My translation.

Let the woman learn in silence with all subjection./ But I suffer not a woman to teach, nor to usurp authority over the man, but to be in silence. (I Timothy 2. 11–12)

Let your women keep silence in the churches: for it is not permitted them to speak, but to be subject, as also the law saith./ But if they would learn any thing, let them ask their husbands at home: for it is a shame for a woman to speak in the church. (I Corinthians 14. 34–5)

When Thomas Aquinas, the thirteenth-century Scholastic theologian, discusses the charism of speech in his *Summa theologiae*, he reinforces the prohibition against women speaking, or teaching in public. He does concede scriptural precedents for women teaching, but maintains that these took place in the privacy of the home, to other women and to children, who are also perceived as subordinate beings. Under no circumstances are women to teach their superiors, or to teach in public.

Speech can be used in two ways. In one way privately, to one or a few, in familiar conversation. In this way the grace of speech becomes a woman. The other way publicly, addressing oneself to the whole Church. This is not conceded to women. First and principally, because of the condition of the female sex, which must be subject to man, according to Genesis. But to teach and persuade publicly in Church is not the task of subjects, but of prelates. Men, when commissioned, can far better do this work, because their subjection is not from nature and sex as with women, but from something supervening by accident.
Secondly, lest men's minds be enticed to lust. Thus Ecclesiasticus, 'Many have been misled by a woman's beauty. By it passion is kindled like a fire.'
Thirdly, because generally speaking women are not perfected in wisdom so as to be fit to be entrusted with public teaching ... women, if they have the grace of wisdom or of knowledge, can impart these by teaching privately but not publicly.[2]

The objective was to keep women under the intellectual and spiritual guidance of men lest they succumb to heterodoxy, and worse still, propagate it. Conveniently, women's subjection to men was also demanded by the natural order, Eve having been created after Adam. Augustine of Hippo (354–430) explains in *Quaestiones in Heptateuchum*:

There is a natural order observed among men, that women should serve men, and children their parents, because it is just that the weaker mind should serve the stronger.[3]

---

[2] Thomas Aquinas, *Summa theologiae, 2a2ae, qu. 171–8*, ed. and trans. R. Potter OP, vol. 45 (London, 1970), pp. 133–5. Hereafter this work will be abbreviated as *ST 2a2ae* followed by the volume and page number.

[3] Cited in K. Børreson, *Subordination and Equivalence: The Nature and Role of Women in Augustine and Thomas Aquinas*, trans. C. Talbot (Washington, DC, 1981), p. 31.

No women were exempt from this stricture; whether they were consecrated virgins, chaste wives or widows, prostitutes or princesses, church and society demanded their subordination to male control.

These beliefs, the ineradicable association of women with body and sensation, with concupiscence and deception, profoundly influenced the transcendental experiences which women had. Women, like men, desired and achieved direct spiritual experiences which transcended the normal order of things and bypassed the hierarchy and order of the Church. Transcendental experiences were understood to take two main forms: mystic and visionary. The impossibility of isolating mystics from their culture is pointed out by Bernard McGinn.

> The mystic as a human subject never perceives experience 'raw', but always within a situation mediated by a host of personal, cultural and religious elements.[4]

Medieval theology generally associated men with intellect, women with the senses; men and intellect were superior, women and sense inferior; the spiritual lives of both sexes were shaped by these assumptions. The evidence of saints' *vitae*, theological writings, visionary accounts and mystical treatises, among other material, suggest that it was predominantly men who embraced mysticism and, for the most part, women who had visions.[5]

Mystics and Visionaries

At this point it is necessary to come to a clear understanding of the terms 'mystic' and 'visionary'. Modern scholars tend to use 'mystic' as a convenient umbrella term under which to shelter all varieties of religious experience.[6] This is not the place to embark on an exhaustive investigation into transcendental life. Nor would it be useful to join the ranks of those whom Bernard McGinn

---

4   B. McGinn, 'Meister Eckhart: An Introduction', in *An Introduction to the Medieval Mystics of Europe*, ed. P. Szarmach (Albany, 1984), p. 247.

5   There are, of course, exceptions to this general state of affairs: for example, Richard Rolle could well be designated a visionary, while Julian of Norwich is certainly on the 'mystic' end of the spectrum. In a forthcoming book, *Vision, Gender, Time*, I conduct a comparative study of two male visionaries – Robert d'Uzès and John of Rupecissa – and two female visionaries – Hildegard of Bingen and Bridget of Sweden.

6   In 1922, Cuthbert Butler claimed that 'there is probably no more misused term in these our days than "mysticism" ' (*Western Mysticism: The Teaching of SS Augustine, Gregory and Bernard on Contemplation and the Contemplative Life*, 2nd edn (London, 1926), p. 3). The situation has not improved a great deal since.

describes as writing laundry lists of the characteristics of mysticism.[7] However, it is vital for this investigation of women and visions to define these terms at the outset, and to do so in a way which reflects medieval understanding. To this end, in this study those who experience intellectual union with the Godhead are designated mystics, and their experiences are mystical. Their experiences are characterised by an inward knowledge of the presence of God which takes no sensory or symbolic form; they correspond to Augustine's third level of vision, intellectual vision, which is defined below.

In contrast, those whose transcendental experiences involve spiritual or imaginary vision are designated visionaries. Their visions are distinguished by seeing or hearing things with the spiritual senses; their experiences conform to Augustine's second level of vision, spiritual or imaginative vision, which is also defined below. The following discussion of medieval theories of vision and mysticism provides the rationale for this distinction. This brief survey of patristic and medieval treatises on what was originally known as the contemplative life,[8] traces the development of these two main forms of transcendental experience, and examines the reasoning behind the hierarchy which privileges mystical experience over visionary.[9]

Augustine's definition of the three forms of vision had a profound and lasting effect.

> Hence let us call the first kind of vision corporeal, because it is perceived through the body and presented to the senses of the body. The second will be spiritual, for whatever is not a body, and yet is something, is rightly called spirit: and certainly the image of an absent body, though it resembles a body, is not itself a body any more than is the act of vision by which it is perceived.[10] The third kind will be intellectual, from the word intellect.[11]

The distinction between these different categories of vision becomes most apparent in Augustine's simple example using Christ's commandment, 'Thou

---

7 McGinn, 'Eckhart', p. 247.

8 Butler, *Mysticism*, p. 3.

9 The two categories – vision and mystical experience – are not mutually exclusive. Visionary experiences are sometimes rungs on the ladder to mystical union, and mystics apprehend the divine in a variety of ways. Those who generally had visions occasionally experienced that annihilation of self into God which characterized *unio mystica*.

10 Note the particular use in this context of 'spiritual', here to be understood as imaginary, that is, employing sensory images to represent ideas. See Augustine, *The Literal Meaning of Genesis: Books 7–12*, trans. J. H. Taylor, Ancient Christian Writers: The Works of the Fathers in Translation XLII (New York, 1982), 301 n. 13 and 302 n. 16. Hereafter this work will be referred to by the abbreviation *LMG*, followed by the volume and page number.

11 *LMG* XLII, 186; *PL* 34, 459.

shalt love thy neighbour as thyself' (Matthew 19. 19). When we hear this, he says, we experience all three kinds of vision simultaneously.

> . . . one through the eyes by which we see the letters; a second through the spirit, by which we think of our neighbour even when he is absent; and a third through an intuition of the mind, by which we see and understand love itself.[12]

Augustine then clearly establishes a hierarchy of vision, and it is this hierarchy which has had such a profound effect on the perception of contemplative experience, indeed of all spiritual experience, by locating the zenith of that experience out of the body and out of this world, by privileging the transcendent over the immanent.

> For spiritual vision is more excellent than corporeal, and intellectual is more excellent than spiritual.[13]

This hierarchy is based on the reliability of each kind of vision. Corporeal and spiritual vision can err, either through the distortions of the natural world, the deficiencies of the viewer, or the deceptions practised by evil spirits. No such misapprehension can occur with an intellectual vision.

> . . . if man has not only been carried out of the bodily senses to be among the likeness of bodies seen by the spirit, but is also carried out of these latter to be conveyed, as it were, to the region of the intellectual or the intelligible, where transparent truth is seen without any bodily likeness, his vision is darkened by no cloud of false opinion . . .[14]

Other Patristic authors adopted Augustine's classification system, varying the terms somewhat, but maintaining both the vital distinction between sensual and intellectual apprehension, and the superiority of the latter over the former. Gregory the Great warns in his *Moralia in Iob*:

> The appearance of corporeal figures the soul has drawn to itself through the infirmity of the body. But to its utmost power it is on its guard that, when it is seeking Truth, the imagination of circumscribed vision shall not delude it, and it spurns all images that present themselves to it.[15]

The preference for intellectual over 'spiritual' vision bestows upon men, who were deemed capable of intellection, a more reliable and more valued spiritual experience than that generally accorded to women, who were seen as irretrievably hampered by the moral and mental distortions and limitations

---

[12] *LMG* XLII, 185; *PL* XXXIV, 458.

[13] *LMG* XLII, 213; *PL* XXXIV, 474.

[14] *LMG* XLII, 216; *PL* XXXIV, 476.

[15] Gregory the Great, *Moralia in Iob* XXIII, 42. Translated in Butler, *Mysticism*, p. 71.

induced by their natures. Women were therefore judged only capable of a spiritual experience which was also sensual, suspect and subordinate.

The discovery of the works of pseudo-Dionysius, and their translation into Latin, first by Hilduin in the ninth century, and then by Johannes Scotus Erigena later in the same century, introduced another concept of transcendental experience. Apophatic mysticism, the *via negativa*, is based on a cerebral, and non-sensual theology. In her introduction to *The Cloud of Unknowing*, Phyllis Hodgson enunciates the central thesis of Dionysian mysticism.

> The spiritual exercise, which was inspired by Dionysius, rests upon the belief in the absolute incomprehensibility of God . . . the natural faculties of intelligence are impotent to comprehend the being of God because God's nature is essentially different from the nature of man . . . any activity of the normal faculties is a hindrance in the prayer of contemplation . . .[16]

The affective aspects of Dionysian mysticism are mere signposts to the ultimate destination of the annihilation of the self in the otherness of God.

> For we contemplate [the divine mysteries] through the perceptible symbols which have grown round them. One must strip these off in order to see them in themselves, naked and pure.[17]

The teachings of pseudo-Dionysius were embraced with enthusiasm by the newly emerging universities, and by the scholastics. This enthusiasm resulted in the proliferation of mystical treatises celebrating the spiritual joys of the *via negativa*.

In marked contrast to cerebral Dionysian mysticism, in the thirteenth century, largely due to the teaching of the Franciscans, there was a popular movement toward the exercise of affective piety in prayer and contemplation. Affective piety was a form of meditation which focused on the nativity and passion of Christ. Worshippers were enjoined to imagine themselves present at the scene, to visualize the events in great detail and living colour, to suffer and rejoice with those who had participated in these scriptural events; in effect, they were encouraged to create a scriptural drama. The purpose was to identify with the life of Christ as a step towards imitating it in one's own life. In the fourteenth-century *Meditations on the Life of Christ*, the meditator is explicitly instructed to give flesh to the bare bones of scriptural narrative.

> It is possible to contemplate, explain and understand the Holy Scriptures in as many ways as we consider necessary, in such a manner as not to contradict

---

[16] P. Hodgson, ed., *The Cloud of Unknowing and the Book of Privy Counselling*, EETS (London, 1944), p. lix.

[17] R. T. Hathaway, *Hierarchy and the Definition of Order in the Letters of Pseudo-Dionysius* (The Hague, 1969), p. 151.

the truth of life and justice and not to oppose faith and morality. Thus when you find it said here, 'This was done and said by the Lord Jesus' and by others of whom we read, if it cannot be demonstrated by the Scriptures, you must consider it only as a requirement of devout contemplation. Take it as if I had said, 'Suppose that this is what the Lord Jesus said and did,' joyfully and rightfully, leaving behind all other cares and anxieties.[18]

Affective piety encouraged worshippers to formulate spiritual experiences in terms of their own everyday lives; they used their senses, their emotions, their imaginations. They identified with Christ in his humanity and it was within their own humanity that they based the concepts of their spiritual understanding and found the words to articulate their devotion. The prologue to the *Meditations on the Supper of Our Lord* (1338) defines its audience, stipulates its varied sources and articulates its objective.

> Now euery man, yn hys degre,
> Sey amen, amen pur charyte.
> . . .
> Y wyl þe lere a medytacyun
> Compyled of crystys passyun;
> And of hys modyr, þat ys dere,
> What peynes þey suffred þou mayst lere.
> Take hede, for y wyl no þyng seye
> But þat ys preued by crystes feye,
> By holy writ, or seyntes sermons,
> Or by dyuers holy opynyons.
> Whan þou þenkest þys yn þy þo3t
> Thyr may no fende noye þe with no3t.[19]

Works such as this were one of the means by which the principles of affective piety were disseminated. 'Holy Writ could be, and had to be, expounded in diverse manners to diverse people for diverse purposes.'[20]

Foremost among the means of expounding Holy Writ were the works of Bonaventure – or pseudo-Bonaventure – in their many translations and variations, as well as Gospel harmonies, sermons, the liturgy, devotional lyrics and visual art. The role of the friars in encouraging the use of material of this kind for devotional purposes is affirmed by Miri Rubin.

---

[18] I. Ragusa and R. Green, ed. and trans., *Meditations on the Life of Christ: An Illustrated Manuscript of the Fourteenth Century* (Princeton, 1961), p. 5.

[19] J. M. Cooper, ed., *Meditations on the Supper of Our Lord, and the Hours of the Passion*, EETS (London, 1875), p. 2.

[20] I. Johnson, 'Prologue and Practice: Middle English Lives of Christ', in *The Medieval Translator: The Theory and Practice of Translation in the Middle Ages*, ed. R. Ellis (Cambridge, 1989), p. 70.

It is in the convergence of these materials and the techniques related to their use that the influence of the mendicant orders was most acute, in the introduction of that which was not strictly biblical, but rather devotional and sometimes apocryphal layers of the religious language.[21]

Because this material was in the vernacular, it was accessible to those people – lay men and women – who knew no Latin. While some women, mainly aristocrats, could read and write, very few even of convent women were Latin literate.[22] Because the transmission of this material did not rely solely on the written word, it was accessible to those who could not read.

The influence on women of vernacular devotional works was profound, and unbalanced by an equivalent exposure to Latin treatises, which is the form in which most theological and mystical works were disseminated.[23] One particularly influential form of affective piety is the *imitatio Christi*, a largely Franciscan model of spiritual exercise based on the threefold way of purgation, illumination and perfection introduced by Bonaventure.[24] *Imitatio Christi* was penitential, and involved emulating the suffering and humility of Christ in one's own life.[25] This devotional model had a profound impact on religious praxis, including that of Margery Kempe. As my work hopefully demonstrates, the idiosyncratic variant of *imitatio Christi* which Margery is represented as compelled to follow contributed toward her ambivalent reception as a visionary.

Variations on the theme of affective piety are to be found in thirteenth-century German *Brautmystik* [Bridal mysticism], a form of transcendentalism mainly experienced by women. It is characterized by nuptial and erotic imagery, by descriptions of marriage between God and the soul, and by representations of the reciprocity of desire between God and the soul.[26] Another variant of affective piety is the development of the devotion to the Sacred

---

21 M. Rubin, *Corpus Christi: The Eucharist in Late Medieval Culture* (Cambridge, 1991), p. 276.

22 W. J. Ong, 'Orality, Literacy and Medieval Textualization', *New Literary History* 16 (1984), 5.

23 A notable exception to this general trend is the fourteenth-century work, *The Cloud of Unknowing*, a masterly exposition of the *via negativa* which was written in English.

24 D. Despres, *Ghostly Sights: Visual Meditation in Late-Medieval Literature* (Norman, 1989), p. 11. This work explores the influence of Franciscan forms of piety on Middle English writing, including *The Book of Margery Kempe*.

25 Sarah Beckwith explores the impact of devotion to Christ's body on late-medieval English religious practices and spiritual identity. She states that, according to the Christocentric piety which Franciscanism elaborates, '. . . the best life was to be a life of *imitatio* encouraged through a proliferation of texts which talked of the loving contemplation of the tortured Christ' (*Christ's Body*, p. 53).

26 An excellent example of *Brautmystik* is *Ein vliessendes lieht der gotheit [A Flowing Light of the Divinity]* by Mechthild of Magdeburg, one of the three visionaries living and writing at the convent of Helfta at the end of the thirteenth century. A modern

Heart, originating in the nunnery of Helfta, Germany, in the late thirteenth century.[27] These spiritual trends, centred around an emotional identification with the humanity of Christ, elicited powerful responses from women.

With the *via negativa* reinforcing and reformulating many of the concepts originally included in Augustine's category of intellectual vision, and affective piety encouraging the involvement of the emotions and senses in contemplation, by the thirteenth century the two categories of vision – spiritual and intellectual – identified by Augustine had crystallized into two distinct types of transcendental experience.

One type is intellectual, cerebral, characterised by *unio mystica*, that union which is by its very nature incommunicable beyond the fact of its occurrence, and which is signalled by an unmistakeable knowing in the soul of the mystic. Works on this type of mystical experience stress the impossibility of misapprehension.

> . . . there is no deception in intellectual vision; for either a person does not understand . . . or he does understand and then his vision is necessarily true.[28]

This being so, it seems that there is perceived to be little need for checks or safeguards, or for examination of the doctrinal correctness of the experience. The spiritual director of a would-be mystic can guide his charge in the right direction, but once he has achieved *unio mystica* his status, spiritual and otherwise, seems to be assured. Mystical episodes are unmediated, incommunicable, and above all, individual. Works which record this kind of experience I designate mystical; those people whose experiences are predominantly mystical I categorize mystics.

The second form of transcendent experience falls into Augustine's category of spiritual or imaginary vision. In these cases the visionary experience

---

English translation of this work is Mechthild von Magdeburg, *Flowing Light of the Divinity*, trans. C. Mesch Galvani, ed. S. Clark (New York, 1991).

[27] Two of the Helfta visionaries, Mechtild of Hackeborn and Gertrude the Great, were instrumental in the inception of the cult of the Sacred Heart. Its influence is marked in their visionary writings: *Legatus divinae pietatis*, by Gertrude, and *Liber specialis gratiae*, by Mechtild. These works can be found in Gertrude the Great, *Revelationes Gertrudianae ac Mechtildianae*, 2 vols., ed. Benedictines of Solesmes (Paris, 1875). The development of the medieval cult of the Sacred Heart is examined in J. Leclercq OSB, 'Le Sacré-Coeur dans la Tradition Bénédictine au Moyen Age', in *Cor Jesu: Commentationes in Litteras Encyclicas PII PP. XII 'Haurietis Aquas'*, ed. A. Bea SJ et al., 2 vols. (Rome, 1959), II, 3–28, and in C. Vagaggini's article in the same volume, '*La Dévotion au Sacré Coeur Chez Sainte Mechtilde et Sainte Gertrude*', II, 31–48. C. Bynum also considers the varieties of devotional and visionary experiences at Helfta in *Jesus as Mother: Studies in the Spirituality of the High Middle Ages* (Berkeley, 1982), pp. 170–262.

[28] *LMG* XLII, 197; *PL* XXXIV, 465.

15

involves seeing things, or hearing things with the inward or spiritual eye or ear. These I classify as visions, and those who principally experience visions I call visionaries.[29] In nearly all cases these visions and locutions feature Christ, the Virgin Mary, the saints, or angels. They are concrete, material and specific. They are a form of prophecy in that the visionary is enjoined to share the experience with others, that the visions reveal matters previously hidden, and that the purpose of the visions is to affect human faith or human behaviour. As Bridget of Sweden is told by God,

> Þow merualles þat I speke and shewe þe swilke grete þinges. Hoppes þowe þat I do it for þiself allone? Nai forsothe, bot for þe edificacion of oþir and hele of oþir.[30]

In other words, God is moving in the ways of his choosing rather than those mapped out by the Church.

While spiritual visions were accepted as a form of direct communication with God, they were undoubtedly perceived as an inferior form of spiritual experience. Aquinas stresses the hierarchy of transcendental experience in his discussion of the divisions of prophecy in his *Summa theologiae*.

> Now it is clear that a manifestation of divine truth which derives from a bare contemplation of the truth itself is more effective than that which derives from images of bodily things. Sheer contemplation is in fact nearer to the vision of heaven, according to which truth is gazed upon in the essence of God.[31]

This privileging of mystical over visionary experiences was virtually universal. In the *Scale of Perfection*, by Walter Hilton (d. 1395), the first part of which is addressed 'Dear Sister in Jesus Christ', Hilton explicitly discounts visionary experiences as having any value in true contemplation.

> By what I have said you will to some extent understand that visions or revelations of any kind of spirit, appearing in the body or in the imagination, asleep or awake, or any other feeling in the bodily senses made in spiritual fashion – either in sound by the ear, or tasting in the mouth, or smelling to the nose, or else any heat that can be felt like fire glowing and warming the breast or any other part of the body, or anything that can be felt by bodily sense, however comforting and pleasing it may be – these are not truly contemplation.[32]

[29] Kathryn Kerby-Fulton offers a similar definition of vision in her discussion of the medieval visionary tradition as it relates to *Piers Plowman*. One of her principal criteria of a visionary writer is that 'such a writer records the ideas presented to him (or her) by the experience in a vividly visual fashion . . . the revelation must be conveyed imagistically' (*Reformist*, 78).

[30] *LC*, p. 155.

[31] *ST 2a2ae* XLV, 75.

[32] Walter Hilton, *The Scale of Perfection*, trans. J. P. H. Clark and R. Dorward (New York, 1991), pp. 83–4.

Nevertheless, women's transcendental experiences generally did include 'feeling in the bodily senses made in spiritual fashion', and these experiences transported them to heights of religious fervour and endowed them with inner fulfilment. They saw, touched, heard, tasted and smelled God, and doing so gave meaning to their lives. Visions gave them a foretaste of the life to come when all their senses would be filled with God.

> And than shall we alle come in to oure lorde, oure selfe clerely knowyng and god fulsomely hauyng, and we endlessly be alle hyd in god, verely seyeng and fulsomly felyng, and hym gostely heryng, and hym delectably smellyng, and hym swetly swelwyng.[33]

The period from the twelfth to the fifteenth century saw the flowering of women's visionary writing. During this period a large number of remarkable women recorded their visionary experiences, experiences which were eagerly read by their contemporaries, both men and women, and which have continued to exert an influence up to the present day. Among them were Elisabeth of Schönau (d. 1165), Hildegard of Bingen (d. 1179), Marie d'Oignies (d. 1213), Hadewijch of Brabant (d. 1269), the three Helfta nuns, Mechthild of Magdeburg (d. 1282), Mechtild of Hackeborn (d. 1298), and Gertrude the Great (d. 1302), Angela of Foligno (d. 1309), Bridget of Sweden (d. 1373), Catherine of Siena (d. 1380), Julian of Norwich (d. *c.* 1416) and Margery Kempe (d. after 1438). Dom Cuthbert Butler, in his study of mysticism, remarks upon the predominance of women visionaries.

> . . . it may be of interest to note the fact that the line of great seers of visions and hearers of revelations is made up almost wholly of women . . . Of course, from SS [*sic*] Peter and Paul and John downwards men too have seen visions and heard words. But it seems to be the case that nearly always it has been women who have had elaborate pictorial visions, often succeeding each other in a sort of panoramic series. It is not suggested that the visions are any the worse for that; but it does suggest that there is something in the mental or psychic make-up of women that renders them susceptible to this kind of quasi-mystical experience.[34]

It is interesting to note that in a passage by a twentieth-century cleric which purports to celebrate 'the great seers of visions and hearers of revelations', there are distinct echoes of the prejudice against both women and visions which can be traced back at least as far as Augustine. Although 'it is not suggested that the visions are any the worse for that', nonetheless there is an implication that women's visions are like brightly coloured picture books

---

[33] Julian of Norwich, *A Book of Showings to the Anchoress Julian of Norwich*, ed. E. Colledge and J. Walsh, 2 vols. (Toronto, 1978), I, 481.

[34] Butler, *Mysticism*, p. 126.

which they are incapable of distinguishing from the real thing – but which keep them happy.

In the preponderance of medieval thought, it was only to be expected that women's transcendental experiences would echo their supposedly fleshly, sensual natures and occur in a form prone to deception and error. The association of women and spiritual vision has the effect of reinforcing the suspect, inferior nature of each. Both women and visions are perceived as potentially deceptive and deceiving, subject to the senses, uncontrolled by the restraining powers of the intellect.

> . . . woman is of a nature to be deceived rather than to reflect greatly, but man is the opposite here. But according to the deeper meaning, the object of sense perception deceives and deludes the particular senses of an imperfect being to which it comes; and sense-perception being already infected by its object, passes on the infection to the sovereign and ruling element.[35]

Visions can be tools of the devil, and visionaries his minions.

> For such false apostles are deceitful workmen, transforming themselves into the apostles of Christ./ And no wonder: for Satan himself transformeth himself into an angel of light. (II Corinthians 11. 13–14)

Eve was easily deceived, and acted as the devil's agent.

> For Adam was first formed, then Eve./ And Adam was not seduced; but the woman being seduced, was in the transgression. (I Timothy 2. 13–14)

The senses cannot be trusted, and the soul, like Adam, can be deceived.

> But in spiritual vision, namely in the likeness of bodies seen by the spirit, the soul is deceived when it judges the objects of its vision to be real bodies, or when it attaches some property of its own fancy and false conjecture to bodies that it has not seen but merely conjures up in imagination.[36]

All women are possessed of the proclivities of Eve; they seduce, they deceive, they distort.

> Yes indeed: they are all weak and frivolous . . . For we are told here, not that Eve alone suffered from deception, but that 'Woman' was deceived. The word 'Woman' is not to be applied to one but to every woman. All feminine nature has thus fallen into error . . .[37]

A mind open to visions is a mind open to the devil's deception.

35 Philo, *Questions and Answers on Genesis*, trans. R. Marcus (London, 1953), p. 26.

36 *LMG* XLII, 215; *PL* XXXIV, 475.

37 John Chrysostom. Cited in B. Anderson and J. Zinsser, ed., *A History of their Own: Women in Europe from Prehistory to the Present*, 2 vols. (Harmondsworth, 1988), I, 79.

For the devil gives whatever he sees the mind disposed to desire and receive. So when he sees the mind gluttonous, with its desire set only on spiritual visions and consolations . . . then I say, the devil presents himself to that mind under the appearance of light.[38]

The foregoing quotations give a graphic indication of the pervasive hold of negative perceptions of both women and spiritual visions, the former rooted in a long history encompassing Christian and Classical thought. A review of that history will assist in understanding the controls and limits later to be placed on women's spiritual lives in the Middle Ages, and in understanding why their visionary experiences were viewed as a flawed and suspect expression of a flawed and suspect spirituality.

Classical and Christian Misogyny

The poisoned blossoms of Christian misogyny flourished on a stock of classical thought which consistently defined women as inferior and subordinate to men in intellectual, physical and spiritual attributes. 'The male is by nature superior, and the female inferior; the one rules and the other is ruled', declaims Aristotle.[39] For the most part, women were perceived solely in the light of their generative function and regarded as walking wombs. Augustine writes: 'I do not see what other help woman would be to men if the purpose of generating was eliminated.'[40] Consequently, treatises on women frequently focused on matters connected with reproduction: menstruation, conception, birth, menopause. Women were defined as material, sensual, passive, moist and cold, therefore susceptible to the heat of lust. They were seen as prevented by their physical nature from pursuing the intellectual, rational path of spirituality. Women were perceived as irredeemably hampered by their bodies in a way that men clearly were not. Classical theories of conception promulgated the view of women as defective or imperfect males – in effect, as men turned outside-in. Galen's treatise on the generative organs is a good example.

> Now, just as mankind is the most perfect of all animals, so within mankind the man is more perfect than the woman, and the reason for his perfection is his excess of heat, for heat is nature's primary instrument . . . the woman is less perfect than the man in respect to the generative parts. For the parts were formed within her when she was still a fetus, but could not because of the defect in the heat emerge and project on the outside, and this, though making the animal itself that was being formed less perfect than one that is complete in all respects, provided no small advantage for the race; for there must

---

38 Catherine of Siena, *The Dialogue*, trans. and ed. S. Noffke OP (New York, 1980), p. 133.
39 Aristotle, *Politics*. Cited in Anderson and Zinsser, *History*, I, 27.
40 *LMG* LXII, 96; *PL* XXXIV, 397.

needs be a female. Indeed, you ought not to think that our Creator would purposely make half the whole race imperfect, and, as it were, mutilated, unless there was to be some great advantage in such a mutilation.[41]

Understanding of woman's role in conception reflected the generally pejorative view of women. Although there were some differences in the details of the process of conception[42] – details which encompass every possible variable from the sex of the child to its temperament as an adult – generally it was held that the male sperm imparts movement, force and spirit to the raw and imperfect matter supplied by the mother. The reproductive capacity of women stimulated a whole host of beliefs, most of which reflected negatively on the sex. The menstrual blood, though linked with pregnancy and the nourishment of the foetus, in non-pregnant women was thought to be the product of a purifying process. This gave rise to the idea that the fluid itself was poisonous, and that menstruating women were unclean.[43] In a statement which reveals an implicit belief in the inherent threat of female physicality, Pliny the Elder wrote:

> Contact with it [menstrual blood] turns new wine sour, crops touched by it become barren, grafts die, seeds in gardens are dried up, the fruit of trees falls off, the bright surface of mirrors in which it is merely reflected is dimmed, the edge of steel and the gleam of ivory are dulled, hives of bees die, even bronze and iron are at once seized by rust and a horrible smell fills the air; to taste it drives dogs mad and infects their bites with an incurable poison . . .[44]

Classical theories of medicine and classical philosophy conspired in the development of an understanding of the nature and role of women *vis-à-vis*

---

41 Galen, *On the Usefulness of the Parts of the Body (Deus partium)*. Cited in V. Bullough, 'Medieval Medical Views of Women', *Viator* 4 (1973), 492. For a recent, incisive study of Galen's theories of conception, see J. Cadden, *Meanings of Sex Difference in the Middle Ages: Medicine, Science and Culture* (Cambridge, 1993), pp. 30–7.

42 There were two major strains of conception theory which survived into the Middle Ages, and which had implications for both medical and moral thought. Briefly, theories which followed Aristotle held that women were passive receptacles for male sperm – there are claims that women could become pregnant merely by bathing in water into which a man had ejaculated. Alternatively, those theories founded on Galenic thought hold that both males and females emit sperm, both of which are necessary for conception. The relevant point here is that the emission of sperm was believed to be a pleasurable act, for both sexes, so that pregnancy branded the woman as having enjoyed the sexual act. For a clear and concise treatment of this topic, see D. Jacquart and C. Thomasset, *Sexuality and Medicine in the Middle Ages*, trans. M. Adamson (Oxford, 1988), pp. 8–39.

43 Bullough, 'Medical Views', 490.

44 Cited in Anderson and Zinsser, *History*, I, p. 17.

men which parallels the body/soul dichotomy. Under this dualistic scheme of things, women were equated with the body, with material concerns and fleshly obsessions, while men represented the rational soul, the mind and the spirit. Pythagoras's division of the universe into two opposing principles allied women with dark and evil, men with light and good. Certain classical philosophers held that the purpose of life was the development of one's spiritual nature, and that the way to achieve this was to identify and follow the path of reason and to divorce oneself from the material world. Not only were women doomed right from the start, but contact with women could severely imperil a man's spiritual quest.

In the Judaic tradition, women were similarly seen as subordinate. Elaborate and specific taboos around menstruation and childbirth are codified in Leviticus 12–15.[45] Women were not educated in the Sacred Books as boys and men were, and their role in religious ceremonies and prayers was strictly limited. The Palestinian Talmud states that it is preferable to burn the words of the Torah rather than put it into a woman's keeping. The Babylonian Talmud argues 'There is no wisdom in woman except with the distaff.'[46] In one of the morning prayers of traditional Jewish liturgy – a prayer still in use, incidentally – men thank God for not having made them a woman.

Philo of Alexandria, a Hellenized Jew writing in the first century AD, defines the respective roles of men and women as follows:

> For just as the man shows himself in activity and the woman in passivity, so the province of the mind is activity, and that of the perceptive sense passivity, as in woman.[47]

This association of women with the senses and with passivity, and of men with intellectual activity, is one which surfaces continually in discussions of gender in Western civilization, and which is present even today. In the Middle Ages, this belief was of fundamental importance in defining and limiting the spiritual aspirations of women.

Philo further explores the innate carnal and dangerous aspects of women, and of association with women, in a treatise on pleasure.

> Pleasure does not venture to bring her wiles and deceptions to bear on the man, but on the woman, and by her means on him. This is a well made point: for in us mind corresponds to man, the senses to woman; and pleasure encounters and holds parlay with the senses first, and through them cheats with her quackery the sovereign mind itself.[48]

---

[45] The appropriate treatment for postpartum and menstruating women is specified along with the exclusionary rituals to be observed for lepers and men with a 'running issue'.

[46] Both examples cited in Anderson and Zinsser, *History*, I, 32.

[47] Philo, *On the Creation*, trans. F. H. Coulson and G. H. Whitaker (London, 1956), p. 249.

[48] Philo, *Creation*, p. 131.

Philo holds Eve responsible for the entry of sin into the world, and argues that the consequence of that sin is that man is distracted from his growth towards spiritual excellence by the companionship of women.

> But since no created thing is constant, and things mortal are necessarily liable to changes and reverses, it could not but be that the first man too should experience some ill fortune. And woman becomes for him the beginning of blameworthy life.[49]

This argument, along with its many and varied expositions, has a profound impact on women's freedom to pursue a spiritual vocation, to explore theological and doctrinal matters, to teach and be taught. As will be shown, these were all areas which required the association of men dedicated to spirituality with women who wanted the same, but who were condemned as daughters of Eve to be suspected and shunned.

The Classical and Judaic traditions, both of which enshrine in their everyday practices and in their respective world views belief in the subordinate nature and status of women, supply the philosophical foundation on which Christianity is built. It is not surprising that it is Paul, originally a Hellenized Jew, who formulated in the New Testament a definition of the nature of women and their role in the Church which has shaped Christian attitudes ever since. That the seeds Paul scattered should have flourished so well argues for the receptivity of the culture to a message with which it was familiar. When the Pauline injunctions are taken together with the Old Testament proscriptions, warnings and horrible examples, they constitute a formidable scriptural armoury. These weapons were refined by the Church Fathers, and then by centuries of Christian theologians and clerics into instruments designed to keep women subordinate, controlled and convinced of their own inferiority.

> But I would have you know, that the head of every man is Christ; and the head of the woman is the man; and the head of Christ is God. . . . The man indeed ought not to cover his head, for he is the image and glory of God: but the woman is the glory of the man. (I Corinthians 11. 3 and 7)

This statement by Paul confirms the subordinate status of women both in relation to men and to God. Paul's attitude toward women is implicit in his incidental exhortations and statements about them, rather than explicit in a treatise directed to the topic. Many of these precepts actually form part of Paul's attempt to define roles and appropriate conduct for both women and men in the newly emerging Church.[50] This material, scattered throughout his

---

[49] Philo, *Creation*, p. 119.
[50] Elaine Pagels argues that Paul was acutely aware of the dangers of social disorder, and that he feared the radical liberty which could be engendered by belief in the new

writings, did, however, provide ample grist for the mill of the exegetes who propounded Christian doctrine in subsequent centuries.[51]

The Early Church Fathers generally manifest the dualistic concepts of the Classical world, in that they promulgate doctrines based on a clear division between flesh and spirit, a division in which women are associated with the flesh and men with the spirit. Jerome says, '. . . as long as woman is for birth and children, she is different from men as body is from soul'.[52] Although the Church Fathers actively promote women committing themselves to chastity and to a life of ascetic spirituality, at the same time they perceive even the best-intentioned, most innocent of virgins as capable of inciting and experiencing lust. In their view, the nature of women makes this inevitable. Consequently, women's pursuit of a spiritual life is fraught with peril, and the spirituality of any men with whom they come into contact is endangered. The African Church Father, Tertullian (*c.* 160 – *c.* 225), in his tract 'On the Veiling of Virgins', warns virgins to go abroad thickly veiled in order to '. . . rear a rampart for your sex', which must neither allow your own eyes egress nor ingress to other people's'.[53] Convictions such as these made it imperative that women be rigorously controlled, and held in continual suspicion.

In addition to woman's natural inferiority – 'flesh must be subject to spirit in the right ordering of nature'[54] – in the eyes of the Church Fathers, Eve's role as the original sinner further debased all women. As Rosemary Radford Ruether writes:

> This double definition of woman as submissive body in the order of nature and 'revolting' body in the disorder of sin, allows the Fathers to slide somewhat inconsistently from the second to the first and attribute woman's inferiority first to sin and then to nature.[55]

freedom and equality in Christ which he proclaims. One of Paul's main concerns in this respect would be that women would throw off the shackles of their oppression ('Paul and Women: A Response to Recent Discussion', *Journal of the American Academy of Religion* 42 (1974), 546). See also B. Brooten, 'Paul's Views on the Nature of Women and Female Homoeroticism', in *Immaculate and Powerful: The Female in Sacred Image and Social Reality*, ed. C. W. Atkinson, C. H. Buchanan and M. R. Miles (Boston: Beacon, 1985), pp. 75–8.

51 See, for example, Augustine's exegesis, cited below, of the passage from Corinthians.

52 Jerome, *Commentariorum in epistolam et ephesios libri 3, PL* XXVI, col. 533. Cited in J. Salisbury, *Church Fathers, Independent Virgins* (London, 1991), p. 26.

53 Tertullian, *Tertullian: A Select Library of the Ante-Nicene Fathers of the Christian Church*, ed. A. Roberts and J. Donaldson (Grand Rapids, 1951), p. 37.

54 Augustine, *De continentia* 1:23. Cited in R. R. Ruether, 'Misogynism and Virginal Feminism in the Fathers of the Church', in *Religion and Sexism: Images of Women in the Jewish and Christian Traditions*, ed. R. R. Ruether (New York, 1974), p. 157.

55 Ruether, 'Misogynism', p. 157.

In other words, even if women could somehow manage to transcend their carnal, physical natures – and many spiritually inclined women literally killed themselves trying to eradicate through zealous asceticism all evidence of their female physical characteristics – they could never escape the stain of the sin of their foremother.

> You are the Devil's gateway. You are the unsealer of that forbidden tree. You are the first deserter of the divine Law. You are she who persuaded him whom the Devil was not valiant enough to attack. You destroyed so easily God's image, man. On account of your desert, that is death, even the Son of God had to die.[56]

Foremost amongst the Church Fathers is Augustine, whose influence on Christian attitudes towards women, sexuality and marriage was profound.[57] Although Augustine does believe in the equality of male and female souls, he argues vehemently and consistently that the natural inferiority of women is represented in the essential carnality of her body which she is not only incapable of escaping, but which acts as a snare for men. He does eschew the dualistic world-view of his earlier colleagues, largely as a result of his rejection of Manichaeism. He accepts sexuality as a part of the divine order, as a human attribute designed to ensure procreation and to fulfil the need for companionship. He also places the locus of lust in the unruly and disobedient male organ, whose disobedience echoes the sin in the Garden, of which it is the direct consequence. However, woman is still the source of sin, and, as Rosemary Radford Ruether puts it, 'the cause, object and extension of [the erection]'.[58]

Augustine's argument for the natural subordination of women is perhaps best represented by his interpretation, in the light of Genesis 1, of the Pauline text, I Corinthians 11. 3–12.[59]

> How then did the apostle tell us that the man is the image of God and therefore he is forbidden to cover his head, but that the woman is not so, and therefore she is commanded to cover hers? Unless forsooth according to that which I have said already, when I was treating of the nature of the human mind, that the woman, together with her husband, is the image of God, so that the whole substance may be one image, but when she is referred to separately in her quality as a helpmeet, which regards the woman alone, then she

---

56 Tertullian, p. 147.

57 There is much debate on Augustine's views of sexuality and marriage, on his interpretation of the Fall and of the role of women in perpetuating sin. For some varied treatments of the issue see: E. Pagels, *Adam, Eve, and the Serpent* (New York, 1988); K. Børreson, *Subordination and Equivalence*; Ruether, 'Misogynism'; P. Brown, *The Body and Society: Men, Women and Sexual Renunciation in Early Christianity* (London, 1988); Salisbury, *Church Fathers*.

58 Ruether, 'Misogynism', p. 163.

59 See above, p. 22.

is not in the image of God, but, as regards the man alone, he is the image of God as fully and completely as when the woman too is joined with him in one.[60]

Even in her God-given role of helpmeet, woman is not in God's image. She can never achieve the image of God unless she is merged with her husband. Alone, she is spiritually invisible, and irrelevant to the spirituality of men.

Augustine's interpretation has profound implications for the independent spirituality of women, as well as for the kind of spiritual experience they can expect to have. According to Augustine, man, in and of himself, is already closer to God than woman can ever hope to be. Any spiritual pursuit that a woman may undertake must be under the guidance, and with the consent, of her husband, or, in the case of virgins and widows, of the male clergy who are the representatives of the Divine Husband here on earth.

> And just as in the soul there is an element which rules by taking decisions and another which is submissive and obeys, so we see that woman has been made for man, in such wise that in her spirit she should have a rational intelligence equal in nature to his, and, nevertheless, in her body and by her sex she should be subject to the male sex, just as the desire for action is subjected to the rational mind so that it begets a right disposition for acting well.[61]

Women's bodies and all that pertains to them should be subject to male guidance and control.

This brief survey has so far dealt with pre-Christian and early Christian views of women in medical and theological treatises, and has demonstrated the extent to which perceptions of the physical, 'natural' inferiority of women and the seductive danger of their bodies restricted and dictated their access to a spiritual life. One millennium later, in the High Middle Ages, medical and theological treatises are dealing with the same issues about women, and promulgating many of the same perceptions.

Medieval theories of conception continue to assign a largely passive role to women and therefore reinforce belief in their essential inferiority. Thomas Aquinas echoes Aristotelian thought in his theory of conception which holds that the prime movers in procreation are the father, who accounts for the individuality of the child, the movements of the heavenly bodies, which account for the child's membership in the human species, and an angel, who accounts for the child's corporeal nature by yoking together body and spirit.[62] The woman's role is limited to providing the internal space and the nourishment for the foetus. As Kari Børreson points out, '. . . strictly speaking [the woman] does not generate: it is only the forming power of the male seed which is the

---

[60] Augustine, *De Trinitate* XII, 7, 10. Cited in Børreson, *Subordination*, p. 28.

[61] Augustine, *Confessiones* XIII, 32, 47. Cited in Børreson, *Subordination*, p. 34.

[62] Jacquart and Thomasset, *Sexuality*, p. 57.

agent of generation'.[63] The denigration of the woman's role to that of a passive
auxiliary to man's superior function is as remarkable here as it was in Augustine's interpretation of I Corinthians 11. 3–12. Albertus Magnus believed that if a
female was conceived it indicated that the father's sperm had been vanquished
by the matter of the mother.[64] Since the male sperm was held to contribute
light, spirit and intellectual force to the child, presumably if this had been
vanquished then these qualities would be missing in the resultant female. In a
statement which reveals the inextricable connection which was believed to
exist between a woman's body and her spiritual health, Rabanus Maurus, in
the ninth century, comments in *De Universo* on the word *menses*:

> It is not permitted to approach menstruating women nor to have intercourse
> with them, because a Catholic man is not permitted to have anything to do
> with the idolatry of pagans or with the heresy of heretics [*haeresi haereti-
> corum*].[65]

This apparent non-sequitur implies that heresy is as innate a part of all women
as menstruation, and that they are as powerless to control the one as the other.
This may seem to be stretching the point somewhat, but when one looks at the
many arguments which promulgate women's predisposition to deceit,
deception and heresy, it does not seem so very far-fetched. There were
proscriptions against menstruating women, or women who had just given
birth, approaching the altar, taking the eucharist, sometimes even entering a
church. Part of the argument against the ordination of women rested on her
periodic 'uncleanness'.

Because a woman was defined almost completely in terms of her generative
functions, she was perceived in those same terms as a being who by nature was
totally bound up with procreation, that is with concupiscence, lust and sin.

The biological consequences of marriage – the loss of virginity, the getting
and bearing of children – are for the woman, in the medieval perspective, not
simply natural processes but poignant and painful symbols of her status as the
daughter of Eve and of the inferior nature of her body.[66] It was beyond either
her ability or that of the men of the age to escape this perception. Even consecrated virgins, women who, by denying their gender, strove to transcend it
and become as men – or at least, as men were perceived to be – were not
exempt. Only the strictest external controls could help them to restrain the
animal lusts which lurked within, ready to devour them and any man, no

---

63 Børreson, *Subordination*, p. 193.
64 Jacquart and Thomasset, *Sexuality*, pp. 140–1.
65 *De Universo* XXII, 6. Cited in Jacquart and Thomasset, *Sexuality*, p. 14.
66 E. C. McLaughlin, 'Equality of Souls, Inequality of Sexes: Woman in Medieval
   Theology', in *Religion and Sexism: Images of Women in the Jewish and Christian Traditions*, ed. R. R. Ruether (New York, 1974), p. 223.

matter how spiritual, who ventured too close.[67] Women are not only subordinate to men, they are also subordinate to their bodies, and to the urges of those bodies.

Aquinas claims that because of the influence of the female nature of her body, the woman is more imperfect than man as regards intellection.[68] The link which he perceived between body and soul, the link which condemns women to spiritual as well as physical subordination is further explicated in the following passage.

> The human soul is the substantial form of the body and has certain powers which work in and through bodily organs. Their operations contribute to those performed without bodily organs, that is to intellect and will, inasmuch as the intellect receives from the sensation and will is impelled by emotion. Hence the fact that because of their frail physique, women seldom keep a firm grip on things . . . Aristotle regards women as lacking in firm rational judgement . . . and therefore not to be called continent, since their conduct is not based on solid reason, but easily swayed by feeling.[69]

Thus it can be seen that from earliest Christian times – and lamentably up to and including our own day – the spiritual subordination of women rests on two fundamental beliefs: their inferior status in the natural order of things, deriving from their creation after Adam, and Eve's responsibility for original sin. This latter not only branded women for ever as gullible and duplicitous, it also had the effect, through the curse which God laid upon Eve, of reinforcing both her subordinate status and the primacy of her reproductive nature.

> I will greatly multiply thy sorrow and thy conception; and thy desire shall be to thy husband, and he shall rule over thee. (Genesis 3. 16)

The Medieval Church and Women's Spirituality

This survey has so far examined the attitudes and cultural assumptions which developed in the Christian West out of the paradigmatic belief in the subordinate status and inherent inferiority of women. These attitudes and assumptions took effective form in social mechanisms and behaviour. Foremost among the institutions creating and supporting such mechanisms was the Church. It was dedicated to the belief that women must be kept under male control, ostensibly to maintain the natural order and to assist the movement of

---

[67] Given the popularity and promulgation of hagiographical accounts of virgin martyrs, one could argue that in the eyes of the medieval Church, the best virgin is a dead virgin. Certainly, death was generally believed to be the only certain remedy for the fires of concupiscence.

[68] Børreson, *Subordination*, p. 175.

[69] *ST 2a2ae* XLIV, 21.

women from the subordination of the order of creation to the equality of the order of salvation. It could be argued that, in actual fact, church control of women was designed to protect male spirituality from female contamination, rather than to promote the spiritual growth and eventual salvation of those women.

In the High Middle Ages, this is evident in the response of male monastic orders to the growing demand for more women's houses. Given the prevailing views on the nature and status of women, it was virtually unthinkable that women should be allowed to regulate their own religious lives; female houses were placed under the auspices of a male order. Initially the response to the demand was positive, though perhaps more from apprehension of the consequences of refusal than from an embracing of the opportunity to enhance women's spiritual lives. It was feared that unless they were brought under the control of the Church, these female aspirants to a spiritual life would have recourse to heretical sects, to which, as women, they were believed to be always susceptible. In time, however, as the flood of women clamouring for admission to religious houses showed no sign of slackening, and as the administration of women's houses became a drain on both the economic and spiritual resources of the male monastic orders, lukewarm acceptance became outright rejection.[70] Bernard of Clairvaux (1090–1153) shared the general distrust of women, as exemplified in his statement that it is easier to raise the dead than to be constantly with a woman and avoid intercourse.[71] Nevertheless, many women sought the shelter of the Cistercian order, often on an informal, unofficial basis, and in the late twelfth and early thirteenth centuries, female houses following the Rule of Citeaux proliferated. Opposition was soon mounted. Initial attempts to control the women read suspiciously like attempts to make the life of a nun so difficult and unappealing that others would be deterred. Enclosure was strictly enforced, nuns were forbidden visitors, and their opportunities for confession were limited. In effect, they were placed under a much more severe regimen than their male brethren. This is despite the fact that one of the explanations for discouraging women from following the Cistercian Rule was that it was too austere. Jacques de Vitry (1170–1240), himself a supporter of holy women, particularly of Beguines, said

---

[70] McLaughlin, 'Equality', pp. 238–42. B. Bolton, '*Mulieres Sanctae*', in *Women in Medieval Society*, ed. S. M. Stuard (Philadelphia, 1976), p. 143.

[71] Cited in R. W. Southern, *Western Society and the Church in the Middle Ages* (Harmondsworth, 1970), p. 314. J. Leclercq, in *Women and St Bernard of Clairvaux*, trans. M. Saïd (Kalamazoo, 1989), pp. 139–58, purports to deal with the question of Bernard's alleged misogyny. In actual fact, he acts as an apologist for Bernard, explaining as misunderstanding or misrepresentation incidents which could be construed as indicating hostility to women.

'It was not thought desirable that the female sex submit itself to such rules of austerity and approach such summits of perfection.'[72]

The desire of women to seek the summits – even the foothills – of spiritual perfection was at times perceived as threatening the spiritual health of men. This is evident in the measures taken to repress, discourage and control the tide of spiritual feminism which swept Europe from the twelfth to the fourteenth centuries. The Fourth Lateran Council of 1215 forbade the founding of new orders, effectively putting an end to any hope women may have entertained of starting their own religious communities. Women's houses were dependent on the generosity of the male orders for their very existence. This generosity was not always forthcoming. In 1228 the General Chapter of the Cistercians forbade the attachment of more nunneries to the order, and refused pastoral care and visitation to those already in existence.[73] In effect, the clergy exercised their power to deny to women who had dedicated themselves to a spiritual life those elements which the Church itself defined as vital to religious health and spiritual growth – pastoral care, teaching, confession, communion – and which the Church had ruled could only be provided by the clergy, that is, by men.

The Cistercians were by no means the only order to restrict and reject female aspirants. Even those orders which set out to attract or to provide for women ended up evading their responsibilities or bemoaning the onerous burden which female houses had become. Norbert of Xanten in 1120 founded the Premonstratensian order, and assumed the care of pious women in double monasteries founded to enable the monks to provide for the needs of the sisters. It was reported that by 1150 there were more than a thousand women 'serving God in such severity and silence that you could scarcely find the like in the strictest monasteries of monks'.[74] Such devotion and piety did them little good, for pressure was already being mounted to exclude them from the order. In 1137, soon after the death of Norbert, the General Chapter forbade the foundation of any more women's houses, a first salvo in the battle to exclude women entirely. Despite the fact that a succession of popes intervened on their behalf, insisting that adequate provision be made for those women who had dedicated themselves – and their often considerable dowries – to the Premonstratensian order, ultimately the papacy was unable, or unwilling to stem the tide of hostility from the established male order.

In 1198 Innocent III's bull, *De non recipiendis sororibus*, supported the decision of the General Chapter to admit no more women.[75] That the hostility to women in the order was misogynistic is revealed in the statement by one of

---

72 McLaughlin, 'Equality', p. 242.
73 Bolton, *'Mulieres'*, p. 143.
74 *PL* CLVI, 996–7. Cited in Southern, *Western Society*, p. 313.
75 Bolton, *'Mulieres'*, p. 142.

the abbots at the time of this Bull, Conrad of Marchtal, in which he rationalizes the exclusion of women religious.

> We and our whole community of canons, recognizing that the wickedness of women is greater than all the other wickedness of the world, and that there is no anger like that of women, and that the poison of asps and dragons is more curable and less dangerous to men than the familiarity of women, have unanimously decreed for the safety of our souls, no less than that of our bodies and goods, that we will on no account receive any more sisters to the increase of our perdition, but will avoid them like poisonous animals.[76]

The Dominicans and Franciscans, both of which orders initially encouraged women, ended up by condemning their presence in the orders, and by excluding them. The power which male orders had to facilitate or inhibit the spiritual development of women is demonstrated in the enthusiasm with which both these monastic reformers, Dominic (1170–1221) and Francis (1181–1226), embraced the cause of women religious at the beginning of their mission, contrasted with the virulent antipathy to women which both exhibited towards the end of their lives. It seems likely that the original intention was to provide spiritual care for a select group of women. When the number of women seeking admission to the order increased beyond expectations of the founders, these women were then perceived as a direct threat to the spiritual lives of the men in the order. On his deathbed, Dominic warned his followers against communion with women, especially young ones.[77] In 1228, the general chapter of the Dominicans prohibited the incorporation of nunneries, and threatened with censure any brother who gave women religious any pastoral care whatsoever, including allowing them to wear religious habits.[78] This was despite papal pressure on the mendicant orders to assume responsibility for the women in their care.

Papal action to protect the rights of women in the new orders and to ensure their physical and pastoral care can be viewed as part of a power struggle between the papacy and the mendicant orders. The religious fervour which had been stimulated amongst women by the examples of Dominic and Francis meant that someone had to take responsibility for their spiritual and economic welfare. Who better than those who had set the movement in motion? In attempting to force the mendicant orders to assume functions and responsibilities which older orders had, the Pope could hope effectively to curtail some of the revolutionary aspects which threatened the established ecclesiastical order. For example, if friars were tied to providing pastoral care for enclosed nuns, the itinerant nature of their mission would be severely restricted.

76 E. L. Hugo, *Annales Praemonstratenses* II, 147. Cited in Southern, *Western Society*, p. 314, and in McLaughlin, 'Equality', pp. 242–3.
77 Bolton, '*Mulieres*', p. 151.
78 Bolton, '*Mulieres*', pp. 151–2.

Similarly, the burden of economic care for communities of women would make the vow of poverty of the mendicant orders difficult to sustain.[79]

Some of the areas of conflict between pope and friars could have been avoided had the sisters been allowed to follow the life of mendicant poverty which they originally wanted. However, this was unthinkable, and strict claustration was demanded. The consequence was that women became a burden on the economic and spiritual resources of the order, because of restrictions dictated by perceptions of the subordinate and defective nature of women. When the needs of women threatened to affect the spiritual life of the men in the order, the women were often abandoned. Francis was obdurate in his refusal to recognize his obligation to those women who had flocked to follow his example and emulate the poverty of Christ. In 1218 he was asked by Cardinal Hugolino to assume formal responsibility for the large numbers of women clamouring to create communities like that of the Poor Clares at St Damian's, which Clare (1194–1253) had established with Francis's assistance. He flatly refused, demanding that no female community other than St Damian's be attached to his order in any way, and denying pastoral care to any other community.[80] His *volte face* from his early attitude to women is summed up in his statement, 'God has taken away our wives, and now the devil has given us sisters.'[81]

There were undoubtedly churchmen who were champions of female religious, who admired them and supported them. Unfortunately, such support was personal and arbitrary, within the power of the individual to give or withhold, rather than institutionalized and reliable, a right on which women could call at need. Religious women were as much at the mercy of male caprice for their spiritual sustenance as their secular sisters were for their physical needs.[82] With Robert d'Arbrissel in France at the beginning of the twelfth century and Gilbert of Sempringham half a century later in England, men who deliberately set out to provide for women religious, the initial impulse seems motivated as much by spiritual self-interest as by concern for women.

Robert's foundation at Fontevrault was established in 1100. His mission was to found a double order in which the community of women would be supported and cared for by the monks, whose service to the women would enable them to imitate the humility of Christ and symbolically fulfil his dying command to John the Evangelist to care for the Virgin Mary. It seems that the women function as vehicles for male spiritual growth, and that their own spiritual welfare is but a byproduct.[83] This becomes even more evident on

---

79 Bolton, 'Mulieres', pp. 151–2.
80 Bolton, 'Mulieres', p. 150.
81 Bolton, 'Mulieres', p. 150.
82 For further discussion of this topic see R. Bell, *Holy Anorexia* (Chicago, 1985), p. 55.
83 McLaughlin, 'Equality', p. 240.

consideration of Robert d'Arbrissel's habit of performing as penance for the sins of his youth a *martyrium*, that is sleeping among the women of his order, thereby exhibiting his supernatural control over the flesh.[84] The rationale for the founding of Fontevrault derives from the stereotype of women as subordinate and weak. Robert's extraordinary use, in his *martyrium*, of the women in his care is predicated on the stereotype of women as instruments of the devil, whose lustful advances can only be resisted by the truly holy, and whose natural concupiscence provides a convenient test for that holiness.

Gilbert of Sempringham (*c.* 1083–1189) originally had the intention of founding a male priory. However, as his *vita* records, he was unable to find enough men willing to dedicate themselves to God. His rationale for setting up a house for women, in 1131, is given in his *vita*.

> When he did not find men who wanted to live so strictly for God, he considered it worthy to confer all his wealth for the use of such who were truly poor in spirit [i.e. women] and who might purchase for himself and others the kingdom of heaven . . . [Gilbert] repeatedly said, and divine counsel admonished, that the more fully should be benefitted those who are naturally weaker and more compassionate, and thus more fully could reward be hoped for.[85]

There are three significant facts here. First, women are Gilbert's second choice, only to be considered when no men were available to enable him to fulfil his mission. Second, women are 'the truly poor in spirit'. Third, the pastoral care of the women is undertaken to earn their benefactors greater reward and a place in the kingdom of heaven. The primary role of the women is to be instruments for the salvation of the men; as with the community at Fontevrault, their own salvation is incidental.[86]

Many women, frustrated in their quest for access to a life of committed

---

[84] McLaughlin, 'Equality', p. 240. The question of the spiritual threat to those women so used seems not to occur, nor of the risk to them if Robert's self-control should lapse.

[85] Cited in S. K. Elkins, *Holy Women of Twelfth-Century England* (Chapel Hill, 1988), p. 133.

[86] It should be noted that the communities of monks and nuns in Gilbertine houses were rigidly separated at all times, including during the celebration of mass. Any communication or transfer of goods between them took place through a turning-door which left each side invisible to the other. The only exception was at the death of a nun, when a male cleric would enter the women's house to administer extreme unction – presumably at this point she was not deemed likely to seduce. The strictness of the separation is a measure of the fear and suspicion in which men held women, and of the depth of their conviction that the two could not be in even minimal contact without dire consequences. For a detailed treatment of the Gilbertine Order, see Elkins, *Holy Women*, pp. 81–3 and 105–138, and C. H. Lawrence, *Medieval Monasticism: Forms of Religious Life in Western Europe in the Middle Ages*, 2nd edn (London, 1989), pp. 224–7.

piety, formed loosely-knit, informal communities within which they pursued spiritual fulfilment. In northern Europe, foremost amongst these groups were the Beguines, who were largely clustered in the Low Countries, northern France and Germany.[87] The movement began in the early years of the thirteenth-century, and attracted urban women, often from the middle and lower classes, who wished to espouse the *vita apostolica* while remaining in the world. It grew at an astounding rate – between 1260 and 1400, 169 Beguine convents, housing around 1,500 women, were established in Cologne, the centre of the movement.[88] They were affiliated with no order, and supported themselves by their own labour. Initially, they were much admired for their piety. During the 1230s, Robert Grosseteste compared them favourably with the Franciscans, declaring that the Beguines had a higher form of poverty and the most perfect and holy kind of religious life because they lived by their own efforts, and did not burden the world with their demands.[89] Robert de Sorbon, the French theologian who founded the Sorbonne in 1257, claimed that at the last judgement the Beguines would do better than many learned theologians.[90] However, disenchantment set in, partly perhaps because of the sheer numbers involved and the enthusiasm of the response. To have so many women operating in visible groups with a high degree of autonomy and minimal supervision by husbands, fathers or clergymen seemed to violate the natural order of things. The reality of so many women living a pious life, free to seek pastoral care where they would, and therefore relatively unhampered by ecclesiastical control, became profoundly threatening to the Church. It was also feared that these women were prime targets for heretical leaders, and that if left to themselves they would develop heterodox views and stray far from the paths of righteousness. In 1273, Bruno, Bishop of Olmutz, complained in a letter to Pope Gregory X that the Beguines used their religious commitment as a means of evading 'the yoke of obedience to their priests and the coercion of marital bonds'.[91] His solution: 'I would have them married or thrust into an approved order.'[92] Opposition to the Beguines continued to mount, as did the

---

[87] For a full examination of the Beguine movement, see E. W. McDonnell, *The Beguines and Beghards in Medieval Culture: with special emphasis on the Belgian scene* (New Brunswick, 1954). Miri Rubin discusses the Beguines' emphasis on eucharistic devotion and their role in the development of the feast of Corpus Christi in *Corpus Christi*, pp. 10 and 167–70.

[88] Southern, *Western Society*, p. 325.

[89] Cited in Southern, *Western Society*, p. 320.

[90] Bolton, *'Mulieres'*, p. 145.

[91] Southern, *Western Society*, p. 329.

[92] Cited in Southern, *Western Society*, p. 329, also Lawrence, *Medieval*, p. 234. It should be kept in mind that, as demonstrated above, the established orders did not want women, certainly not in such vast numbers, and certainly not from the poorer classes, whence came many Beguines.

popularity of the movement. In 1312, the Council of Vienne gave official voice to this opposition.

> We have been told that certain women commonly called Beguines, afflicted by a kind of madness, discuss the Holy Trinity and the divine essence, and express opinions on matters of faith and sacraments contrary to the catholic faith, deceiving many simple people. Since these women promise no obedience to anyone and do not renounce their property or profess an approved Rule, they are certainly not 'religious' although they wear a habit and are associated with such religious orders as they find congenial . . . We have therefore decided and decreed with the approval of the Council that their way of life is to be permanently forbidden and altogether excluded from the Church of God.[93]

Following this proclamation by Pope John XXII in 1317, beguinages were ordered disbanded, their members to be absorbed into regular orders. A virtual witch-hunt ensued, as churchmen actively sought out and persecuted those who resisted this command, branding them as heretics in their zeal to dissociate themselves from those women whose piety they had earlier admired.

There is a distressingly similar pattern to all the instances cited in this general survey of women's religious movements from the twelfth to the fourteenth centuries. A small number of women seeking to dedicate themselves to a religious life manage, either through their own efforts, or with the assistance of a religious reformer, to establish a community. Other women, frustrated in their own efforts, flock to join. The males in question, possibly alarmed at the response, and certainly disturbed at the propinquity of so many women, feel their own spirituality threatened. They then turn on the women, dissociate themselves as much as possible, and eventually exclude the women altogether from the variety of religious experience which they had sought, and which the men were still free to enjoy.

Women, Vision and *discretio spirituum*

The preceding survey demonstrates that the commentaries on the nature of women not only define women, but also, either implicitly or explicitly, define men, because the human norm is believed to be male. Women are consistently identified with sensuality, with emotion, with passivity and with corporeality. Men are equally consistently identified with rationality, with intellect, with activity, and with spirituality. Where the 'natural' tendencies of each sex are so rigidly defined, the forms of transcendental experiences to which each can aspire are in consequence also rigidly defined. Women were assumed to be

---

93 Cited in Southern, *Western Society*, p. 330.

only capable of a sensual, inferior form of transcendental experience, such as that found in visions. Women's spirituality was seen to be focused on a divinity which was quantitatively, rather than qualitatively different, as befitted their perceived lack of abstract rationality. For males, on the other hand, the signposts to spiritual growth led through the paths of the mind, to an intellectual experience of the Godhead as qualitatively different, unimaginable and unknowable.

Consequently, it was difficult for medieval women to follow the paths which led to intellectual vision, that is, mystical experience. In part this was due to cultural and religious conditioning, in part due to the lack of exposure and opportunity to discover alternative forms of spirituality. One of the foremost factors in this restricted opportunity was briefly mentioned above. The majority of religious and theological works were written in Latin, thereby limiting their audience to the Latin-literate, a category which excluded most women. In the cultural diglossia of the western Middle Ages, Latin was a tool of the educated male, as Walter Ong points out.

> The Latin of the Middle Ages, which I have styled Learned Latin, had a commitment to writing that went far beyond that of the literary language of ancient Rome: Learned Latin was a fully textualized language, tied to the text as simple literary languages are not . . . everyone who knew Latin [in the Middle Ages] had learned it through writing.[94]

In addition to being written in Latin, many of the mystical treatises were developed and studied in the monastic schools and universities; their understanding demanded a mind trained in the complexities of philosophy and theology. Women did not have this kind of education. Not only were there proscriptions against women teaching, but also against their being taught. Paul's injunction 'But if they will learn anything, let them ask their husbands at home': (I Corinthians 14. 35) is evident in the subsequent restrictions on women's education. Predictably, in Michael Goodich's survey of 518 thirteenth-century saints, not one of the female saints had attended university.[95] Women read, or had read to them, mostly devotional material, gospel harmonies, saints' lives and accounts of visions. The bulk of this material was in the vernacular, and had those qualities which made it attractive for reading aloud: it was vivid, simply presented, colourfully described, repetitive and concrete. It had elements familiar to women from their own lives: domestic images, liturgical settings, descriptions of clothing and food, representations of family relationships. This material had a practical focus; it was largely designed to inspire pious behaviour and spiritual fervour. It is not surprising therefore that women found in this material, much of which featured female

---

[94] Ong, 'Orality', 6.
[95] M. Goodich, *Vita Perfecta: The Ideal of Sainthood in the Thirteenth Century* (Stuttgart, 1982), pp. 213–41.

protagonists, the models for their transcendental experiences. Caroline Bynum's studies of women's eucharistic devotion[96] and of the religious significance of food for women[97] demonstrate dramatically how women influenced each other in spiritual expression, and how this mutual influence served to unite and strengthen them. In much the same way that little girls earlier in this century were encouraged by example and precept, by educational opportunities and societal expectations, to become nurses and teachers rather than doctors and university professors, medieval women with a yearning for direct experience of the divine became visionaries and prophets rather than mystics or speculative theologians.

The link between prophecy and vision is clear. In his discussion of the grades of prophecy, Aquinas states: '. . . we term "prophets" in the more proper sense, those who see in imaginative visions'.[98] Later he elaborates:

> . . . a yet higher grade of prophecy obtains when the prophet not only sees symbols, words, or deed but also perceives, while awake or asleep, someone speaking with him or showing him something – because in this way it is shown that the prophet's mind is nearer to the cause of revelation . . . Still higher is that grade of prophecy, when, awake or asleep, there appears the very guise of God himself . . .[99]

Prophecy is the communication of that which had been hidden but which has been divinely revealed with the intent of influencing human behaviour or belief. 'But he that prophesieth speaketh unto men to edification and exhortation and comfort' (I Corinthians 14. 3). Aquinas states:

> The gift of prophecy is granted to a man both for the utility of others and the enlightenment of his own mind.[100]

Bernard of Clairvaux affirms both the relationship of vision to prophecy as well as the perception of vision as inferior to mystical experience in one of his sermons on the Song of Songs.

> But when the spirit is ravished out of itself and granted a vision of God that suddenly shines into the mind with the swiftness of a lightening flash, immediately, but whence I know not, images of earthly things fill the imagination, either as an aid to understanding or to temper the intensity of the divine light. So well adapted are they to the divinely illumined senses, that in their shadow the utterly pure and brilliant radiance of the truth is rendered more

96 C. W. Bynum, 'Women Mystics and Eucharistic Devotion in the Thirteenth Century', *Women's Studies* 11 (1984), 179–214.
97 Bynum, *Holy Feast*.
98 *ST 2a2ae* XLV, 77.
99 *ST 2a2ae* XLV, 81.
100 *ST 2a2ae* XLV, 41.

bearable to the mind and more capable of being communicated to others. My opinion is that they are formed in our imaginations by the inspirations of the holy angels, just as on the other hand there is no doubt that evil suggestions of an opposite nature are forced upon us by the bad angels.[101]

It is worth noting here that Bernard also indicates the danger posed by visions, that is, of deception by 'bad angels'.

Paradoxically, given that women generally experienced visions because of cultural limitations on their spirituality, it was as visionaries and prophets that women were empowered. Visions and prophecy provided them with an arena where they were authorized, through scripture, to operate with some degree of autonomy or independence. As Eleanor McLaughlin says:

> The equivalence of the female soul to that of the male here on earth is acknowledged only in the admission of the possibility of a woman receiving gifts of the Holy Spirit, gifts of prophecy.[102]

Women's authorization to prophesy rests in part on Old Testament precedents: Deborah (Judges 4. 4), Miriam (Exodus 15. 20), Huldah (II Kings 22. 14; II Chronicles 34. 22) and Anna, in the New Testament (Luke 2. 36–8), for example, were all chosen by God to be prophets.[103] Further authorization is offered when Paul speaks of women praying and prophesying (I Corinthians 11. 5) and seems to find this quite acceptable as long as they keep their heads covered. Prophecy is one of the special graces of the Holy Spirit, conferred at God's will and not part of the natural order of things (I Corinthians 12. 10).[104] Paul ranks prophets second in value in the Church, after apostles: 'And God hath set some in the church, first apostles, secondarily prophets, thirdly doctors, after that miracles, then the graces of healings, helps, governments, kinds of tongues, interpretations of speeches' (I Corinthians 12. 28).

Aquinas argues that while a woman cannot be ordained, she can be a prophet.

> Now, in the reality of the soul there is no distinction between man and woman, and sometimes a woman is better in her soul than a man. So she may well receive the gift of prophecy and other gifts like it, but she cannot receive the sacrament of Order.[105]

[101] *On the Song of Songs*, trans. K. Walsh OCSO (Kalamazoo, 1979–83), II, 206–7.

[102] McLaughlin, 'Equality', p. 236.

[103] See the discussion of Alfonso of Jaén's use of these women to supply a precedent for Bridget of Sweden's visionary activities, below, pp. 82–5.

[104] The fact of precedent did not in any way end the debate. There was continual discussion in patristic and medieval theology as to whether the medium affects the validity of the message; i.e. whether fools and madmen can speak moral sense, or unregenerate sinners give voice to sacred truths. Obviously, the role of women had a place in this debate.

[105] Cited in Børreson, *Subordination*, pp. 237–8.

Similarly, Hildegard of Bingen recounts a vision which suggests a complementarity between the roles of priest and visionary. God tells her that, while women cannot administer the sacraments, those who have dedicated themselves to Christ can experience union with him, which endows them with the equivalent spiritual graces.

> So too those of female sex should not approach the office of My altar; for they are an infirm and weak habitation, appointed to bear children and diligently nurture them . . . A virgin betrothed to My Son will receive Him as Bridegroom, for she has shut her body away from a physical husband; and in her Bridegroom she has the priesthood and all the ministry of My altar, and with Him possesses all its riches.[106]

An issue related to the ordination of women, which also has implications for women as prophets and visionaries is that of women preaching. Visionaries are divinely enjoined to communicate their revelations, but women are enjoined to keep silent. This matter excited considerable debate in the late Middle Ages. Proscriptions against women preaching were generally based on the Pauline injunctions that women should keep silent in the church (I Corinthians 14. 35–4) and should neither teach nor have authority over men (I Timothy 2. 12). Other arguments cited in support of female silence were the disastrous example set by Eve's teaching Adam, woman's perceived lack of intellection and susceptibility to heretical teaching, and the seductive qualities of the female voice.

One of the principal participants in this debate at the end of the thirteenth century was Henry of Ghent. After considering, in his *Summa quaestionum ordinarium*, the issues involved, he concludes that women are not suited to teach or preach in public, and that in private such activities should be limited to other women and girls.[107] A century later in England, the debate intensified in

---

[106] *Scivias*, trans. C. Hart and J. Bishop (New York, 1990), p. 278. Latin source CC XLIII, part 1, 290.

The complementarity of priest and visionary is explored by John Coakley in relation to Catherine of Siena. He writes '. . . one of her main uses of the supernatural power arising from her intimacy with Christ . . . was to provoke in people the contrition that brought them to make confession to priests' ('Friars as Confidants of Holy Women in Medieval Dominican Hagiography', in *Images of Sainthood in Medieval Europe*, ed. R. Blumenfeld-Kosinski and T. Szell (Ithaca, 1991), p. 238). This same phenomenon is noted by Caroline Bynum, who writes that while Mechthild of Magdeburg is acutely conscious of lacking priestly authority and learning, she is simultaneously convinced of 'her counseling, mediating, pedagogical and prophetic role as authorized by Christ' (*Jesus*, p. 245).

[107] A. J. Minnis, 'The *Accessus* Extended: Henry of Ghent on the Transmission and Reception of Theology', in *Ad litteram: Authoritative Texts and their Medieval Readers*, ed. M. D. Jordan and K. Emery Jr (Notre Dame, 1992), pp. 311–16 . This essay offers an illuminating analysis of Henry of Ghent's thought on the whole issue of who has

response to the claims of Walter Brut, tried for heresy before the Bishop of Hereford from 1391 to 1393. One of Brut's arguments was that women should be allowed to preach, and since, as he asserted that preaching was more important than administering the sacraments, that this office should also be open to women.[108]

The question of women's right to speak or teach in public is obviously crucial as far as visionaries and prophets are concerned. It was a contentious issue for Margery Kempe, and led to her being charged with Lollardy. It also dictated the careful presentation and justification of Bridget of Sweden's prophetic ministry which her editor, Alfonso of Jaén undertook in the *Epistola solitarii ad reges*.

Nevertheless, it was as visionaries and prophets that medieval women found a voice, and words to speak, words that were listened to because of their divine origin, not automatically discounted because of the body which uttered them. It is under the shelter of this grace that the great women visionaries influenced the lives and faith of their contemporaries and of subsequent generations. The charism of prophecy bestowed upon women a status and authority quite exceptional in this male-dominated world. Women visionaries were able to influence events to an extent that few other women could. Bridget of Sweden and Catherine of Siena actively worked for the return of the papacy to Rome. Joan of Arc was instrumental in driving the English out of France. Other visionaries criticized ecclesiastical corruption and political immorality. Because the woman visionary spoke as God's mouthpiece, she was able temporarily to transcend her gender.

Nevertheless, although prophecy is a suspension of the natural order, it does not supersede it; women, even those with the gift of prophecy, must still be subservient and subject to the will and wisdom of men. The gift of prophecy, like any other of the special graces, cannot be controlled. What can be controlled is the use to which those gifts are put. Aquinas sums this up when he discusses the crucial space between the receipt and transmission of prophetic revelation. God's voice speaks to the spirit, but it is the human mind which understands and gives words to the revelation. In all cases, prophetic utterances need to be carefully examined. Aquinas says that a prophet's mind is a deficient instrument [*mens prophetae est instrumentum deficiens*].[109] When the mind in question is female, and therefore perceived as intellectually weak and morally defective, the examination must be more severe.

---

the right to preach, teach or learn theology. For related issues concerning female ordination, see A. J. Minnis, '*De impedimento sexus*: Women's Bodies and Medieval Impediments to Ordination', in *Medieval Theology and the Natural Body*, ed. P. Biller and A. J. Minnis (York, 1997), pp. 109–40.

108 A. Blamires and C. W. Marx, 'Woman Not to Preach: A Disputation in British Library MS Harley 31', *The Journal of Medieval Latin* 3 (1993), 37.

109 *ST 2a2ae* XLV, 67.

Every teaching of women, especially that expressed in solemn word or writing, is to be held suspect, unless it has been diligently examined by another . . . and much more than the teaching of men.[110]

The gift of prophecy was not seen to make a woman less dangerous, less ready to deceive or more capable of intellection. The conjunction of deceitful woman and deceiving visions demanded very stringent checks and controls by ecclesiastical authorities. The mechanism, through which visionaries were authorized, controlled as well as empowered is *discretio spirituum*, the discernment of spirits. *Discretio spirituum* defined the visionary experience, it decreed the virtue and deportment of the visionary, it established forms of expression and criteria for assessment. And it facilitated – or restricted – dissemination of the writing of visionaries, under an implicit *imprimatur*.

The doctrine of *discretio spirituum* was not only of use to the clergy, but also provided a means for visionaries themselves to examine their visions; they were no less aware than the ecclesiastical authorities that Satan can appear as an angel of light. The sin lay not so much in having a false vision, as in communicating it to others. Only if visionaries conformed to the precepts of *discretio spirituum* could they effectively communicate their visionary experiences and execute their divine mission to influence human behaviour and belief. The consequences of communication without conformity were severe; Marguerite Porete (d. 1310) and Joan of Arc (1412–31) were burned at the stake, ostensibly because the visionary accounts which they had transmitted to others were deemed to be of demonic origin.

Conclusion

Visions and prophecy gave women a voice; that voice could be effectively raised only if the speaker and the words spoken submitted to the guidance of the church, and conformed to its precepts. Awareness of this requirement affected the ways in which women visionaries articulated their spiritual experiences. In the next chapter, I examine the development, up to the late Middle Ages, of the doctrine of *discretio spirituum* and argue that the doctrine became, in effect, a discourse, a discourse which provided both a vocabulary to articulate visionary experience and a set of criteria to evaluate the vision and the visionary. In Chapter Three, I then consider the influence of *discretio spirituum* on the *Revelaciones* of Bridget of Sweden, who was constructed according to its precepts and emerged as an exemplary visionary. The fourth chapter examines *The Book of Margery Kempe* and the problematic nature of Margery's presentation as a visionary, which, I argue, was due in part to her inconsistent fashioning according to *discretio spirituum*.

---

[110] Gerson, *Oeuvres* IX, 468. See also above, p. 7.

CHAPTER TWO

Seducing Spirits

> Dearly beloved, believe not every spirit, but try the spirits if they be of
> God: because many false prophets are gone out into the world.
>
> (I John 4. 1)

Introduction

In 1959 a Benedictine scholar, Paschal Boland, completed a dissertation for a
doctorate in Sacred Theology, entitled 'The Concept of *discretio spirituum* in
Jean Gerson's *De probatione spirituum* and *De distinctione verarum visionum a
falsis*'.[1] In his prologue, the author writes that this topic had been suggested to
him because 'of a need in our times . . . and because this subject of the discernment of spirits is so little known'.[2] His intention, he continues, is 'to draw up
two sets of concise rules . . . that priests could use as definite sets of norms in
making a judgement should someone come to him for advice concerning
visions or revelations'.[3] To accomplish this, Boland returns to the early
fifteenth-century writings of Jean Gerson, arguing that, despite much progress
in theology, very little has been added to the understanding or expression of
discretio spirituum since Gerson.

Boland's statements about his rationale are of interest to this study for two
reasons. First, that knowledge of *discretio spirituum* is so esoteric in modern
times that even parish priests need instruction in the concept; this is a different
state of affairs from that which existed in the late Middle Ages, when
knowledge of *discretio spirituum*, to a greater or lesser extent, was disseminated
through all levels of society.[4] Second, that the best source for modern instruction is perceived to be a medieval theologian, a medieval theologian,

---

1 Washington, DC, 1959. For *De probatione spirituum*, see Gerson, *Oeuvres* IX, 177–85;
for *De distinctione verarum revelationum a falsis*, see Gerson, *Oeuvres* III, 36–56. Note
that the *Opera Omnia*, ed. Ellies du Pin (Paris, 1706), on which Boland has based his
translation, uses the title *De distinctione verarum visionum a falsis* as opposed to the
Oeuvres Complètes title, *De distinctione verarum revelationum a falsis*.

2 Boland, *Concept*, p. ix.

3 Boland, *Concept*, p. x.

4 This is not to say that all medieval parish priests were necessarily experts in *discretio*

moreover, who was motivated, in 1415, to write one of his treatises, *De proba-tione spirituum*, in reaction to Bridget of Sweden's claims to visionary status. Gerson in turn based part of *De probatione spirituum* on the *Epistola solitarii ad reges* of Alfonso of Jaén. This treatise was written by Alfonso, Bridget's spiritual director and editor of her books of revelations, in 1375 or 1376,[5] to support and authorize Bridget by instructing his readers – her potential supporters in the canonization process – in the fine art of *discretio spirituum*.[6]

A similar didactic motive informs this chapter. Pascal Boland asserts a pastoral need to revive the knowledge of *discretio spirituum*. I assert a critical need. As I stated in my introduction, *discretio spirituum* has hitherto attracted little interest from medievalists, and its function in the writing of medieval visionaries has not been adequately recognized. As a result, the components of the doctrine have not been examined in recent scholarly literature. It will therefore be useful to identify the sources of the doctrine and to trace its evolution, thereby supplying a context for examination of its particular focus and especially stringent application to the visionary experiences and narra-tives of medieval women.

Alfonso's treatise is a synthesis of previous doctrine on *discretio spirituum* and like Gerson after him, and, nearly six centuries later, Pascal Boland, he provides his readers with a concise set of rules for judging visions and vision-aries. The *Epistola solitarii* is an example of applied *discretio spirituum*. Gerson's triad of works – there is also a 1423 treatise entitled *De examinatione doctri-narum*[7] – is a theoretical exposition of the topic. However, both authors draw on essentially the same sources, and, as mentioned above, Gerson recycles Alfonso's work for his own purposes, which included attempting to discredit Bridget of Sweden as a visionary.[8] This rather audacious borrowing brings to mind Alain de Lille's comment, that a certain authoritative passage 'has a wax nose, which means that it can be bent to take on new meanings'.[9]

---

spirituum. Ignorance and corruption amongst the lower ranks of the clergy were the targets of many of the reforms of the Fourth Lateran Council of 1215.

5   A. Jönsson, *Alfonso of Jaén: His Life and Works with Critical Editions of the Epistola solitarii, the Informaciones and the Epistola serui Christi* (Lund, 1989), p. 108.

6   E. Colledge, '*Epistola solitarii ad reges*: Alphonse of Pecha as Organizer of Birgittine and Urbanist Propaganda', *Mediaeval Studies* 43 (1956), 45.

7   Gerson, *Oeuvres* IX, 458–75.

8   Eric Colledge claims that Gerson borrowed his discussion of the sensation of 'sweet-ness' as a mark of divine favour, and his citation of his source, Hugh of St Victor's *De arrha animae*, directly from Chapter VI of the *Epistola solitarii*. Colledge also notes that Chapter II of the *Epistola* is very close to Gerson's *considerationes* VII–VIII ('*Epistola*', p. 45).

9   *De fide catholica*, PL CCX, 333. This was not the only time that Alfonso's words were bent into taking on new meanings. The author of *The Chastising of God's Children*, written quite soon after the *Epistola*, probably soon after 1382, borrows his material in

Bridget of Sweden's canonization and the establishment of her religious Order provoked considerable controversy and generated a number of works either attacking or defending her, in addition to those by Alfonso and Gerson. Most of these works deal with the issue of *discretio spirituum* to some degree, a fact which demonstrates the importance of this vital and pervasively influential force in medieval spiritual life. Its prescriptions, designed to let the angels rush in while keeping the demons howling outside, were specifically aimed at visions and visionaries, and for this reason it was a doctrine of particular importance to spiritual women. As discussed in Chapter One, women predominantly experienced spiritual visions, and both women and visions were believed to require rigorous testing.[10] *Discretio spirituum* established the forms which a vision could take which were acceptable to the Church, and outlined acceptable behaviour for a visionary. It therefore created expectations in both visionary and society, expectations which shaped the visionary experience, the form in which it was articulated, the behaviour of the visionary, and the way in which the visionary was perceived, particularly when the visionary was a woman. Consciousness of these expectations, in other words an awareness of the requirements of *discretio spirituum*, is evident in the writings of visionary women. It is also a significant factor in men's writing about visionary women, especially in the ways in which they authorize holy women by pointing to their virtuous behaviour, behaviour which conforms to the well-known and all-powerful criteria of *discretio spirituum*.

It is important to realize that *discretio spirituum*, although supremely influential, is not necessarily, or only, a restrictive factor in the experience of women visionaries. It can also empower them. Because it was so familiar a concept, with knowledge of its components disseminated widely, in a variety of ways, it provided visionary women with a complete model for behaviour and communication, a model which facilitated the communication and acceptance of their divine message. In this sense, *discretio spirituum* offered a means for visionary women to use the prescriptions and proscriptions of ecclesiastical authorities to accomplish their own ends, ends that they understood as divinely ordained. Certainly, visionaries whose lives and works are presented as abiding scrupulously and consciously by the principles of *discretio spirituum* fare better than those who, for one reason or another, fell short of its standards.

Chapters 19 and 20 almost verbatim from the *Epistola*. However, he uses the material to deter rather than inform; in his hands it becomes a warning as to how easily the unwary may be deceived by devils. See *The Chastising of God's Children and the Treatise of Perfection of the Sons of God*, ed. J. Bazire and E. Colledge (Oxford, 1957), p. 48. My forthcoming essay discusses this issue; see 'Rewriting the Letter: Variations in the Middle English Translation of the *epistola solitarii ad reges* of Alfonso of Jaén', in *The Translation of St Birgitta of Sweden's Works into the European Vernaculars*, ed. B. Morris and V. O'Mara (Turnhout, 1999).

[10] See above, pp. 34–7.

Where a visionary, for example, Bridget of Sweden, accepts the restrictions imposed by *discretio spirituum*, she is empowered. Where she does not conform, as Margery Kempe does not, her credibility as a visionary is diminished and she is disempowered. The last two chapters of this study consider the 'degrees of discretion' represented by Bridget of Sweden and Margery Kempe and relate this factor to their power as visionaries, measured in terms of perceived holiness or heresy, the distribution and influence of their visionary accounts and their subsequent reputation.

The Discourse of *discretio spirituum*

It is a central argument of this work that *discretio spirituum* constitutes a discourse which shaped the transcendental experience of the visionary, the articulation of that experience, and the expectations of her audience. This audience included the institutional Church, as well as interested, devout – and not-so-devout – religious and lay people.

It may be helpful at this point to offer a definition of discourse to assist in understanding this way of viewing *discretio spirituum*.[11] Discourses are systems of language use, with characteristic vocabularies and signifiers which establish and define themselves in contention with other discourses. Their boundaries are fluid and are continually being negotiated.

> [A discourse] defines the subjects it will treat in distinctive ways, formulating and giving prominence to particular problems and effectively excluding others from consideration. In doing so each [discourse] develops a characteristic vocabulary, establishes a particular order of priorities in its discussion and implies particular ideological valuations of the subjects it has defined.[12]

The discourse depends on where, and in relation to what it is operating, and on the position which its speaker holds within the institution or hierarchy generating the discourse. A discourse can also be non-verbal. As Diane Macdonell puts it, 'Whatever signifies or has meaning can be considered part of discourse.'[13] She cites Foucault, who writes that meanings are 'embodied in technical processes, in institutions, in patterns for general behaviour and in

---

[11] It is beyond the confines of this work to deal with the definition of discourse in depth; I wish here merely to clarify terminology and establish a basis for my own analysis of *discretio spirituum* as a discourse. A vast literature exists on the topic. A useful introduction, which contains a fairly comprehensive bibliography, is D. Macdonell, *Theories of Discourse: An Introduction* (Oxford, 1986).

[12] Stephen Copley, *Literature and the Social Order in Eighteenth-Century England* (London, 1984), p. 18.

[13] Macdonell, *Theories*, pp. 3–4.

pedagogical forms'.[14] This last statement is particularly relevant to under-standing *discretio spirituum* as a discourse. Much of what is measured and recorded in the writing of and about women visionaries relates to their behaviour and demeanour, to their bodies, to the submission and obedience which are believed to demonstrate their inward holiness.

The discourse of *discretio spirituum* perpetuates the ideological valuations of revelation developed by the Church. It is concerned exclusively with vision and visionaries, and although of course it is part of a larger religious discourse – a whole made up of many such parts – it is distinct and separable from that larger discourse. Simple religious orthodoxy – if there is such a thing – is not the same as conformity to *discretio spirituum*, and vice versa. Skill in the discourse of *discretio spirituum* is a discrete ability. At times aspects of the larger religious discourse are incorporated in the discourse of *discretio spirituum*, for example, when discussing the orthodoxy of specific revelations. However, the ruling discourse for matters to do with visions and visionaries is *discretio spirituum*. Knowledge of the discourse creates a community of under-standing.[15] It establishes a language in which the ineffable can be articulated[16] – and in which those articulations are examined, and either endorsed or condemned. It also formulates the criteria for those examinations, endorse-ments and condemnations. It stipulates how the visionary experience should be expressed, and, most important, who can speak and who should be heard.

Because the discourse of *discretio spirituum* derived from ecclesiastical doctrine, it was a discourse developed and defined by men. It was formulated by church fathers and male theologians and disseminated, usually in Latin, the men's language, through ecclesiastical networks. Through this discourse men define both the visionary experience and the visionary. A medieval woman who wanted recognition as a visionary, a recognition vital to accomplishing her divinely ordained task, had to have knowledge of the discourse in order to conform to the definition; she had to be able to translate her experience into the masculine discourse. While male visionaries also needed to operate within the discourse, there is a different emphasis when the discourse is employed by, or about, women visionaries. The emphasis in the construction of women vision-aries is on living virtuously under the rule of a spiritual director. Alfonso of Jaén gives this as the first and most definite sign of *discretio spirituum*.[17] As

---

[14] Macdonell, *Theories*, p. 4.

[15] See, for example, Brian Stock's discussion of textual communities in *The Implications of Literacy: Written Language and Models of Interpretation in the Eleventh and Twelfth Centuries* (Princeton, 1983), pp. 88–92.

[16] Augustine wrote of the burning desire to speak of God, and the simultaneous impos-sibility of doing so because any experience of God is ineffable. *De doctrina Christiana*, *PL* XXXIV, 21.

[17] References to the *Epistola soilitarii* will be given for two sources. The first is to the

stated above, for medieval women visionaries the discourse encompasses a mode of behaviour as well as of expression and articulation.

In order to identify the characteristics of *discretio spirituum*, this chapter will survey the main components of the doctrine, a survey which will fall into four sections. First, it will define the doctrine and look at its development during the patristic and scholastic periods; this survey will be organized around the sources used by Alfonso of Jaén in his *Epistola solitarii*. Second, it will consider the all-important role of the spiritual director of the visionary. Third, it will discuss popular knowledge of *discretio spirituum*. Fourth, it will examine how and why *discretio spirituum* was a discourse with particular application and relevance to women.

Discretio spirituum: Definition and Development

But when a good spirit seizes or ravishes the spirit of a man to direct it to an extraordinary vision, there can be no doubt that the images are signs of other things which it is useful to know, for this is a gift of God. The discernment [*discretio*] of these experiences is certainly a most difficult task when the evil spirit acts in a seemingly peaceful manner and, without tormenting the body, possesses a man's spirit and says what he is able, sometimes even speaking the truth and disclosing useful knowledge of the future. In this case he transforms himself, according to Scripture, as if into an angel of light, in order that, once having gained his victim's confidence in matters that are manifestly good, he may then lure his victim into his snares. This spirit, so far as I know, cannot be recognized except by that gift mentioned by St Paul, where he speaks of the different gifts of God: . . . 'to another the distinguishing of spirits' [*alii dijudicatio spirituum*].[18]

As Saint Augustine states above, *discretio spirituum* is the ability to distinguish spirits sent by God from those sent by the devil. This facility is a fundamental requirement for a religion which, as Christianity does, believes in the immanence of supernatural forces and the possibility of their irruption into everyday life. It is even more necessary in a culture which perceives God and

Latin version, printed by Bartholomaeus Ghotan in 1492, and edited by Arne Jönsson in *Alfonso of Jaén*, pp. 115–71. This will hereafter be abbreviated as Lat. followed by the chapter and sentence number. The second reference will be to my edition of the Middle English translation of the *Epistola* which forms an Appendix to this book. This reference will be given as Appendix, followed by the manuscript folio number and line number. So, for the above reference to the *Epistola solitarii*, see Lat. VI: 16; Appendix fol. 252v: 8–10.

18 *LMG* XLII, 196; *PL* XXXIV, 465. Augustine cites St Paul as speaking of the 'distinguishing' [*dijudicatio*] of spirits. The Vulgate (I Corinthians 12. 10) gives the verse as *alii discretio spirituum*.

the devil in a constant struggle for souls, and which believes that trickery and deceit are the devil's most potent weapons against God's absolute power. In this context, the ability to distinguish between the will of God and the wiles of the devil is a spiritual survival technique. Genesis teaches that Satan can assume any guise, and the history of post-lapsarian humanity is a testimony to the dire consequences of faulty discernment. The fact that it was Eve, a woman, who lacked *discretio spirituum*, discernment, is not immaterial.

Discretio spirituum is not intended to demonstrate whether or not visions occur, and spirits appear; that is a given of the Christian faith. *Discretio spirituum* is a means of control, intended to test the origin of the vision, the provenance of the spirit. Mystical, as opposed to visionary, experiences were not believed to be susceptible to demonic influence.[19] However, the visionary was thought to be particularly vulnerable, and needed to be always on guard against the devil's deceits. Fear of demonic delusion is evident in the writing of virtually all visionaries. Teresa of Avila, writing of her first transcendental experiences, demonstrates typical fears.

> [I] began to be afraid . . . and would begin to wonder if it was the devil who wanted me to believe it was a good thing, so that he might deprive me of mental prayer, and prevent me from thinking about the Passion and making use of my understanding.[20]

Their acute awareness of the snares placed for them made visionaries look for means to validate their experiences, to measure what they had seen and heard and felt against authoritative criteria. The desire for validation was particularly urgent for women visionaries, who had internalized the Church's teaching that women were by nature gullible, deceitful, and not to be trusted by others or even by themselves. This need of the visionaries was reinforced by the need of the ecclesiastical authorities to test the spirits, in order to protect both the faithful and the Church from the potentially demonic elements which lurked in vision and prophecy, without closing its collective ear to the voice of God. These authoritative criteria are embodied in the Church's doctrine of *discretio spirituum*, which attempts to respond to the imperative of the visionary experience while recognizing the presence of evil in the world. It acknowledges and enumerates the forms of evil which can beset the visionary, and expounds upon those virtues which the Church believes will enable the visionary to achieve her, or his, task of mediating between human and divine. As a discourse, *discretio spirituum* both facilitates the articulation and understanding of the visionary experience, defines its dangers and limitations, and controls what are deemed to be deviant forms of that experience.

19 See above, p. 11.
20 E. A. Pears, trans. and ed., *The Life: The Complete Works of St Teresa of Avila* (London, 1963), p. 145.

St Paul includes *discretio spirituum*, the discerning of spirits, among the charisms, or gifts given by the Holy Spirit.

> And the manifestation of the Spirit is given to every man unto profit./ To one indeed by the Spirit is given the word of wisdom: and to another the word of knowledge, according to the same Spirit./ To another, faith in the same spirit: to another, the grace of healing in one Spirit./ To another, the working of miracles: to another, prophecy: to another, the discerning of spirits: to another, diverse kinds of tongues: to another, the interpretation of speeches.
>
> (I Corinthians 12. 7–11)[21]

All of these are gifts of grace given for the general good of the whole church.[22] The public nature of *discretio spirituum* is most significant. It posits the existence of experts in the discernment of spirits, who can correctly identify spirits which they themselves encounter and spirits which are encountered by others. Although theoretically it was as possible for the charism of *discretio spirituum* to be visited upon a woman as upon a man, in practice the Church's perception of women as inferior and its sanctions against their teaching or preaching meant that women were unlikely to be permitted to exercise *discretio spirituum* publicly for the general good.[23] Additionally, by the late Middle Ages, it had come to be understood that *discretio spirituum* could be acquired through learning combined with grace.[24] In fact, Jean Gerson explicitly states in *De probatione spirituum* that the official method of discerning the spirits is achieved through a combination of ecclesiastical office and interior grace.[25] Grace alone without learning is not sufficient. This effectively appropriates the charism to ordained men, and deems all women and lay men incapable of exercising *discretio spirituum* without the guidance of an expert.

Despite its reservation to experts, essentially *discretio spirituum* is a simple concept. It originates in the belief that good and evil spirits, which may at first seem indistinguishable because the devil is a master of disguise, can in fact be distinguished by observing the virtue of the recipient, the circumstance of the apparition, the orthodoxy of the revelation, and the 'fruits' of the experience – that is, striving after goodness or succumbing to temptation. However, as the Church developed the doctrine, the components of *discretio spirituum* were

---

21 Scriptural roots for *discretio spirituum* are also found in Mark 7. 16; Romans 12. 1–2; Ephesians 5. 10–11; Philippians 1. 9–10; Galatians 5. 22–3; I John 2. 24 and 4. 1–6.

22 Boland, *Concept*, pp. 14–15.

23 It is significant that Julian of Norwich is identified in *The Book of Margery Kempe* as an expert in *discretio spirituum*, and that she is the only person whom the text records as teaching Margery the signs of *discretio spirituum* (*BMK*, p. 42). See below, pp. 126–8.

24 For an additional survey of medieval writing on *discretio spirituum* see D. Elliott, 'The Physiology of Rapture and Female Spirituality', in *Medieval Theology and the Natural Body*, ed. P. Biller and A. J. Minnis (York, 1997), pp. 141–74 (pp. 151–6).

25 Gerson, *Oeuvres* IX, 178; translation, Boland, *Concept*, p. 27.

elaborated through complex dissertations on such topics as the quality of virtue, the nature of visions, and the purpose of revelation. Accordingly, *discretio spirituum* became a very far-reaching concept, holding within its purview matters as diverse as the degree of humility proper to a visionary, and the nature of mystical union itself. This is reflected in writings on *discretio spirituum* which range from the anecdotal, such as Cassian's account of the solitary monk deceived by a demon,[26] to the analytical, for example, Bernard's twenty-third *Sermo de diversis*.[27] The multi-faceted nature of the concept means that its evolution was somewhat uneven, with different eras focusing on different aspects. Writers in the early Church tend to look to the fruits of spiritual revelation as the most important measure of validity, while the scholastics are more concerned with the virtue of the visionary. In the late Middle Ages the importance placed on the virtue of the recipient has particular relevance for the Church's attitude towards women visionaries, and is reflected in the emphasis in the discourse on meekness and submission.

The transmission of the principles of *discretio spirituum* takes two fundamental forms. First, as a formal doctrine, it is discussed, described and embodied in scriptural sources, and therefore appears in subsequent patristic and scholastic treatises, although, as mentioned above, the treatment is uneven. Secondly, by the late Middle Ages, the criteria which constitute *discretio spirituum* have become so fundamental to Christian belief and behaviour that they form a cultural substratum which informs and pervades spiritual experience. The multifaceted nature of the concept assists in this absorption, with some of its aspects overlapping with folklore: identifying a demon by its stench, knowing that the devil can quote scripture.[28] This chapter will first examine the formal treatment of *discretio spirituum*, by reviewing the source material cited by Alfonso of Jaén in the *Epistola solitarii*, and then consider some of the possible sources for lay familiarity with the discourse.

The *Epistola solitarii ad reges* of Alfonso of Jaén is a convenient place to begin an investigation of the medieval understanding of the concept of *discretio spirituum*, by enumerating the principles of the doctrine. In the *Epistola solitarii* Alfonso wrote that there are seven signs whereby one may tell a true visionary. The first, and most definite sign is whether the person lives a virtuous life under the rule of a spiritual director.

---

[26] John Cassian, *Conferences, A Select Library of Nicene and Post-Nicene Fathers*, ed. P. Schaf and H. Wace (Grand Rapids, 1978), XI, 310.

[27] *PL* CLXXXIII, 600–603. Both these texts are discussed below.

[28] Although such signs were not part of the doctrine of *discretio spirituum*, they perform the same function and were widely used. Julian of Norwich realized, by the smoke seeping under the door and the residual stink, that the fiend had come to tempt her (Julian of Norwich, *Showings*, 1, 267). Bridget of Sweden was overwhelmed by a nauseating stench when in the presence of blasphemers and sinners (*A&P*, p. 24).

The ferst most serteyn sygne is yat ye vision is of god when yat persone seinge visions is really meke and levis undir obediens of sum spiritual fadir vertuos and expert in spiritual lyff.[29]

The second sign is that, as a result of the vision, the soul feels inflamed by God's love and charity, and her faith, obedience and reverence to Holy Mother Church are strengthened. Third, that the visionary feels a deep inward knowledge of the truth of the revelation. Fourth, that the revelations are always and only of true things, and accord with Scripture and accepted teachings. Fifth, a true vision is known by the fruit which it bears. Sixth, true visionaries will have the day and hour of their death revealed to them. And finally, seventh, posthumous miracles will establish the status of the visionary beyond all question.

Alfonso's listing of these signs is actually a summary of his review of the principal authorities on *discretio spirituum*. The theologians and works to which Alfonso refers are: Cassian (360–435), *Collationes*; Augustine (354–430), Book XII of *De Genesi ad litteram*; Chrysostom (347–407), *Super Matheum Homilia XIX*; Jerome (342–420), *Prologus Apocalypsis*; Athanasius (296–373), *Vitae patrum: Vita beati Antonii abbatis*; Gregory the Great (540–604), *Moralia* and *Dialogi*; Hugh of St Victor (d. 1142), *Soliloquium de arrha animae*; Thomas Aquinas (1225–74), *Summa theologiae 2a2ae*; and Nicholas of Lyra (1270–1340), *Prologus super psalterium*. Alfonso examines each of the components of *discretio spirituum* by referring to his sources; the following survey will follow his organization.

Cassian in his *Collationes II* states that the only virtue which will preserve a monk from the 'snares and deceits of the devil' is *discretio spirituum*. All other virtues – fasting, vigils, solitude, charity and so on – can fail if discernment is wanting. It is *discretio spirituum* which informs thought and judgement and enables one to discern the presence of evil.

> You see then that the gift of discretion is no earthly thing and no slight matter, but the greatest prize of divine grace. And unless a monk has pursued it with all zeal, and secured a power of discerning with unerring judgement the spirits that rise up in him, he is sure to go wrong, as if in the darkness of night and dense blackness, and not merely to fall down dangerous pits and precipices, but also to make frequent mistakes in matters which are plain and straight forward.[30]

Not only is *discretio spirituum* the only protection against error; it is also the means to achieve union with the divine.

---

[29] Lat. VI: 16; Appendix fol. 252v: 7–10. The seven signs are given fully in the *Epistola solitarii* cap. VI, and recapitulated briefly in cap. VII. For the Latin see Lat. VI: 16 – VII: 7; for the Middle English translation see Appendix fols. 252v–254r.

[30] Cassian, *Conferences*, p. 308.

... it is discretion which leads a fearless monk by fixed stages to God, and preserves the virtues ... continually intact, by means of which one may ascend with less weariness to the extreme summit of perfection, and without which even those who toil most willingly cannot reach the heights of perfection.[31]

Having established the vital significance of *discretio spirituum*, Cassian explains how to achieve it.

True discretion ... is only secured by true humility. And of this humility, the first proof is given by reserving everything (not only what you do but what you think) for the scrutiny of the elders, so as not to trust at all in your own judgement but to acquiesce in their decisions in all points, and to acknowledge what ought to be considered good or bad by their tradition.[32]

Cassian's cautionary tale, mentioned earlier, of how a monk was deceived by the devil, demonstrates how a life of heroic virtue can come to nothing if discernment is lacking. The monk in question had lived an ascetic life in the desert for fifty years. However:

... having too little of the virtue of discretion he preferred to be guided by his own judgement rather than to obey the counsels and conferences of the brethren and regulations of the elders.[33]

His excessive devotion to his own solitude and his fear of relaxing his virtuous observance in the company of his fellow monks lead him to receive a demon disguised as an angel and to obey the demon's command to throw himself down a well; he is assured that his virtues are so great that he can come to no harm. Even when he does come to harm, and has to be rescued, he still maintains his belief in the supposed angel, and dies in a state of delusion and sin. In spite of his fifty years of great virtue, his lack of *discretio spirituum* brought him to a bad end.

Given that the purpose of *discretio spirituum* is to distinguish demonic illusions from angelic manifestations, the circumstances of the apparition must be considered. Alfonso appeals to the wisdom of Gregory the Great, for a pronouncement on the ways in which visions can be received, and in particular, on visions experienced during sleep. Visions received in dreams are especially problematical, since the senses are less guarded by the soul in sleep.[34] Generally, visions in sleep, or dreams, are held to be much less reliable

---

31 Cassian, *Conferences*, p. 310.
32 Cassian, *Conferences*, p. 312.
33 Cassian, *Conferences*, p. 310.
34 Avicenna, however, sees dreams as one of many sources of inspiration which assist the soul. Prophetic dreams 'result from a direct action of angelic intelligences upon

than those experienced while awake.[35] Nevertheless, dreams and sleeping visions cannot be dismissed out of hand; after all, an angel appeared to Joseph while he slept.[36] Gregory the Great addresses this problem in his *Dialogues*.

> Seeing, then, that dreams may arise from such a variety of causes, one ought to be very reluctant to put one's faith in them, since it is very hard to tell from what source they come. The saints, however, can distinguish true revelations from the voices and images of illusions through an inner sensitivity.[37]

Another factor which was of great importance in *discretio spirituum* is the nature of the vision: corporeal, spiritual (or imaginative), or intellectual. This hierarchy of vision derives from the taxonomy devised by Augustine based on the reliability of the various types of vision.[38] Alfonso refers to Augustine's *De Genesi ad litteram*. Summarizing his hierarchy of vision, Augustine writes:

> In one and the same soul, then, there are different visions: by means of the body it perceives objects such as the corporeal heaven and earth and everything that can be known in them in the degree that they are capable of being known; with the spirit it sees likenesses of bodies . . . and with the mind it understands those realities that are neither bodies nor the likeness of bodies. But there is, of course, a hierarchy in these visions, one being superior to another. For spiritual vision [*visio spiritualis*] is more excellent than corporeal [*corporalis*], and intellectual vision [*visio intellectualis*] more excellent than spiritual.[39]

The rationale behind this hierarchy is quite simple: 'Corporeal and spiritual vision can err, but not intellectual vision.'[40] Alfonso also cites Jerome, *Prologus Apocalypsis*, in support of the three principal kinds of vision, and the hierarchy of vision.

Next, Alfonso turns to Augustine for his definition of ecstasy, that state into which the soul is swept up by the immediate experience of the divine.

> But when the attention of the mind is completely carried off and turned away from the senses of the body, then there is rather the state called ecstasy. Then

---

the mind in sleep, acting upon the imagination'. Cited in M. Carruthers, *The Book of Memory: A Study of Memory in Medieval Culture* (Cambridge, 1990), p. 59.

[35] Steven Kruger, in *Dreaming in the Middle Ages* (Cambridge, 1992), examines patristic discussion of dream visions, and develops a useful hierarchy to demonstrate Gregory's relation of the varied causes of dreams to their benignity or malevolence. For example, dreams caused by overeating are morally neutral, whereas dreams which are demonically inspired are deceptive and malevolent (pp. 43–53).

[36] Matthew 2. 13 and 19.

[37] Gregory the Great, *Dialogues*, trans. O. J. Zimmerman OSB (New York, 1959), p. 262.

[38] See above, p. 11.

[39] Augustine, *LMG* XLII, 213; *PL* XXXIV, 474–5.

[40] Augustine, *LMG* XLII, 212; *PL* XXXIV, 475.

any bodies that are present are not seen at all, though the eyes may be wide open; and no sounds at all are heard. The whole soul is intent upon images of bodies present to spiritual vision or upon incorporeal realities present to intellectual vision without benefit of bodily images.[41]

This definition is particularly significant when dealing with visionaries, as Alfonso is doing, because it distinguishes between corporeal vision as a bodily sense and the other two forms of vision, spiritual and intellectual, as faculties of the soul. In this way spiritual vision is linked with intellectual vision as a valid means of communication with the divine, and ecstasy becomes an indication of the receptivity of the soul.[42] Within the category of spiritual vision, Alfonso argues that there are levels of excellence.[43] He states that the value of the vision is commensurate with the status of the apparition; if the likeness is of God, it is of a higher order than a likeness of a human messenger, or an angel, and appeals to Nicholas of Lyra's prologue to his commentary on the psalter for support.

As discussed in Chapter One, visions and prophecy are related phenomena in that both have a community orientation, both carry the injunction to communicate the message, both involve seeing and hearing things with the spiritual senses, and both, according to scriptural and theological tradition, are visited upon women as well as upon men. This aspect of *discretio spirituum*, which is concerned with the fruits of revelation and with discovering false prophets, develops in concert with doctrine on prophecy. Alfonso cites extensively from Thomas Aquinas's reflections on prophecy.[44] This reference to one of the most influential scholastic theologians has the dual effect of further authorizing Alfonso's treatise on *discretio spirituum* and preparing the ground for establishing Bridget as a prophet as well as a visionary.

One of the signs of a false prophet is, naturally enough, a false prophecy. In his *Summa Theologiae*, Aquinas states:

Demons manifest to men what they know, not by enlightening their intelligences, but by giving them imaginative vision, or even by addressing them in terms of sense impressions. In this way, this type of prophecy falls short of true prophecy.Certain signs, even external signs, make possible the discernment of true prophecy from false. So it is said, 'Some prophesy in the spirit of

---

[41] Augustine, *LMG* XLII, 186; *PL* XXXIV, 464.

[42] See pp. 86–8, below, for Alfonso's exploitation of this association of spiritual and intellectual vision in order to enhance the presentation of Bridget's visions.

[43] It is spiritual vision which is of particular concern to Alfonso, since this is the type of vision which Bridget generally experiences.

[44] Aquinas is not really concerned with determining the provenance of inspiration; his major interest in this area is judging false prophets. See *ST 2a2ae* XLV, 43–9. Paschal Boland notes that while Aquinas discusses the charisms of prophecy and of miracles in great detail, he scarcely mentions *discretio spirituum* ('Concept', p. 13).

the devil, and these are diviners: but we can distinguish these, because at times the devil proclaims something untrue, the Holy Spirit never'.[45]

Alfonso also cites Chrysostom, *Super Matheum, Homilia XIX* on the fact that false prophecies come from the devil, whereas the prophecies of the Holy Spirit never prove untrue.

In addition to true prophecies, a significant fruit of revelation is the positive emotional reaction of the visionary. Happiness and joy are signs of the divine, fear a sign of the devil. Often, it is true, the initial reaction to a divine apparition is fear, but this is inevitably followed by intense joy, which is usually long lasting. A demonic presence, on the other hand, either invokes continual fear, or initial joy followed by fear and panic. Alfonso cites Hugh of Saint-Victor, *De arrha animae*, and Athanasius, *Vita beati Antonii abbatis*, on the sensation of sweetness and joy which is an identifying feature of true visions.[46] As Athanasius writes:

> The distinguishing of good from evil spirits is not difficult: if fear is followed by joy, we know that the help of God has come to us. The security of the soul is a mark of the presence of divine majesty. If, on the contrary, the fear remains, then the enemy is present.[47]

These are the sources which Alfonso cites specifically in the *Epistola solitarii* in support of some of the principles which he includes in the doctrine of *discretio spirituum*.[48] It is significant, though, that his discussion of the virtue of the visionary is not so closely tied to the sources. He does use Cassian's anecdote of the deluded monk to emphasise the need to submit visions to outside judgement. However, Alfonso's insistence that the 'first most certain' sign of a true visionary is her meekness and her humble obedience to her spiritual director is largely supported by examples of Bridget's own meekness and submissive behaviour. Given that Alfonso is advocating Bridget as an

---

45 Aquinas, *ST 2a2ae* XLV, 43–5. This reference is to q. 172. However, in both the Latin and the Middle English texts of the *Epistola* this source is mistakenly given as *2a2ae*: 173. See Lat. VI: 48; Appendix fol. 253r: 4.

46 *PL* CLXXVI, 970.

47 Athanasius, *The Life of St Anthony*, trans. R. Meyer (Westminster, Md, 1950), p. 43.

48 Other earlier treatments of *discretio spirituum* to which Alfonso does not allude directly include *The Shepherd of Hermas*, a second-century Greek account of revelations given for the edification of the Church, a work which had wide distribution in its Latin version; John Climacus (*c.* 570–649), *Scala paradisi*; the fifth-century bishop of Photike, Marcus Diadochus, *De perfectione spirituali*; Richard of St Victor (d. 1173), *Benjamin minor*; Henri de Freimar (d. 1340), *De quatuor instinctibus: divino, angelico, diabolico, mundano*; and Bernard of Clairvaux, *Sermo XXIII de diversis*. While Alfonso did not refer specifically to these works, they form part of the canon on *discretio spirituum*, reiterating and reinforcing the same doctrines as the sources that Alfonso does use.

exemplary visionary, this is hardly surprising, but the lack of reference to authoritative sources does suggest that Alfonso's focus on the virtue of the visionary is a relatively new one. Although Alfonso adopts this focus in relation to Bridget, it is Jean Gerson, a near contemporary of Alfonso's, who was responsible for formally articulating, on a general level, the appropriate demeanour for a visionary and for delineating the role of the spiritual director of a visionary.

Jean Gerson was Chancellor of the University of Paris from 1395 until his death in 1429. He was one of the most prominent theologians of the era and an extremely powerful conciliarist.[49] His work on *discretio spirituum* is of particular interest to this study because some of it was written in reaction to the acclamation accorded to Bridget of Sweden, an acclamation chiefly orchestrated by Alfonso, through his editing of her revelations and his promotion of her cause. In 1415 the 1391 canonization of Bridget was presented to the Council of Constance for confirmation. The extremely volatile state of papal politics throughout the decades following the initial submission and approval of Bridget's cause made her followers somewhat nervous, and desirous of an ironclad acknowledgement of her sainthood.[50] Although Gerson, a delegate to the Council, did not argue with Bridget's claim to sanctity, he did question the veracity of her visions, and felt compelled to write *De probatione spirituum* in an attempt to refute *unius quae Brigitta nominatur*[51] and to clarify the Church's teaching on visions. He had already produced an earlier treatise on *discretio spirituum*, *De distinctione verarum revelationum a falsis* (1400–1401) and later wrote *De examinatione doctrinarum* (1423).[52] In his systematic assembly of the accumulated wisdom and scattered teachings on *discretio spirituum* with the

---

[49] Gerson's pastoral teaching as well as some of his writings on mysticism are explored in C. Brown, *Pastor and Laity in the Theology of Jean Gerson* (Cambridge, 1987). With regard to Gerson's treatises on *discretio spirituum*, Brown points out that he is drawing on a well-established tradition for his material (p. 173). This tradition is the same, and derives from the same sources, as that which Alfonso draws on. However, Gerson organized and codified the material.

[50] Bridget's canonization was duly reconfirmed by John XXIII on 1 February 1415. However, her supporters were still not satisfied, and a further confirmation was given by Martin V at Florence on 1 July 1419. Eric Colledge summarizes what he terms 'The great Birgittine debate' in '*Epistola*', 42–6. André Vauchez also examines the circumstances surrounding Bridget's triple canonization in *The Laity in the Middle Ages: Religious Beliefs and Devotional Practices*, ed. D. Bornstein, trans. M. J. Schneider (Notre Dame, 1993), p. 249.

[51] Gerson, *Oeuvres* IX, 179.

[52] Gerson deals with *discretio spirituum* peripherally in several other works. These include: *De diversis diaboli tentationibus*; *De arte audiendi confessiones*; *De modo inquirendi peccata in confessione*; *De correptione proximi*; *De officio pastorum*; *Judicium de vita sanctae Erminae*; *De vitae spirituali animae*; and *Regulae morales*. Brief annotations of these works are given in Boland, *Concept*, pp. 20–21. A justifiable addition to this

intention of establishing the criteria for the discernment of spirits, Gerson deserves the recognition which Paschal Boland bestows upon him.

> Although Gerson is never specifically credited with being the first to treat the subject of discernment of spirits *ex professo* and to formulate a set of norms for discernment, we attribute this oversight to the gradual development of the teaching regarding the discernment of spirits, for our research shows him to be the first one to do this.[53]

Gerson even developed a rhetorical *circumstantia* for *discretio spirituum*:

> *Tu, quis, quid, quare*
> *Cui, qualiter, unde, require.*
>
> *Who* is it to whom the revelation is made? *What* does the revelation itself mean, and to what does it refer? *Why* is it said to have taken place? *To whom* was it manifested for advice? *What kind* of life does the visionary lead? *Whence* does the revelation originate?[54]

In addition to its synthesis of previous teaching on *discretio spirituum*, the main features of interest in Gerson's writing on the doctrine are his delineation of the role and character of the spiritual director of the visionary, and his recognition of the significance of the individual circumstances of each visionary in relation to *discretio spirituum*. Among the factors which Gerson recognized as influencing the visionary experience are the social and economic status of the seer, and his or her gender. The significance of the former in relation to Bridget of Sweden and Margery Kempe, and their familiarity with the discourse of *discretio spirituum* will be examined in the last two chapters. The latter issue, of course, informs my entire study. Gerson demanded greater care in testing the spirits of women visionaries, and delineated a variety of problems associated with their pastoral treatment; his attitude to female visionaries will be examined later in the chapter. However, his discussion of the role and character of the spiritual director serves as a useful introduction to an examination of the principal way in which *discretio spirituum* was institutionalized, and functioned as a control mechanism for medieval visionaries. This chapter will now consider how *discretio spirituum* functioned as a discourse disseminated and reinforced by the churchmen who served variously as confessors, directors, editors and amanuenses to visionaries.

---

list is Gerson's 1429 treatise on Joan of Arc, *De puella aurelianensi*, in which he argues that her revelations were genuine.

[53] Boland, *Concept*, pp. 74–5.

[54] Gerson, *Oeuvres* IX, 180; trans. Boland, *Concept*, p. 30. *Circumstantiae* were based on the teaching of the ancient rhetoricians that everything which could form the subject of a dispute or discussion could be reduced to a series of basic questions. Alastair Minnis discusses this topic in *Medieval Theory of Authorship: Scholastic Literary Attitudes in the Later Middle Ages* (Philadelphia, 1988), pp. 16–17 and 19.

The Role of the Spiritual Director of Visionaries[55]

By the late Middle Ages, the spiritual director is seen as absolutely vital to *discretio spirituum*. The charism of *discretio spirituum* is effectively reserved to the clergy, and one of the principles repeatedly emphasized is the danger of visionaries relying on their own judgements. This last is undoubtedly a recognition of the psychologically distorting effects of the ascetic life, and of solitude. It is equally undoubtedly a recognition by the Church of the charismatic power of visions and visionaries and of its need to harness such forces. The spiritual director is the instrument by which the visionary can be both counselled and controlled. His function is to examine the spiritual life of the visionary and to assess the nature and content of vision and revelation according to the principles of *discretio spirituum*. Gerson uses the image of the testing of coins.

> Just as is the case with gold, this spiritual coin of revelation ought to be examined on five special points: weight, malleability or impressibility, durability, truth of shape and design and charity of colour.[56]

The relationship between spiritual director and visionary is, of necessity, complex, since *discretio spirituum* is not a single test. It involves continual evaluation and validation of visionary and vision on multiple levels. It is also fallible.

> . . . so far as man is concerned, there is no general norm or natural ability for distinguishing always and infallibly the revelations that are genuine from those that are false and illusory.[57]

Nevertheless, the spiritual director constitutes the first line of defence in the Church's battle against demonic infiltration.

The spiritual director is always described as an older, wiser man, although the mention of age is generally more of an honorific than a chronological reality. For example, Alfonso uses the terms 'discreet senior' and 'religious spiritual men'.[58] The ability to exercise *discretio spirituum* can be acquired, with, of course, the assistance of grace, through study and reflection, through familiarity with mystical theology, the lives of ascetics, and the teachings of Holy Writ and Holy Church. Ideally, however, the spiritual director should

---

55 This discussion will focus largely on the role of the spiritual director of women visionaries. Although there are factors common to the supervision of both male and female visionaries, there are enough significant differences to warrant a separate study of male visionaries.

56 Gerson, *Oeuvres* III, 39; trans. Boland, *Concept*, p. 81.

57 Gerson, *Oeuvres* III, 37; trans. Boland, *Concept*, p. 78.

58 Lat. II: 4 and III: 9; Appendix fol. 248v: 5 and 8 and fol. 249v: 7.

also possess the charism of *discretio spirituum*. Both Alfonso and Gerson argue that the director should himself have had transcendental experiences; Gerson writes that at the very least, he should be a sound theologian and an advanced contemplative.[59] As stated earlier, all these qualifications effectively define the ability to exercise *discretio spirituum* as male.

The understanding, skill and knowledge of a visionary's counsellor are therefore of paramount importance, since the spiritual director of a woman visionary is in the position of supplying what she lacks. As well as exercising *discretio spirituum*, he is likely to be required to give devotional instruction to his charge, to assist in the writing and translation of her revelations, and to be instrumental in their distribution. In other words he performs those tasks which gender hinders the female visionary from doing herself; his involvement is crucial and bestows a kind of *imprimatur* on the writings and, indeed, on her life.[60]

In addition, a spiritual director who is socially adept and well-versed in ecclesiastical politics can make a great deal of difference to the acceptance of a visionary who, as a woman, is restricted in promoting herself. For example, Alfonso of Jaén was from the Spanish nobility and had risen to the rank of bishop.[61] He had friends in high places, and his social background would have been a valuable asset in addressing the kings and princes, of the Church and of the realm, who were the principal focus of many of Bridget's visions. Jacques de Vitry (1170–1240), director, confessor and biographer of Marie d'Oignies, eventually became a cardinal. He used his power in the Church hierarchy to enhance her memory and to support the Beguine movement in Liège.[62] It is interesting to speculate what might have become of Margery Kempe had she been allied with a similarly influential spiritual director.[63]

---

[59] For Alfonso see: Lat. I: 15; Appendix fol. 247v: 1–5. For Gerson see: Gerson, *Oeuvres* IX, 179; Boland, *Concept*, p. 29. Catherine Brown expresses doubt that Gerson had mystical experiences, because he states that he is not qualified to write about such matters (*Pastor*, p. 205). He was undoubtedly, though, 'a sound theologian and an advanced contemplative'.

[60] This latter effect of the spiritual director is evident in Richard Kieckhefer's comment about Dorothea of Montau, a late fourteenth-century holy woman who undertook horrifying austerities, and spent the last year of her life as an anchoress at Marienwerder: '. . . in submitting herself to a respected spiritual director [John of Marienwerder] she obtained ecclesiastical legitimation for her austerities and her alienation from the world; no longer merely signs of eccentricity, they became marks of sanctity' (*Unquiet Souls: Fourteenth-Century Saints and their Religious Milieu* (Chicago, 1984), p. 31).

[61] Jönsson, *Alfonso*, p. 42; Colledge, 'Epistola', p. 20.

[62] Brenda Bolton discusses de Vitry's involvement with the Beguines and his work to protect them from charges of heterodoxy in 'Mulieres', 144–9.

[63] For Margery Kempe's difficulties with her spiritual directors, and in finding an amanuensis, see below, pp. 113 and 122–8.

While the spiritual director obviously plays a crucial role in the life and work of a female visionary, she supplies something the director lacks.[64] He is an ordained cleric, with sacerdotal power to which the visionary, because of her sex, cannot aspire. However, she has been chosen by God as his intermediary, and this mark of holiness is something which the director is unlikely to achieve. Often, this gives rise to intense admiration and leads to a remarkably close relationship between the visionary and her spiritual director.[65]

It seems that some churchmen specialized in the pastoral care of women visionaries.[66] Often the association lasted until the death of either visionary or spiritual director. Sometimes the director remained active in the service of the visionary after her death, promoting her canonization, or editing and disseminating her writings. Such was the case with Alfonso and Bridget, for example, and with Catherine of Siena and Raymond of Capua, who was her confessor and confidant from 1374 until her death in 1380, and who then assumed the responsibility for editing her *Dialogue*. Sometimes the cleric sought out the holy woman, as Guibert of Gembloux did with Hildegard of Bingen. He was inspired by his correspondence with her, and on the death of her previous secretary, came to Bingen in 1177 and remained with her until her death in 1179.[67] It also seems that certain clerics would administer to a number of holy women, evidently gaining both expertise and something of a reputation in the field. Jacques de Vitry is a case in point. As noted above, he was confessor to

---

64 Paul Strohm discusses the concept of holy women supplying what he terms 'a male lack'. He argues that medieval queens also perform the same function. *Hochon's Arrow: The Social Imagination of Fourteenth-Century Texts* (Princeton, 1992), p. 103.

65 John Coakley has compared the *vitae* of holy women and male saints written by Dominicans between the thirteenth and sixteenth centuries. He writes: 'As confidants [the spiritual directors of holy women] have no counterparts in *vitae* of Dominican men. On the other hand, neither are they unique to their order; Dominicans had no monopoly on attachment to holy women . . .'. See 'Friars', p. 223. Brian Patrick McGuire examines the mixed nature of the relationship between holy women and their confessors in 'Holy Women and Monks in the Thirteenth Century: Friendship or Exploitation?', *Vox Benedictina* 6:4 (1989), 343–73.

66 A list of some of the better known medieval women visionaries and their confessors is given in Valerie Lagorio, 'The Continental Women Mystics of the Middle Ages: An Assessment', in *The Roots of the Modern Christian Tradition*, ed. E. R. Elder (Kalamazoo, 1984), pp. 74–5. It could be argued that in their alliance with individual holy women, these clerics are continuing an honourable tradition beginning with St Paul and Priscilla, continued through Jerome and his female disciples, Augustine and his mother and so on. These alliances demonstrate that it was possible for individual women to separate themselves, or be separated, from their suspect sisters; however, the accomplishments of these individuals seems not to have affected the general perception of women.

67 B. Newman, *Sister of Wisdom: St Hildegard's Theology of the Feminine* (Berkeley, 1987), p. 14.

Marie d'Oignies, whom he apparently admired greatly, and whose *vita* he wrote.[68] After her death in 1213 he continued to be an advocate and supporter of other Beguines in Liège.[69] After the death of Bridget, Alfonso of Jaén visited Catherine of Siena in 1374, at the request of Pope Gregory XI, to ask her to discern God's will for the pope.[70] He also visited Clara of Gambacorta in 1378 and was instrumental in her dedication to a holy life, against the wishes of her family.[71]

In more ways than one the fortune of the spiritual director was tied to the success of the visionary: a cleric who promoted a visionary who was then perceived to be deluded – or worse, heretical – was unlikely to make great career gains; his fate in the hereafter hardly bears thinking of. The problems inherent in hitching one's wagon to a visionary star are exemplified in the doubts and internal debate which consumed Fra Arnaldo, director of Angela of Foligno, a late thirteenth-century Italian visionary, before he committed himself to promoting her status as a visionary. He was at first embarrassed by, and suspicious of, her extravagant devotion, and began to write her revelations with the intention of submitting them to 'some wise and spiritual man' who would, Arnaldo was sure, judge them to be delusions.[72] He was eventually convinced of the truth of her visions, but admits that he failed to write everything down 'out of my fear of my brothers who opposed my work'.[73] Similar doubts are also evident in the reluctance of Margery Kempe's amanuensis to take on the task, until he is given signs which he can interpret as divine authorization.[74]

Up to this point, this chapter has been primarily concerned with the dissemination of *discretio spirituum* through institutional ecclesiastical

---

[68] Jacques de Vitry, *The Life of Marie d'Oignies*, trans. and ed. M. H. King (Toronto, 1989).

[69] Bolton, '*Mulieres*', pp. 144–9.

[70] *Epistolario di Santa Caterina da Siena*, ed. Eugenio Dupré-Theseider, 2 vols. (Rome, 1940), I, 85.

[71] Colledge, '*Epistola*', p. 34. Richard Kiekhefer examines Clara's life and spirituality in detail in *Unquiet*.

[72] Angela of Foligno, *Works*, pp. 136–7.

[73] Angela of Foligno, *Works*, p. 138. See also C. M. Mooney, 'The Authorial Role of Brother A. in the Composition of Angela of Foligno's Revelations', in *Creative Women in Medieval and Early Modern Italy: A Religious and Artistic Renaissance*, ed. E. A. Matter and J. Coakley (Philadelphia, 1994), pp. 34–63.

[74] See below, pp. 111–13. It is interesting to note that this state of affairs still obtains. In his study of canonization past and present, Kevin Woodward cites a contemporary member of the Congregation for the Causes of Saints as saying '. . . the servants of God experience much misunderstanding and detraction in their pursuit of holiness. Those who undertake to promote the causes of the Servants of God must expect the same.' *Making Saints: How the Catholic Church Determines Who Becomes a Saint, Who Doesn't, and Why* (New York, 1990), p. 22. For a discussion of issues which arose between scribe and visionary over the writing of revelations, see my article 'Words

channels, that is, through the writings of the Church Fathers and later theologians, and through the offices of the spiritual director. However, knowledge of *discretio spirituum* was by no means limited to those with a formal theological training. As Colledge remarks, 'It was a commonplace to use the Scriptural allusion, which hardly any medieval writer on the subject can resist, that the Devil knows well how to disguise himself as an angel of light.'[75] This chapter will now consider some of the vehicles whereby knowledge of *discretio spirituum* was made available to a wider spectrum of the medieval population. It was through this wider diffusion of awareness of the means of discerning the spirits that the discourse of *discretio spirituum* pervaded society.

Popular Knowledge of *discretio spirituum*

Belief in the omnipresence of good and bad spirits meant that Christians, both lay and religious, had a profound interest in distinguishing between the two. In his study of apparitions in late medieval Spain, William Christian traces the roots of lay familiarity with discerning the spirits.

> It is not difficult to see how . . . familiarity with divine spirits, which first grew in Christian culture among the desert saints, could pass from monastic to lay culture. With it came a series of techniques for distinguishing good spirits from false ones.[76]

Popular knowledge of *discretio spirituum* was acquired largely through such media as scriptural stories, saints' lives, collections of *exempla*, stories of otherworld journeys, cautionary tales and advice manuals, many of which formed the basis for sermons and pastoral instruction. Sometimes discerning the spirits overlapped with magic in the popular mind, particularly as regards the appearance and activities of demons. Herbal remedies and amulets are recommended for those troubled by evil spirits.[77] In order to prescribe such remedies, however, one needed to identify evil spirits in the first place. Medieval iconography made graphic clues as to the appearance of demons readily available to those concerned with such matters, as did accounts of otherworld journeys such as *The Treatise on the Purgatory of St Patrick*. This late twelfth-century narrative of the extraterrestrial adventures of the Knight Owen was translated into most European vernaculars, rendered in verse, and

of Flame and Moving Cloud: The Articulation Debate in the Revelations of Medieval Women Visionaries', in *The Medieval Translator* VI, ed. R. Ellis and R. Tixier (Turnhout, 1998), pp. 159–74.

75 Colledge, '*Epistola*', pp. 39–40.

76 Christian, *Apparitions*, p. 6.

77 See Richard Kieckhefer, who describes the composition and hoped-for effect of some of these amulets in *Magic in the Middle Ages* (Cambridge, 1989), pp. 75–7.

used by preaching friars as a vehicle for lay religious instruction, particularly for evoking dread of purgatory.[78] It contains vivid descriptions of demons howling and shrieking, as well as instructions for avoiding their clutches.Some romances, the Arthurian cycle for example, provided models for appropriate behaviour by penitent sinners, and gripping accounts of the lengths to which the devil will go to capture a soul. The early thirteenth-century *Queste del Sainte Graal* in particular, with its allegorical underpinning of the soul's quest for union with the divine, demonstrates the dangers of demonic entrapment inherent in trusting one's own spiritual judgement, and advocates frequent and honest consultation with holy men, especially over the interpretation of visions. Holy men (and one holy woman) and hermits are conveniently encountered by the Quest knights whenever they have experienced a troubling dream or some form of temptation. These 'older, wiser, spiritual men' then discern the spirits and advise the knights. Such tales and romances exposed the lay audience to the habits, behaviour and appearance of both demons and angels; the protagonists provided models for avoiding the former and allying with the latter. The moral of the tale always emphasized the importance of vigilance and virtue in combating the power of the devil.

Popular knowledge of *discretio spirituum* was not restricted to its more lurid aspects. A Catalan sermon of Vincent Ferrer, delivered in the early years of the fifteenth century, describes the terror felt by Zacharias at the appearance of the angel Gabriel, despite being told not to fear. Ferrer explains:

> You see that the doctrine is correct that when the good angel or a soul appears to a person, at first they make him terrified, because the flesh cannot bear so much; but then they console him; hence, 'Fear not'.[79]

This sermon demonstrates that it was believed to be important to communicate to the laity the criteria for evaluating visions – here, that one of the fruits of a true vision is fear followed by joy.

Other more or less informal treatments of *discretio spirituum* appear in a wide variety of works which circulated among both lay and religious readers. Advice manuals, treatises written for spiritual instruction, often included teachings on *discretio spirituum* along with instructions for contemplation, with the hope, undoubtedly, of providing an antidote should the medicine have an adverse effect. For example, *Ancrene Wisse*, an early thirteenth-century English advice manual originally written for three anchoresses, had a wide circulation and a strong impact on popular devotional prose.[80] Its author warns that visions are devices of the devil:

---

[78] Carol Zaleski, *Otherworld Journeys: Accounts of Near-Death Experience in Medieval and Modern Times* (Oxford, 1987), p. 35.

[79] Cited in Christian, *Apparitions*, p. 200.

[80] M. B. Salu, trans., *The Ancrene Riwle* (Notre Dame, 1955), p. xxiv.

Na sihðe þ ȝe seoð, ne i swefne ne waken, ne telle ȝe bute dweole. for nis hit
bute his gile. he haueð wise men of hali & of heh lif ofte swa bichearret . . .[81]

That the author was deliberately using cautionary tales to teach the principles
of *discretio spirituum* is evident. After telling various anecdotes about devils in
disguise, he concludes:

Of mon þe spekeð wið ow þulliche talen hereð. hu ȝe schulen witen ow wið
þes deofles wiltes. þ he ow ne bichearre.[82]

The author of *The Cloud of Unknowing* was similarly aware of the educational power of anecdotes. This fourteenth-century English treatise on contemplation, although addressed to a young monk, had immediate popularity and
a wide and continuing circulation.[83] The author explicitly refrains from giving
sensational examples, presumably from fear of over-stimulating his audience.

For what schuld it profite to þee to wite hou þees greet clerkis, & men &
wommen of oþer degrees þen þou arte, ben disceyuid? Sikerly riȝt nouȝt. &
þerfore I telle þee no mo . . .[84]

However he is definitely concerned to warn that 'þe deuil haþ his contem-
platyues, as God haþ his'.[85] To this end he sets out to provide his charge with
knowledge of *discretio spirituum* so that he will not mistake the false feelings
that come to those who strain after ecstasy and neglect the proper preparation
of the soul. He is specifically teaching him to identify the fruits of vision, which
provide one of the signs of *discretio spirituum*.

For as fast after soche a fals felyng comeþ a fals knowyng in þe feendes scole,
riȝt as after a trewe feling comeþ a trewe knowing in Gods scole . . . Þis
disseite of fals felyng, & of fals knowyng folowyng þer-on, haþ diuerse &
wonderful variacions, after þe dyuerste of states & þe sotyl condicions of
hem þat ben disceyuid; as haþ þe trewe felyng & knowyng of hem þat ben
sauid.[86]

Contemporary with *The Cloud of Unknowing*, and very probably written by

---

81 J. R. R. Tolkien, ed., *Ancrene Wisse*, EETS (Oxford, 1962), p. 116. It would seem that
    despite his evident fondness for his charges, the author accepts the prevailing
    misogynistic view that women are deficient in reason. Such a perception could well
    account for his wholesale dismissal of visions – if wise, noble and holy men cannot
    identify the devil, then women would have little chance. It is better to eliminate the
    possibility of deception altogether by avoiding visions.

82 Tolkien, *Ancrene*, p. 116.

83 Hodgson, *Cloud*, p. lxxxii.

84 Hodgson, *Cloud*, pp. 86–7.

85 Hodgson, *Cloud*, p. 86.

86 Hodgson, *Cloud*, p. 86.

the same author, is a work called *A Tretis of Discrecyon of Spirites*.[87] It is part of a collection of treatises on contemplative prayer, of which the best known is *Deonise Hid Diuinite*. Like *The Cloud*, these vernacular works are addressed to a young disciple, but they probably had a more limited circulation than did *The Cloud*. *A Tretis of Discrecyon of Spirites* is largely based on two sermons of Bernard of Clairvaux, *sermo xxiii* and *sermo xxiv, de diversis*, which deal exclusively with *discretio spirituum*.[88] The author of *A Tretis of Discrecyon of Spirites* wishes to educate his audience both in contemplation and in the behaviour appropriate to a contemplative. He is quite specific about some of the manifestations of false holiness inspired by the devil. He cites the familiar caution, which reflects the essential rationale for *discretio spirituum*, that the devil can appear as an angel of light. The writer then identifies some of the signs of the devil's machinations: a fair vision that produces the bitter fruits of discord, and ostentatious piety which is really a disguise for pride and love of power.

> And it is ful needful & speedful to knowe his queintyse and not for to vnknowe his doelful deseites. For somtyme he wol, þat wickeid cursid wiȝt, chaunge his licnes into an aungel of liȝt, þat he may, vnder colour of vertewe, do more dere. Bot ȝit þanne, and we loke rediliche, it is bot seed of bittirnes and of discorde þat þat he schewiþ, seem it neuir so holi ne neuer so feire at þe first schewing. Ful many he steriþ vnto singuleer holines, passing þe comoun statute and costume of here degree, as is fastyng, wering, and many oþer deuote obseruances and outward doinges, in open reprouing of oþer mens defautes, þe whiche þei haue not of office for to doo.[89]

This description gives some idea of the fine line that holy men and women were treading, and the difficulties encountered in establishing that their piety was authentic. It is certainly possible to see here the roots of the suspicion with which Margery Kempe was viewed. She is frequently encouraged by Christ to eschew the outward signs of piety, such as fasting and telling beads, which he, like the author of *A Tretis*, warns can be hypocritical in favour of inward devotion and contemplation.[90] On the other hand, she alienates numerous people by 'open reprouing of oþer mens defautes', as when she chides the archbishop's retinue for their swearing.[91]

---

[87] *Deonise Hid Diuinite and Other Treatises on Contemplative Prayer Related to The Cloud of Unknowing*, ed. P. Hodgson, EETS (London, 1990).

[88] Hodgson, *Deonise*, p. xxxvi. For Bernard's sermons see *PL* CLXXXIII, 600–605. For information about Bernard's influence on later devotional writers, see Giles Constable, 'The Popularity of Twelfth-Century Spiritual Writers in the Late Middle Ages', in *Renaissance Studies in Honour of Hans Baron*, ed. Anthony Molho and John A. Tedeschi (Dekalb, Ill., 1971), pp. 5–26.

[89] Hodgson, *Deonise*, pp. 85–6.

[90] *BMK*, p. 205: 28–35.

[91] *BMK*, p. 36: 6–15.

A Tretis of Discrecyon of Spirites argues strongly that arming oneself against the wiles of the devil calls for meticulous observation of the principles of *discretio spirituum*. Like Alfonso and Gerson, and the other writers on the topic, he urges submission to a spiritual director, as the most effective course.

> ȝif þou be in doute or in were of þees iuel þoutes whan þei come, wheþer þat þei be þe speche of þin owne spirite or any of þe toþer of þin enemyes, loke than besily by þe witnes of þi counsel and þi conscience . . .[92]

Walter Hilton's *Scale of Perfection* is a late-fourteenth century devotional treatise, widely circulated and profoundly influential. The nominal addressee of Book One is an anchoress, but, as with *The Cloud* and *Ancrene Wisse*, the actual readership was much broader. It was written in English, to the extent that even Latin quotations from scripture are translated; this certainly made it accessible to those readers who lacked even rudimentary Latin. In the *Scale of Perfection* Hilton considers the question of sensual visions, but, unlike the earlier *Ancrene Wisse*, he does not advocate rejecting such experiences out of hand. Instead, he advises treating them with caution, and not striving to achieve such encounters.

> . . . visions or revelations of any kind of spirit, appearing in the body or in the imagination, asleep or awake or any other feeling in the bodily senses made in spiritual fashion . . . these are not truly contemplation. They are only simple and secondary – though they are good – compared with spiritual virtues and the spiritual knowledge and loving of God.[93]

Hilton attempts to give his readers the skills necessary to form their own initial judgement. His advice derives from the argument that the emotional fruit of a vision is testimony to its provenance. If a sensual spiritual experience results in abandonment of spiritual thoughts and longing for virtue, or in an excessive longing for such experiences, then it has clearly come from the devil. In addition to giving this advice, however, Hilton encourages the submission of visions to one who is experienced.

> . . . just as a good angel comes with light, so can the devil, and so with the other senses. Anybody who had felt both kinds should know how to tell which is good and which evil, but a person who never felt either, or only the one, can easily be deceived.[94]

Whereas devotional treatises often featured the signs of *discretio spirituum* as an adjunct to instruction in contemplation, discerning the spirits was central to visionary narratives. Written accounts of visions, which were generally

---

[92] Hodgson, *Deonise*, p. 88.
[93] Hilton, *Scale*, pp. 83–4.
[94] Hilton, *Scale*, p. 84.

nd enjoyed a wide and diverse readership, nearly always included validation, and are probably the most concentrated reflection of the)f *discretio spirituum*. The credibility of the visionary depended on a ____ demonstration of her, or his, ability to distinguish good spirits from evil ones. This deliberate display of knowledge meant that a lay person such as Margery Kempe, for example, hearing the visions of Bridget of Sweden, would also hear how Bridget distinguished true visions, feared demons, identified angels, exhibited the appropriate virtues, and above all, how she merited this mark of divine favour. The various functions of the discourse of *discretio spirituum* in the vision narratives of Bridget of Sweden and Margery Kempe will be examined in the next two chapters. Before doing so, however, it is useful to consider the evidence of a specialized application of *discretio spirituum* to women.

Discretio spirituum and Women Visionaries

In addition to the major risk of woman as devil's gateway, the risks which women visionaries posed can be divided into three categories: (i) the gullibility of women; (ii) the desire of women for attention, even notoriety; (iii) the contaminating effect of women.

Although the first category obviously would include women duped by the devil, it also, perhaps more realistically, includes those who inflate their own imaginings to the level of divine revelation. The Spanish visionary and nun, Teresa of Avila (1515–82), addresses this issue in a markedly self-denigrating statement, written totally in the discourse of *discretio spirituum*. In this statement, Teresa is meek, acknowledges the 'natural' inferiority of women, and implies that she needs guidance.

> It should be remembered that the weakness of our nature is very great, espe-cially in women, and that it shows itself most markedly in this way of prayer; so it is essential that we should not at once suppose every little imagining of ours to be a vision.[95]

---

95 Teresa of Avila, *Book of the Foundations* III, Ch. 8: 43. Cited in Boland, *Concept*, p. 69. Boland cites this passage as his sole commentary on Gerson's strictures against women visionaries in *de probatione*, a citation which can only be seen as support of Gerson's position. It is unfortunate that Boland did not also quote the following passage from Teresa of Avila's *Life*, and attempt to reconcile the two. 'The Lord gives these favours [transcendental experiences] far more to women than to men: I have heard the saintly Fray Peter of Alcantar say that, and I have also observed it myself. He would say that women made much more progress on this road than men, and gave excellent reasons for this, which there is no point in my repeating here, all in favour of women.' (*Life*, Ch. XL. Cited in Mary Daly, *The Church and the Second Sex*

Gerson, in *De probatione spirituum* links the gullibility of women with that of the young.

> The ardour of adolescents and women is too great, too eager, unstable, unbridled and therefore suspect.[96]

In a misogynistic culture it is not a great leap from thinking that women imagine they are having visions to thinking that women deliberately feign visions to attract attention or to gain power. This is the second risk posed by women visionaries. Because women's paths to power were so few, there must have been an awareness, on the part of both women and men, of the possibilities offered by visionary power; there were undoubtedly those who succumbed to the temptation.[97] However, even if they were not perceived as deliberately counterfeiting visions, women were seen as exploiting visionary status in order to get attention. Gerson warns that women visionaries need to be deterred from lengthy time-wasting conversations about their visions with their confessors.

> All the more is it true if these women, itching with curiosity, are the kind whom the Apostle describes: 'Silly women who are sin-laden and led away by various lusts: ever learning yet never attaining knowledge of the truth' (II Timothy 3. 7). For where truth is absent, it follows that vanity and deception are present.[98]

These remarks are provoked more by the physical presence of women visionaries and the attention they receive than by their visions; this was a common

---

(New York, 1975), p. 100.) These two seemingly opposing statements by Teresa exemplify her internalized misogyny at war with her empirical knowledge of women's virtue, strength and power. Alison Weber argues that Teresa found herself in a classic 'double bind' situation. 'Even if she could convince her confessors that the favours were not diabolical delusions, how could she do so without appropriating the male prerogative in theological disquisition.' See *Teresa of Avila and the Rhetoric of Femininity* (Princeton, 1990), p. 46. Virtually all women visionaries find themselves in this same double bind – and one way out is through intelligent employment of the discourse of *discretio spirituum*.

96 Gerson, *Oeuvres* IX, 180; translation, Brown, *Pastor*, p. 222.

97 William Christian, in his study of apparitions and visions in late-medieval and renaissance Spain writes of 'a general feeling that women were tempted to have visions as a way of gaining the power and attention they lacked in society' (*Apparitions*, p. 197). Judith Brown has written a fascinating account of a late-sixteenth-century Italian nun who was accused – and convicted – of falsifying visions. During her trial, it apparently emerged that she was also engaged in lesbian activities with her companion. See *Immodest Acts: the Life of a Lesbian Nun in Renaissance Italy* (Oxford, 1986).

98 Gerson, *Oeuvres* IX, 184; trans. Boland, *Concept*, p. 37.

response. Bridget is encouraged to get back to her spinning, as is Margery Kempe, who is also told that she should be 'shut up in a house of stone'. Both these examples reveal the speaker's perception that the proper place for a woman is at home or enclosed in a nunnery rather than out in the world communicating visions.

It was difficult to keep women who claim to speak the word of God in their proper womanly place, and this fact evoked traditional fears of the contaminating effect of women visionaries, the third risk women visionaries create. Gerson claims that, at the very least, garrulous women will waste their confessor's time relating lengthy accounts of visions.[99] At worst, they will – again – provide entrée for the devil. Gerson cites a cautionary tale of a certain holy man who entered into a close spiritual friendship with a nun, a friendship with absolutely no trace of sensuality in it. However, the devil took advantage of the security which the two friends felt in their chaste relationship, and soon the holy man realized that 'if God had not prevented it, he might have fallen into serious evil'.[100] It has been suggested that this anecdote was drawn from Gerson's own experience.[101] In fact, a very similar episode occurs in the early thirteenth-century English *Life of St Margaret* found in the Katherine Group.[102] In it, a demon recounts how he allows a chaste woman and a chaste man to converse together of spiritual things, to feel comfortable together in their shared virtue and chastity, until, lo and behold, soon they are neither virtuous nor chaste any longer. Although this episode is an addition to the sources used by the English author, the editors of the text argue that the expansions were adaptations of traditional material.[103] This would strongly suggest that, rather than drawing on his own experience, Gerson was playing a minor variation on a traditional theme – woman as the 'devil's birdlime', as Jerome puts it. This homily from *The Life of St Margaret*, as well as Gerson's anecdote, is specifically directed at the situation of the holy woman and her spiritual director.[104] They are further examples of the widespread belief in the danger posed to religious men by prolonged contact with women, be they ever so holy.

These three categories – the credulity of women, their desire for attention, and their contaminating effect – provide the rationale for those who advocate particularly stringent application of *discretio spirituum* to women. The actual articulation of suspicion of women visionaries, however, is only the tip of the iceberg. The pervasive assumptions in medieval society about the nature of women elevate the issue of gender to the most important factor in the commu-

---

99 Gerson, *Oeuvres* IX, 184; trans. Boland, *Concept*, p. 36.
100 Gerson, *Oeuvres* III, 52; trans. Boland, *Concept*, pp. 99–100.
101 J. Huizinga, *The Waning of the Middle Ages* (New York, 1954), p. 196.
102 B. Millett and J. Wogan-Browne, ed., *Medieval English Prose for Women: Selections from the Katherine Group and Ancrene Wisse* (Oxford, 1992), p. 67.
103 Millett and Wogan-Browne, *Prose*, p. xxiii.
104 Millett and Wogan-Browne, *Prose*, p. xxiii.

nication and reception of the transcendental experiences of a woman visionary.[105] It is important to remember that *discretio spirituum* was the primary discourse for articulating and assessing all visions. However, for four reasons, all arising out of the traditional perception of the female, *discretio spirituum* loomed larger, and had a different emphasis, in the spiritual life of women than in that of men.

First, as argued in Chapter One, the prevailing religious and cultural factors meant that women principally had visionary experiences, whereas men tended toward apophatic mysticism. Since intellectual vision was believed to be always true, it was not subject to judgement in the same way as spiritual vision. Therefore, women more than men were subject to the constraints of *discretio spirituum*. Second, the ability of women to make discerning judgements was believed to be inferior to that of men; women's judgements, beginning with Eve, were perceived as flawed and needed to be checked. Hence there was a greater degree of doubt about women's visions, and a commensurately greater demand for a careful testing of the spirits. Third, women were believed to be a natural target for the devil – he presumably thinks that if it worked once, it might work again – and so it was thought more likely that women's visions were diabolically inspired. For these reasons, *discretio spirituum* had a particularly vital importance to women.

The fourth factor which must be considered is the requirement of *discretio spirituum* that a visionary be under the guidance of a spiritual director. This meant that in most cases, the first point of contact for women visionaries were men, whose sense of women as 'other', and whose culturally determined understanding of the female inevitably distorted their recognition of the visionary in a way which did not happen with male visionaries. As discussed above, there are two principal aspects to the medieval understanding of the female: on the one hand, she is carnal, irrational and dangerous; on the other, the female is synonymous with humility, marginalization, and suffering. This bilateral understanding results in a unilateral expectation for women's behaviour: they should be obedient and submissive. The negative female qualities must be controlled by demanding and enforcing obedience – to husband, father and Church; the positive female qualities will naturally result in obedience and submission to others.

Here a significant factor should be noted. The quality of submission and obedience of a woman to a man was quite different from that of man to a man, even when both occured in an ecclesiastical context under the guise of religious obedience. Even those spiritual directors who fervently admired

---

[105] This fact is very much in line with other aspects of women's spirituality. Caroline Bynum states that recent scholarship supports a claim that gender was the overriding factor in shaping medieval women's piety ('Religious Women in the Later Middle Ages', in *Christian Spirituality: High Middle Ages and Reformation*, ed. Jill Raitt (New York, 1988), p. 134).

their charges, and who were in awe of their holiness and direct experience of the divine, expected, as a matter of course, obedience and submission from the holy women they were counselling.[106] These qualities are primary among those virtues which establish the woman's holiness, and are enshrined in the discourse of *discretio spirituum*. A deficiency in this area could be enough to bring her holiness – and her visions – into doubt. Margery Kempe is an obvious case in point.

The same set of prejudices that required a woman's submissive demeanour also affected the judging of the veracity of women's visions. It is not so much that there were special tests which had to be applied to women's visions as opposed to those of men. It is that women visionaries were handicapped by the inherent suspicion attached to them, and that there was minimal room for deviation from the criteria of *discretio spirituum*. An excellent proof of the negative assumptions about women visionaries is found in Gerson's trilogy of works on *discretio spirituum*.[107] Every example of false or deluded visions is illustrated by an anecdote about a woman. This is the only capacity in which women feature in these works. All the examples that he gives of true visions and positive spiritual experiences feature men. Whether this bias is unconscious or deliberate, it exemplifies the dominant attitude towards women's visions and visionary women.[108]

Although Jean Gerson is explicit about the particular risks which women visionaries pose he was certainly not alone in his perception. Alfonso of Jaén, concerned as he is to present Bridget of Sweden and her visions in the most positive light, states that he is driven, in part, to write the *Epistola solitarii* to counteract the predominant inclination of most authorities.

> Therefore many men erringe as blinde men in this mateer ar turned to contempne . . . simpl spiritual personys ydiotes and the kende of a woman as ignoraunt and of a light capacite and reputacoun and yerfore to be taken on worthy on to godly visions or profecyes . . .[109]

---

[106] This could, of course, result in complex and continuing negotiations for authority and power. This issue is evident in Margery Kempe's relationship with her clerical advisors, and is explored below, pp. 122–8. See also the brief discussion of Teresa of Avila's 'double bind' above.

[107] See above, p. 55.

[108] It is interesting to observe that Gerson's twentieth-century amanuensis and translator has no cavil with Gerson's pronouncements on women visionaries. He does take issue – albeit mildly – with other of Gerson's stands, citing later authorities or different interpretations of various aspects of *discretio spirituum*. However, when it comes to women and visions, Boland reiterates and reinforces Gerson's pronouncements. Boland's work, it should be remembered, was designed to serve as an aid to parish priests.

[109] Lat. I: 21; Appendix fol. 247v: 7–18.

Discretio spirituum offered women visionaries a vehicle to counteract the automatic presumption that they were unworthy of divine favour. Conformity to the restrictions it imposed could result in their empowerment as visionaries. Familiarity with the discourse was a determinant of success.

Conclusion

All visionaries had to confront the problems inherent in having visions and being visionaries: spiritual visions were an inferior form of transcendental experience; they could be manipulated, misconstrued, misunderstood; there was a constant danger of deviating from accepted doctrine and incurring charges of heresy; it was difficult, if not impossible, to articulate the ineffable and to ensure the accurate transmission of divine communication; visionaries became identified with what they communicate, and their lives and spiritual practices were expected to reinforce and exemplify the divine locution.[110] All visionaries faced these difficulties; but it was only women who, in addition, had to contend with their gender, and who had to defuse the automatic suspicions which surfaced with the conjunction of woman and vision.

That women, and those who wrote for and about them, were well aware of this pervasive suspicion is evident in the pre-emptive defences raised and strategies of validation offered. These include the recitation of female antecedents – Old Testament prophetesses, classical sibyls and Desert Mothers – which often accompanies the revelations of women visionaries. Such lists established precedents – something which was not thought necessary with male prophets and visionaries. Another defence was establishing the woman's virtue, in the teeth of the reigning assumption to the contrary. *Vitae* of women visionaries and accounts of their visions placed enormous emphasis on the humility, obedience, chastity, patience, and prudence of the visionary, and her willing submission to her spiritual director; these qualities, of course, are all important criteria of *discretio spirituum*. The argument of negative capability is a further strategy of validation which is frequently invoked. This argues that God's choice of a seemingly inappropriate instrument – a fool, a madman, or a woman – is evidence of his absolute power, and a reminder of the inscrutable ways of the Divine.[111]

However, the most important and effective of all these defences is the deliberate display of conformity to *discretio spirituum*, the intelligent employment of the discourse, which is evident in the writings of and about visionary women. The following chapter will analyze how, in the *Epistola solitarii ad reges*, Alfonso of Jaén presents Bridget as an impeccable visionary by establishing the criteria

---

110 This last is surely a prime early example of Marshall McLuhan's famous dictum, 'The medium is the message.'

111 Newman, *Sister*, pp. 35 and 255 n. 10.

of *discretio spirituum* and measuring her against them. It will then examine the way in which Bridget's *Revelaciones* are couched in the discourse of *discretio spirituum*, and how she is presented as accepting the restrictions it imposes. Her construction within the discourse is as a disembodied voice, uttering the word of God. She is a vanishing visionary, and therefore she is empowered.

Chapter Four will focus on *The Book of Margery Kempe*. Whereas Bridget was widely known for her visions, was eventually canonized, and can be seen as an exemplary visionary in her representation within the discourse, Margery's reception by both layfolk and clergy was ambivalent. Her status as a visionary and holy woman elicited controversy and involved her in conflict. It will be argued that much of this conflict was due to the inconsistent employment of the discourse of *discretio spirituum* in *The Book of Margery Kempe*. Margery is not represented as accepting the restrictions of *discretio spirituum*. Unlike Bridget, she is the woman who will not go away, and consequently, to that extent, she is disempowered as a visionary.

CHAPTER THREE

The Lady Vanishes:
Bridget of Sweden, Exemplary Visionary

> Hear what I speak, and go to your confessor, magister Mathias, who is
> expert at discernment of spirits, and say to him on my behalf what I say
> to you, that you will be my bride and my channel, and you will hear
> and see spiritual things, and my spirit will remain with you even unto
> your death.[1]

In this manner Bridget of Sweden describes her summoning vision. So began a
spiritual odyssey which was to elevate an obscure Swedish noblewoman into
one of the best-known and most powerful holy women of her time.[2] It is surely
no accident that Bridget should represent God's first command to her as a
command to seek guidance from an expert in *discretio spirituum*, the discerning
of spirits. Stating that God's revelations to Bridget are to be verified by an
expert in *discretio spirituum* is the first step in constructing Bridget within the
discourse of *discretio spirituum*; she is thereby presented as under the guidance
of a spiritual director, as passive, and obedient. Bridget's vision narratives,
treatises which support her or those which attack her, her canonization process
and the debate at the Council of Constance in 1415 over the provenance of her
visions, are all articulated in that discourse. This chapter will examine the
function of the discourse in Alfonso of Jaén's treatise arguing for her credibility
as a visionary, the *Epistola solitarii ad reges*, and in some of Bridget's vision
narratives collected in the *Revelaciones*.

In this discourse of *discretio spirituum* it is possible to see the paradox at the
heart of the medieval woman visionary's experience; *discretio spirituum* both
restricts and empowers. Conforming successfully to its principles means that
the visionary's voice will be heard, that she will accomplish her God-given

---

1 *A&P*, p. 80. My translation. This incident is described in almost identical form in the
   vita composed by the Swedish Archbishop Birger Gregersson (d. 1383). See I. Collijn,
   ed., *Birgerus Gregorii Legenda S. Birgitte*, SSFS, ser. 2 (Uppsala, 1946), p. 19. It also
   appears in the *defensorium*, written by the Spanish Dominican theologian Cardinal
   Juan de Turrecremata (1388–1468), which serves as a prologue to the Ghotan edition
   of the *Revelationes* (Lübeck, 1492), fols. 2v–6v.
2 Colledge writes that Bridget was recognized by the men of her own age as 'a factor
   far from negligible in the affairs of Christendom' ('*Epistola*', p. 20).

purpose, that she will be effective, often in secular as well as religious matters. Paradoxically, conforming successfully to *discretio spirituum* has the effect of making the visionary herself disappear. To reverse the aphorism, visionary women should be heard and not seen. The ideal visionary or prophet is one who is perceived purely as a channel for the voice of God. Humility, submission, obedience, meekness, ignorance and passivity, as noted above in Chapter Two, are qualities central to the discourse of *discretio spirituum*. These qualities all encourage extreme self-effacement and self-abnegation. The effect of *discretio spirituum* is to make the body of the visionary vanish; then her voice can be clearly heard. A woman visionary who conforms so completely to the principles of *discretio spirituum* as to render herself invisible makes it more likely that the ecclesiastical authorities will hear and accept God's message, and in this way she is empowered. Bridget of Sweden was a woman and a visionary whose acceptance of the restrictions of *discretio spirituum* enabled her to fulfil her divine mandate. Constructed as voice alone – albeit a strong and powerful voice – speaking the words of God, Bridget enters the public sphere, a sphere forbidden to women by tradition and scriptural edict.[3] It is possible to see in the *Epistola solitarii* and in the *Revelaciones* just how this vanishing act is accomplished and how Bridget is empowered as an authentic visionary.

In the section *The Woman Behind the Visionary*, this chapter will consider the background of Bridget of Sweden and her relationship with her spiritual director and the editor of the *Revelaciones*, Alfonso of Jaén. As discussed above, a spiritual director was a necessity for a visionary; one with the theological training and political acumen of Alfonso could also be a definite asset. The chapter will then, in *Epistola solitarii ad reges*, assess Alfonso's contribution to Bridget's reception as a visionary by analysing his use of the discourse of *discretio spirituum* in his construction of Bridget in the treatise. The third section of the chapter, *Sancta Birgitta Revelaciones*, will examine the *Revelaciones* itself for evidence of Bridget's conformity to the doctrine of *discretio spirituum*, and assess her fluency in the discourse. Bridget's skilful use of the discourse, resulting in her extreme self-effacement, works in concert with Alfonso's presentation of her as exemplary visionary to effectively establish her as disembodied voice, as mouthpiece of God.

The Woman behind the Visionary[4]

Bridget of Sweden was born in 1302 or 1303 in the province of Uppland, north of Stockholm. Her mother was related to King Magnus of Sweden, and both her parents were pious. Bridget experienced her first vision, of a beautiful

---

3   For example, I Corinthians 14. 34–5.
4   Unlike Margery Kempe, about whom her book is our only informant, there are a

woman who called her and placed a crown on her head, at the age of seven. Her life thereafter was marked by spiritual devotion; after her marriage at thirteen she persuaded her husband, Ulf Gudmarsson, to live chastely for the first two years. She eventually bore eight children, and spent several years as lady-in-waiting to the queen. During her years at court she acquired some influence and understanding of power and politics, which undoubtedly stood her in good stead in the future when conveying the word of God to men of power.[5] In 1341 Ulf and Bridget went on pilgrimage to Santiago de Compostela. On the return journey, Ulf fell ill, his health never recovered, and after their return to Sweden he died in 1344. Bridget then retired to the monastery at Alvastra to devote her life and her love to God. It was here that she experienced a vision summoning her to be bride of Christ, and mouthpiece for the divine word. Obedient to what she believed to be the will of God, she espoused several causes. She fought against clerical corruption, she worked for the return of the papacy to Rome from Avignon, and she campaigned for peace between France and England. She also felt herself called to establish a religious order, the *Ordo Sanctissimi Salvatoris*, the rule for which, the *Regula Salvatoris*, she had received in a vision sometime in the late 1340s.[6] To achieve these ends she travelled extensively and communicated her revelations to leaders of church and state. Her influence was considerable; she was a widely known and sometimes controversial figure.

At the time of her conversion, her spiritual director was Mathias of Linköping, one of Sweden's foremost theologians.[7] He encouraged her in her vocation, and assisted her with writing down her first revelations. He was responsible for issuing a volume of these revelations around 1346. They were

number of historical sources for various aspects of Bridget's life. The principal references used in this survey are: 'General Introduction', and 'Special Introduction', *Sancta Birgitta Revelaciones*, Book I, ed. C. Undhagen, SSFS (Uppsala, 1978), pp. 1–50. These introductions will henceforward be referred to in the notes as 'Undhagen', to distinguish them from the *Revelaciones* itself, which will be referred to as 'Revs.' plus the book number. Other sources for the survey are: A. Andersson, *St Bridget of Sweden* (London, 1980); B. Bergh, 'A Saint in the Making: St Bridget's Life in Sweden (1303–1349)', *Papers of the Liverpool Latin Seminar* III, ed. F. Cairns (ARCA Classical and Medieval Texts, Papers and Monographs 7, 1981), pp. 371–84; Colledge, 'Epistola'; Jönsson, *Alfonso of Jaén*; M. T. Harris, ed., *Birgitta of Sweden: Life and Selected Revelations* (New York, 1990), 1–52; Birger Gregorsson and Thomas Gascoigne, *The Life of Saint Birgitta*, trans. J. B. Holloway (Toronto, 1991).

5 Andersson, *St Bridget*, pp. 17–18. See also Colledge, 'Epistola', p. 20, who discusses the harsh realities that Bridget faced in the political forum.

6 Harris, *Birgitta*, p. 31.

7 Colledge, 'Epistola', p. 22. For a study of Mathias as theologian, see A. Piltz, 'Magister Mathias of Sweden in his Theological Context: A Preliminary Survey', in *The Editing of Theological and Philosophical Texts from the Middle Ages*, ed. M. Asztalos (Stockholm, 1986), pp. 137–160.

originally published in Old Swedish, and then translated into Latin by Mathias.[8] This volume eventually constituted the first book of the *Revelaciones*.[9] Mathias obviously thought highly of Bridget; in his prologue to Book One of the *Revelaciones*, known by its *incipit* as *Stupor et mirabilia*, he makes the somewhat unwise claim that her visions are a greater indication of God's power than the Incarnation of Christ, a claim which was to fuel some of the subsequent attacks on Bridget.

> For who, unless guided by the grace of the same spirit, could believe that Christ, dwelling in heaven, would speak to a woman [Bridget] still living in this mortal state? . . . To be sure, this appearance is more amazing than that by which he showed himself in the flesh. That brought the external appearance of flesh to fleshly eyes, this brings God and man to the eyes of the spirit.[10]

Mathias influenced Bridget considerably in her early years as a visionary; he instructed her in *discretio spirituum* and guided her reading.[11] She was familiar with the writings of the Church Fathers, Augustine, Ambrose, Jerome and Gregory; with the *Vitae patrum*, *Speculum virginum* and *De modo bene vivendi*. She owned a copy of the Old Swedish *Legendariet*, which recounts the lives of the saints.[12] These works would all have furthered her knowledge of visionary theology.

---

8   Only fragments of this original Old Swedish text survive (Undhagen, p. 10). Bridget Morris examines the implications of the translation and editing of Bridget's revelations, and argues that the *Revelaciones extrauagantes* are the closest to Bridget's original vision narratives. See 'Labyrinths of the Urtext', in *Heliga Birgitta – budskapet och förbilden*, Proceedings of the Symposium at Vadstena 3–7 October, 1991, ed. A. Härdelin and M. Lindgren (Västervik, 1993), pp. 23–33.

9   R. Ellis, '*Flores ad fabricandam . . . coronam*: An Investigation into the Uses of the Revelations of St Bridget of Sweden in Fifteenth-Century England', *Medium Aevum* 52 (1983), 163–4.

10 'Quis enim, nisi eiusdem spiritus gracia preuentus, credere poterit, quod Christus, residens in celo, loquatur femine [Bridget] in hac mortalitate adhuc degenti? . . . Sane stupendior est hec apparicio illa, qua se per carnem monstrauit. Illa carnis superficiem carnalibus oculis ingessit, hec Deum et hominem spiritualibus oculis ingerit' (Revs. I: *Prologus Magistri Mathie*: 18–21). This prologue does not appear in the *Liber Celestis*.

11 See, for example, Undhagen, p. 10; Harris, *Birgitta*, pp. 6 and 17–18. Birger Bergh suggests that there were erotic undertones in the relationship between 'the perhaps very attractive' Bridget and Mathias, citing Professor Hjalmar Sunden, a psychologist of religion, who argues that Mathias replaced Bridget's (then living) husband as her primary source of emotional satisfaction (Bergh, 'A Saint', p. 379). I find little support for this interpretation, although it could be argued that Bridget was very dependent on Mathias in the beginning.

12 B. Klockars, 'St Birgitta and Mysticism', in *Mysticism*, ed. S. S. Hartman and C-M. Edsman (Stockholm, 1970), pp. 109–10.

Bridget originally found favour with the King of Sweden, Magnus Eriksson; he granted her land and a castle at Vadstena to house the order she wished to found. However, there is evidence that conflict arose between them, conflict which possibly came to a head over the crusade which Magnus conducted against Novgorod in 1347–8.[13] At the same time, there is evidence of a break with Mathias, although the reasons for the rupture are not known.[14] These events may have precipitated Bridget's decision to go to Rome for the Jubilee Year. In 1349 she left Sweden, taking with her the Cistercian prior Peter Olavsson of Alvastra and Magister Peter Olavsson from Skänninge as her confessors and amanuenses. She never returned to Sweden, and the two Peters remained in her service for the rest of her life.

While based in Rome, Bridget continued to receive and write her revelations. She also travelled widely, on pilgrimage and in order to accomplish her God-given missions. She was not always well received on these missions; for example, when in Cyprus in 1372 she foretold disaster for the kingdom, she was assailed as a heretic and accused of sorcery. Neither was she always successful. Her representations to the popes that God wished them to leave the fleshpots of Avignon and return to Rome, fell on deaf ears for many years. Nevertheless, Bridget persisted, using all the weapons at her disposal to achieve her goals. She worked to establish alliances with powerful churchmen and statesmen. She wrote letters, she garnered support, she demanded interviews and audiences. She petitioned tirelessly for an end to the war between France and England, for an end to clerical corruption and for the establishment of her order. She negotiated continually with ecclesiastical officials and with three successive popes to get the papacy returned to Rome.[15] All this public activity was uncharacteristic and, of course, deemed undesirable for women of the time. Bridget was able to function in public only behind the shield of her revelations. They served to inspire, protect and empower her. Her familiarity

---

[13] Harris, *Birgitta*, p. 18. See also Bergh, 'A Saint', pp. 379–81. Bridget Morris examines Book IV: 2 of the *Revelaciones* as a possible meditation on Magnus's crusade and offers convincing evidence of Bridget's increasing disapproval, even hatred, of Magnus. See 'Swedish Foreign Policy of the 1340s in the Balance: An Interpretation of Book IV Chapter 2 of St Bridget's *Revelations*', in *Studies in St Birgitta and the Brigittine Order*, 2 vols., ed. J. Hogg (New York, 1993), I, 180–91.

[14] B. Morris, 'The Monk-on-the-Ladder in Book V of St Birgitta's *Revelaciones*', *Kyrkohistorisk Arsskrift* (1982), 101. A number of scholars have speculated that the corrupt monk on the ladder in Book V of the *Revelaciones*, the *Liber questionum*, is based on Mathias, and suggest that this indicates that Mathias and Bridget parted on bad terms. In the above article Morris assesses the textual evidence, concluding that 'the evidence is not so contradictory that it makes the supposition [that Mathias is the monk] altogether unlikely' (105).

[15] As Colledge points out, 'Catherine [of Siena] and Bridget were both acquainted, from long and bitter experience, with the realities of politics . . .' ('*Epistola*', p. 20).

with the discourse of *discretio spirituum*, her fluency in the discourse, identified her as a divine instrument. Bridget the woman vanished and Bridget the visionary and prophet was empowered.

Eventually, many of the goals to which she had dedicated herself were achieved; the papacy was returned to Rome, she was canonized, her Order was established at Vadstena, and her works were widely disseminated. Of her other missions, the church is still fighting the battle against clerical corruption, and it took another woman visionary, Joan of Arc, to bring about peace – of a sort – between France and England. In all, Bridget's accomplishments were exceptional.

Sometime between 1368 and 1370 Alfonso, former bishop of Jaén, joined Bridget's household in Rome. Alfonso was born in Segovia in 1329 or 1330.[16] His family was aristocratic, and both his father and brother were officials at the court. Like Bridget, his family background equipped him with skills and influential contacts which were to contribute to his gaining influence in the higher echelons of the church. In 1359 he was made Bishop of Jaén, a see that he resigned in 1368, possibly with the intention of becoming a Hieronymite hermit.[17] Soon after this, by some process which has not been recorded, he entered Bridget's service. Alfonso became one of Bridget's closest advisors during her last years in Rome; he undertook – by divine edict – the task of editing, organising and censoring the mass of material which constituted the *Revelaciones*. After Bridget's death, he, with her daughter Katherine, initiated and supervised the process for Bridget's canonization, for which the *Revelaciones* were used as evidence.[18]

There is a strong possibility that Alfonso entered the household partly because the Latin of Bridget's Swedish amanuenses was proving inadequate for the standards of the *curia*.[19] The submission for the approval of the *Regula Salvatoris* was corrected at least twice by the ecclesiastical authorities. When it was first approved by Pope Urban VI in 1370, to Bridget's disappointment he authorized only the foundation of two convents at Vadstena, under Augustinian control, not the establishment of a new Order.[20] Alfonso's skill with Latin, his familiarity with the clerical hierarchy, his ability as an editor and his political sophistication were exactly what Bridget needed to accom-

---

[16] Principal sources for information on Alfonso are Colledge, '*Epistola*'; Undhagen; Jönsson, *Alfonso*, and M. Seidlmayer, 'Ein Gehilfe der hl. Birgitta von Schweden: Alfons von Jaén', *Historisches Jahrbuch* 50 (1930), 1–18.

[17] Jönsson, *Alfonso*, p. 40. However, Colledge maintains that there is no firm evidence of Alfonso's ever becoming a professed Hieronymite, or an Olivetan, which is another possibility ('*Epistola*', pp. 26–7).

[18] Colledge, '*Epistola*', p. 20.

[19] Jönsson, *Alfonso*, p. 46; Colledge, '*Epistola*', pp. 24 and 28.

[20] Jönsson, *Alfonso*, p. 46.

plish her goals.[21] The wisdom of her alliance with Alfonso is borne out by his continuing her work after her death in 1373. He collected the revelations of her last years, and assembled them into a single work; he organised the publication of an edition of the *Revelaciones* before 1377, in time for the opening of the canonization process; he was responsible for subsequent redactions of the *Revelaciones*;[22] he wrote the *Epistola solitarii* to defend Bridget's credibility as a visionary; and he wrote an explanatory preface for Book V of the *Revelaciones*, and for the *Sermo Angelicus*.[23] His work as literary editor made the wide dissemination of Bridget's writing possible. It was Alfonso's edition of the *Revelaciones* which constituted the bulk of the evidence in the process for Bridget's canonization. She was canonized in 1391, two years after Alfonso's death.

The *Epistola solitarii* is evidence of the way in which Alfonso's theological knowledge and sophistication supported Bridget. In order to bring about the positive reception of Bridget's text, as the next section of this chapter demonstrates, Alfonso constructs Bridget within the discourse of *discretio spirituum* as an exemplary visionary. His representation of Bridget's conformity to the restrictions of *discretio spirituum* is a vital factor in her empowerment.

Epistola solitarii ad reges

> . . . entrust all of the books of revelations to my bishop, the hermit, who will write them, and elucidate the hidden matters, and preserve the orthodox meaning of my inspiration.[24]

Thus, in a revelation to Bridget, Christ lays out Alfonso's responsibilities as Bridget's spiritual director and editor of her revelations. In fact, Alfonso's contribution goes far beyond this divine ordinance to write and gloss the revelations. His accomplishment is more complex, and more significant, in that he presents Bridget as a visionary whose authority as God's mouthpiece is beyond question. Part of the success of this presentation lay in the editing of the text of the *Revelaciones*. Alfonso selected and arranged Bridget's revelations to ensure that they conformed to received doctrine, that they avoided suspicion of heresy and skirted controversial issues. However, the most important part of Alfonso's task lay in constructing Bridget as a visionary in

---

21 Undhagen, p. 11. For a detailed account of Alfonso's political activities in support of Urban VI, see Colledge, '*Epistola*'.

22 Undhagen examines the history of the various 'Alfonso redactions' in complete detail, with manuscript sources and variants (pp. 14–37).

23 Ellis, '*Flores*', 164–5.

24 '. . . trade omnes libros reuelacionum . . . episcopo meo heremite, qui conscribat et obscura elucidet et catholicum sensum spiritus mei teneat' (*RE*, pp. 165–6).

the terms of the discourse of *discretio spirituum*; this is the central purpose of the *Epistola solitarii*. He locates her within the tradition of visionaries and prophets, presents her in terms which resonate in the ears of the ecclesiastical authorities with familiarity and safety, and reassures his readers of the impeccable qualities of the visionary and the subsequent reliability of her revelations. The *Epistola*, ostensibly intended as an introduction to Book VIII of the *Revelaciones*, is also a demonstration of Alfonso's erudition in the discernment of spirits, and consequently of his well-informed conviction of the veracity and virtue of Bridget and her visions.

The *Epistola solitarii* is a compendium of previous writing on *discretio spirituum*; it lays out a system of knowledge. That system of knowledge provides terminology to assess Bridget of Sweden as a visionary, and supplies criteria to evaluate her revelations. Alfonso uses the discourse of *discretio spirituum* to locate Bridget within the tradition of Christian visionaries, to validate her and to authorize her within that tradition. In addition, in a master-piece of tautology, Bridget herself becomes the *exemplar* for a majority of the criteria of *discretio spirituum*. What she has said or done becomes the standard against which a true visionary should be measured; in effect, her own acts as a visionary serve to authorize her as a visionary.

Alfonso establishes the dual purpose of his treatise at the very beginning.

> ... to schew you the condiciouns and the qualite of the blissid soule of the forseid lady Brigid, and ye maner of wise yat she had the visions of god. Also I intende to write and in writyng to teche boþe ȝou and odir a breff maner of discernyng godly visions from the cursid illusions of Sathan the deule.
>
> (Appendix fol. 247r: 9–11)[25]

Here, it is clear, Alfonso is setting out to control the reception of the *Revelaciones*. To do this he defines the female visionary experience in terms which shift it from the personal to the exemplary. The *Epistola solitarii* is designed to ensure a favourable response by offering the reader a definition of the impeccable woman visionary to which Bridget is then shown to conform absolutely. Her visions and the manner in which she receives them serve as object lessons in the discerning of spirits and in the proper deportment of visionaries. Alfonso does cite the wide range of patristic and scholastic writers on *discretio spirituum* which were mentioned above, but his practical evidence is nearly always provided by Bridget. In fact, Bridget becomes the model, in a kind of circular reasoning which owes little to logic but much to the rhetorical powers Alfonso employs in promoting her as the exemplary visionary.

In this study I examine the manner in which the visionary is constructed in the discourse of *discretio spirituum* under the three categories of Authority,

---

[25] Lat. I: 6–7.

Knowledge and Behaviour.[26] Authority is concerned with authenticating the vision by appealing to a celestial or ecclesiastical interpretation, and by locating the visionary within an ecclesiastically endorsed tradition. The category of Knowledge examines the ways in which the visionary demonstrates her knowledge of the doctrine of *discretio spirituum*. Behaviour covers the manner in which the visionary's behaviour conforms to the principles of *discretio spirituum*. As will be seen, in the *Epistola solitarii* Alfonso constructs Bridget as an exemplary visionary by establishing her authority as a visionary, demonstrating her knowledge of the discernment of spirits and describing her behaviour as an exemplar of visionary virtue. The analysis of both the *Epistola solitarii* and the *Revelaciones* is organized under these same categories, in order more clearly to demonstrate how Alfonso and Bridget both work in relation to the same doctrine, reacting to the same injunctions in the same way. In the next chapter, the analysis of *The Book of Margery Kempe* is similarly organized.

Authority

Part of Alfonso's task is to authorize Bridget, a woman, as a visionary. As a cleric and as her spiritual director, Alfonso's endorsement of Bridget is one vital element in establishing her authenticity according to *discretio spirituum*. This endorsement is found throughout the *Epistola* in the respect and admiration for Bridget which he demonstrates. But, in addition Alfonso employs two explicit strategies of authorization: first, he offers the traditional argument of negative capability, and second, he locates Bridget within the tradition of women visionaries and prophetesses, thereby authorizing her by precedent. As discussed in Chapter One, the question of women and vision was particularly charged for the ecclesiastical authorities because of the suspicion attached to both; woman as the devil's gateway, incapable of intellection; vision as a potential tool of the devil, impossible to verify. Nevertheless, it was accepted

---

26 My use of these three categories was suggested by the fact that the medieval debate over who should preach, which was discussed briefly in Chapter One, pp. 38–9, focused on the issues of the authority, knowledge and virtue of the preacher. Although, of course, the debate over women visionaries was not explicitly structured according to these categories, it seemed to me that those same issues, of authority, knowledge and virtue (or behaviour), were embedded in *discretio spirituum*, especially in relation to women. Therefore, there seemed a certain aptness in employing in my discussion of women visionaries the same classifications used in the debate over who should hold the office of preacher, a debate which nearly always excluded women from that office. For further information on the *officium praedicatoris* see: A. Minnis, 'Chaucer's Pardoner and the "Office of Preacher"', in *Intellectuals and Writers in Fourteenth-Century Europe*, ed. P. Boitani and A. Torti (Cambridge, 1986), esp. pp. 88–92; H. L. Spencer, *English Preaching in the Late Middle Ages* (Oxford, 1993), pp. 49–56; Robert of Basevorn, *The Form of Preaching (Forma praedicandi)*, trans. L. Krul OSB, *Three Medieval Rhetorical Arts*, ed. J. J. Murphy (Berkeley, 1971), pp. 121–8.

that vision and prophecy were visited upon women. Often, the argument of negative capability was used as explanation, and this is indeed one of the arguments that Alfonso offers.

> ... almighty god as weel in the old testament as in ye newe, to shew his gret might has chosin to him as wel in womankende as man kende. to confounde wisemen whedir he made nat a profete of a scheppard and repleshid 30ung ydiotes with sprith of profecie/ And whedir he chose nat rude men and fischeres in to apostolys ... (Appendix fol. 247v: 19–23)[27]

This reasoning not only provides a traditional explanation for God's choice of Bridget, but also confirms her humility, and her inferior status, thereby demonstrating her acceptance of the restrictions of *discretio spirituum*.

The second way in which Alfonso seeks to authorize Bridget's prophetic activities is by citing tradition and precedent. He offers biblical precedents for women as divine instruments and prophets.[28] It is instructive to consider the women Alfonso selects as authorizing precedents for Bridget in terms of the implicit messages which they and their stories convey. All are women who enter the public space only as divine instruments; they are celebrated in this capacity alone, and where their womanhood becomes visible at all it is only inasmuch as it is harnessed and subject to the divine will. The women Alfonso cites are Huldah, Deborah, Hannah, the unnamed wife of Manoah, Hagar, Miriam, Anna, Judith, Esther, Elisabeth, Lucy the Virgin Martyr, the Tiburtine and the Erythraean Sibyls.[29] These women can be grouped into five different categories, all of which have relevance to Bridget and strengthen her claim as a woman to divine inspiration. Although Alfonso did not group the women in this way, nevertheless it provides a helpful way to highlight the implications of his choice of female antecedents for Bridget.

The first group to be considered are women of authority who counselled rulers. Deborah was a prophetess and one of the judges of Israel; her advice was sought by the commander of the army (Judges 4. 4). Huldah, a prophetess, was advisor to King Josiah (II Kings 22. 14; II Chronicles 34. 22). A striking parallel may be drawn between Bridget and Huldah. Huldah condemned the corruption of religious observance which had developed during the reign of the evil king Manasseh, and instructed his successor, King Josiah, to return to

---

27 Lat. I: 22–3.

28 In his *defensorium*, Juan de Turrecremata also calls on this same tradition to support Bridget's claims. He cites Judith advising Ozias and the priests – and also being humble – and draws a specific comparison with Bridget (*Sancta Birgitta Revelaciones* (impressit B. Ghotan, Lübeck, 1492), fols. 2v and 3r). This tradition of Old Testament women – Huldah, Deborah, Judith, Jael – is also cited in the second book of visions of Elisabeth of Schönau as a precedent for her prophetic activities. See E. A. Petroff, ed., *Medieval Women's Visionary Literature* (Oxford, 1986), p. 159.

29 Appendix fol. 247v: 24 – fol. 248r: 3; Lat. I: 24–7.

the Law in order to avert the wrath of God. Similarly, Bridget condemned the moral laxity of a number of courts and nations, notably Cyprus and the papal court at Avignon, warning of disasters unless the people returned to the ways of God.[30] Both Huldah and Deborah, in their biblical contexts, were clearly respected for their prophetic knowledge, and their advice was sought and taken. The Tiburtine and Erythraean sibyls were consulted by statesmen and rulers in classical times on all matters of importance. Their pronouncements were accepted by many of the Church Fathers, who drew from them arguments in defence of Christianity, and their fame continued into the late Middle Ages.[31] The example of these respected authoritative women who advised on political as well as spiritual matters is particularly relevant to Bridget of Sweden in that she sought, through her visions, to influence rulers in the political as well as religious sphere. In fact, the *Epistola solitarii* is directed *ad reges*, and is intended to marshal the support of kings and princes for Bridget's canonization.[32]

The second category of women which can be drawn from Alfonso's list of precedents is women who prophesy or have visions; this is obviously relevant to Bridget. In this group is Miriam, the sister of Moses, who is designated a prophetess (Exodus 15. 20). Hagar, Sarah's handmaid, had a vision of an angel after she had been cast out into the desert by Abraham (Genesis 21. 17). Perhaps the most significant members of the group of women prophetesses and visionaries, in terms of validating Bridget by association, are Anna, the daughter of Fanuel, and Elisabeth, wife of Zacharias and cousin to Mary. Anna was a prophetess at the temple in Jerusalem when the infant Christ was presented, and she recognized him as the Messiah (Luke 2. 36–8). Elisabeth, inspired by the Holy Ghost, recognized the child in Mary's womb as the Messiah (Luke 1. 41–5). The inclusion of these women in the *Epistola solitarii* implies that Bridget, like them, can recognize the Messiah, and is in no danger of being deceived by demonic illusions.

This ability to recognize manifestations of the divine suggested the formation of the third category of women, which I would label women of conviction. Two women in the group saw and believed in visions, or themselves as divine instruments, when men did not. Elisabeth's husband, Zacharias, did not believe the angel who told him that his wife would conceive (Luke 1. 11–20). He was consequently struck dumb, deprived of speech as a punishment for not trusting the evidence of his senses. Reference to this incident is significant in a treatise arguing for belief in spiritual (imaginative) visions, that is, for visions involving sensory awareness of the divine. Manoah

---

[30] See Colledge, '*Epistola*', p. 29, for historical accounts of Bridget's activities in Cyprus.

[31] B. McGinn, '*Teste David cum Sibylla*: The Significance of the Sibylline Tradition in the Middle Ages', in *Women of the Medieval World: Essays in Honor of John H. Mundy*, ed. J. Kirshner and S. F. Wemple (Oxford, 1985), pp. 13–20.

[32] Jönsson, *Alfonso*, p. 108.

did not believe his barren wife when she told him that an angel had appeared to her and told her that she would conceive the child who was to be Samson (Judges 13). Even when he tested the angel himself, by asking its name and offering a sacrifice, he still did not recognize it for a divine manifestation. It was only when the angel 'did wondrously', providing a dramatic demonstration and ascending in the flame of the altar, that Manoah believed (Judges 13. 20). Manoah and Zacharias are precursors of those with whom Bridget struggled, men who do not trust the word of a woman, and will accept only the evidence of their own faulty senses, or who rely upon a rationality which fails to recognize divine omnipotence.

My fourth category of the women cited by Alfonso is a group who served as divine instruments to save their people. Judith seduced and killed Holofernes, the Assyrian general (Judith 8–16). Esther saved the Jews from the machinations of Haman (Esther 2–9). Deborah's foreknowledge determined the successful outcome of the battle, a success which was dependent on Jael, another courageous woman used as an instrument of God (Judges 4). Jael lured Sisera, the Canaanite captain, to her tent and killed him, thus securing the day for the Israelites. Jael, Esther, and Judith form a strong female triumvirate of devout women who were vehicles for miraculous intervention to deliver their people from enemies. They entered the public space, they became visible, only when cloaked in the mantle of divine instrumentality. Significantly, all three were able to achieve their purpose because they were women. Jael offered food and rest to Sisera, her womanly behaviour disarming his suspicions. Esther's beauty and feminine charms captured the attention of King Ahasuerus, who made her his wife, thereby elevating her to a position where she was able to manipulate events to save her people. Judith seduced Holofernes with her beauty and charm, lulling him into false and fatal security. It was their very essence as women which made them appropriate instruments; their gender was the means by which God achieved his end.[33] They were not chosen for an acquired skill, such as David's with the catapult, nor for their devotion, their virtue or their wisdom, although they did possess these latter qualities. It was solely because they were women that they were chosen by God for this endeavour. The importance of these women as precedents for Bridget is clear. They reinforce the argument of negative capability which Alfonso makes, demonstrating that God uses those who best suit his divine purpose, and that sometimes those are women.

My fifth classification of the women in the *Epistola solitarii* is those who have conceived miraculously, or given birth to some sort of miraculous child – or both. This group consists of Manoah's wife, the mother of Samson; Hannah, the mother of Samuel; and Elisabeth, mother of John the Baptist. Hagar, and by association with her, Sarah, mother of Isaac, can be included in this grouping.

---

[33] It is, of course, that same essential nature, directed to the wrong ends, which earned women their reputation as deceivers, manipulators and creatures of lust.

All of these women prefigure the Virgin Mary, in that they are vessels for the divine will. Again, it is only because they are women that they can serve God in this way. These women validate the status of mother, and, by implication, Bridget's own motherhood.

This last grouping points to the salient fact that a large number of these women are wives, mothers, or widows – certainly not virgins. This has particular relevance to Bridget. Given the importance placed on virginity in medieval Christianity – the heavenly reward of virgins was believed to be one hundredfold, that of chaste widows sixtyfold and of wives thirtyfold – Bridget's status as widow and mother needed to be addressed and placed in an acceptable context, that of Christian motherhood and virtuous widowhood. Such an illustrious group of holy women who are also wives or widows reflects well on Bridget. Judith is a widow, as is Anna the prophetess; Esther, Jael, Deborah, Huldah, Hannah, Elisabeth, the wife of Manoah, are all wives, Hagar is a surrogate wife; most of them are mothers. Of the group of women cited by Alfonso, only the Sibyls, Miriam and Lucy the virgin martyr are not identified, in the sources, as married women.

This analysis demonstrates that the group of highly devout, virtuous, biblical women are chosen by Alfonso for a definite purpose. They serve as precedents for Bridget in a number of key areas: as visionary and prophetess; as respected advisor to kings and princes; as divine instrument to save her people; as one who recognizes the divine and who knows God's will where men do not; and as a virtuous wife, chaste widow and Christian mother. Alfonso implies that what was done by women then can be done by a woman now. Placing Bridget within this select context of biblical tradition is an essential step in authorizing her as a visionary.

Knowledge

Thus Alfonso attempts to ensure that Bridget's voice is authorized, is seen to be authorized, and that she is herself empowered, in her own right, and, inevitably, as a model to other women. However, it is not sufficient that Bridget be only externally authorized. It must also be demonstrated that she possesses independent knowledge of *discretio spirituum*. While she is required to be submissive to the judgement of her spiritual directors, in order to reassure her judges she must also be capable of distinguishing an angel from a demonic illusion. The greater her fluency in the discourse of *discretio spirituum* the more her visions are perceived as authentic and authoritative. This increases her credibility as a visionary and effectiveness as a divine instrument. Alfonso's principal concern in his representation of Bridget's knowledge is to validate the types of vision she experiences.

The evidence of Bridget's *Revelaciones* indicates that she has spiritual (imaginative) visions, as well as some corporeal visions, the types of vision which it was believed could be appropriated by the devil and which were consequently held to be suspect. It is therefore crucial that Bridget's visionary experiences be presented in the best possible light, that is, a light which casts Bridget's womanhood, her essential association with the body and senses, into shadow. To this end Alfonso devotes considerable effort to identifying and justifying the type of vision which Bridget experiences, exhibiting at times a certain legerdemain, as will be evident later. A constellation of factors, including scriptural precedent, women's devotional activities and education, meant that spiritual vision was the form of transcendentalism usually experienced by women; intellectual vision was usually experienced by men.[34] The association of a potentially deceptive form of vision with a potentially deceptive woman visionary is an association which Alfonso is concerned to minimize. Consequently, he suggests that Bridget was well aware of the hierarchy of vision, of the dangers posed by bodily and spiritual vision, and that most of her visions were, in fact, of an intellectual nature.

In order to make this argument, Alfonso rather blurs the boundaries between spiritual and intellectual vision.

> ... oure lord spekis be him self or be an aungil creature wordes are schapen to vs. But whan god spekis be himself alonly streinkthe of inwardly inspiracoun to vs is openyd. And whan god spekis be him self he spekis of his word with ought wordes and sillablis the hert is taught for his inwardly vertu is knowen be asertyn leftyng vp . . . Soche an ynwardly godly spekinge this holy lady was taught and informyd of these thinges yat ar conteyned in this celestial boke to spiritual doctrine as it scheuys be þe hool booke.
>
> (Appendix fol. 252r: 2–9)[35]

By insisting that Bridget's visions are intellectual, Alfonso draws on the protection afforded by such visions, which Augustine avers cannot be false.[36] Alfonso's action here implicitly acknowledges the importance of the hierarchy of vision in establishing the credentials of a woman visionary. He shelters Bridget under the mantle of masculinised intellectual vision, with all its masculine associations, diverting attention from her femaleness and its connections with the body and senses.

However, despite Alfonso's casuistry, it can be argued that Bridget nearly always experiences spiritual visions. She sees or hears divine figures with her spiritual senses. When she recounts her experiences she meticulously lists the actors in each of the divine dramas, along with detailed descriptions of the action. Nevertheless, Alfonso often puts a different gloss on Bridget's visions. A very clear example of Alfonso's 'redefinition' of intellectual vision occurs when he states that the *Liber questionum* (Book V of the *Revelaciones*) was an intellectual vision, received by Bridget as instantaneous knowledge as Christ spoke.

---

[34] See above, p. 9.

[35] Lat. V: 41–7.

[36] Augustine, *LMG* XLII, 52; *PL* XXXIV, 475–6.

. . . many things were infused into her mind at the same moment that Christ spoke them, namely . . . the Book of Questions . . . Behold, it was clear and evident to us that through this flood of intellectual, supernatural light, this same person stood there rapt in ecstasy, and then her mind and intelligence were illuminated and enlightened by divine inspiration through super-natural intellectual vision.[37]

Yet in the *Liber questionum* itself, Bridget describes falling into ecstasy, and seeing a ladder reaching from earth to heaven, with Christ seated on a throne, surrounded by saints and angels. The narrative of revelation presents a courtroom scene, with Christ as judge and the corrupt cleric marooned halfway up the ladder, as the accused.[38] This experience, therefore, clearly falls within the category of spiritual vision, not, as Alfonso claims, intellectual vision.

Despite the above mentioned efforts, it is clear that Alfonso knew that Bridget's visions were spiritual as opposed to intellectual. One of the most telling arguments for this inference is Alfonso's statement that Bridget often did not understand her visions, which were then expounded by divine inter-preters, or sometimes by her spiritual directors.[39] Sometimes she feared that visions she did not understand were demonic illusions, and she required reas-surance on this point. Although such behaviour manifests a scrupulous adherence to the principles of *discretio spirituum*, it is also a clear indication that she and Alfonso knew her visions to be spiritual. For intellectual visions are by definition unmistakeable, incapable of deception, and constitute an infused knowledge in the recipient which needs no interpretation. Only corporeal and spiritual visions require the external verification of *discretio spirituum*.

There is a certain amount of silver-tongued smoothness on Alfonso's part here, in manipulating terminology and insisting that a rose could just as well be called a peony, because both are pink flowers which smell pleasant. Never-theless, Alfonso is sufficiently schooled in the discourse of *discretio spirituum* to recognize the need to justify Bridget's having other, inferior types of vision, and to include implicit *apologiae* for them. For example, on the question of corporeal visions he states:

The ferst kende of visions the whech is corporal or bodyli towchis not gretly owre mater. Alþow the seyd blissid Bridgid sum Wylis sy the modir of god

---

[37] '. . . quod in momento erant, Christo loquente, infusa in intellectu eius multa, vt scilicet . . . Liber Questionum . . . per quendam influxum luminis intellectualis super-naturalis ecce quod per hoc clare ostenditur nobis quod ipsa tunc stabat rapta in illo extasi, et tunc illuminabatur et illustrabatur mens et intelligencia eius diuinitus per supernaturalem, intellectualem visionem' (Lat. V: 34–5). This passage does not appear in the Middle English translation of the *Epistola*.

[38] *LC* V: prologue; *Revs.* V: prologus.

[39] Lat. IV: 18–24; Appendix fol. 250v: 8–15.

and hir sone with hir bodily eyin yat is for to sey whan she was a maydin.
(Appendix fol. 251r: 17–20)[40]

Alfonso then details other occasions of bodily vision: when she was in peril during childbirth, two occasions of eucharistic miracles, and on her deathbed. The suggestion is that for Bridget, bodily vision was an aberration due to her youth, or to physical crisis, or within an accepted tradition of eucharistic miracles.[41] The deathbed vision is valorized by the fact that Christ informed Bridget of the time of her death; according to the principles of *discretio spirituum*, only a true visionary is the recipient of such privileged information.[42] By citing these visions Alfonso testifies to Bridget's knowledge of the different levels of vision, but by downplaying them he reduces the association of Bridget and body.

Alfonso is similarly concerned to establish that Bridget knows that only waking visions can be trusted. Received wisdom held that visions experienced while sleeping or in dreams were extremely suspect. It was believed that while reason was off-guard, the devil had easy access to the senses. Alfonso initially denies that Bridget had such visions.

This sompnial vision touchis nat oure mateer for yat lady sey all hir visions in prayour wakinge and not slepynge. (Appendix fol. 251v: 14)[43]

Not only does she not have sleeping visions, she has her visions awake and at prayer, thus affirming the acceptability of those visions.

Nevertheless, Alfonso does recount one occasion when Bridget saw a vision of the crucified Christ while she was asleep.[44] Although he asserts that 'sumtyme dremys ar trewe and good and of god' (Appendix fol. 251v:11),[45] he also insists that this inferior, suspect form of vision occurred only once, and when she was a maiden. As with the bodily visions, it is implied that her youth was responsible for the lower form of vision. In making this defence, Alfonso is of course tacitly upholding the belief that youth and gender affect the quality of spiritual experience.[46] While it is possible to claim youth as an excuse – one does, inevitably, grow older – womanhood can only be an indictment, unless placed within a tradition of divinely empowered women. Alfonso's successful

---

40 Lat. V: 10.

41 It is possible that the argument for her youth (*puella*) also implies that at the time she was a virgin, and so possibly less suspect in the eyes of the authorities. For examples of eucharistic miracles, and their association with women, see Bynum, 'Women Mystics', pp. 122–34.

42 Lat. V: 16–18; Appendix fol. 251v: 1–4.

43 Lat. V: 24.

44 Lat. V: 22; Appendix fol. 251v: 13.

45 Lat. V: 22.

46 But see Gerson on the ardour of adolescents and women, p. 67 above.

presentation of Bridget depends on demonstrating that in her visionary experiences she transcends the essential handicaps of her femaleness, thereby elevating her as an ungendered, disembodied voice.

Behaviour

In his authorization of Bridget, Alfonso uses her womanhood to its best advantage by locating her in a tradition of holy women and by employing the argument of negative capability. In his presentation of Bridget's knowledge he attempts to masculinise her, by implying that her visions are intellectual and by minimizing associations with the body and senses. Femaleness was also construed as a handicap when virtue was judged as manifested in the behaviour and way of life of the visionary. In the *Epistola solitarii* Alfonso focuses mainly on two aspects of Bridget's behaviour. One is her submission to her spiritual directors. The second is her behaviour while in ecstasy. He demonstrates Bridget's exemplary virtue so as to suggest that in behaviour as well as knowledge she transcends her sex. This he achieves by presenting her so that almost nothing of Bridget's personality emerges. Alfonso's portrait of Bridget is a portrait of an empty vessel to be filled by God. He employs the discourse of *discretio spirituum* to such effect that the lady vanishes; only the words she speaks remain.

The quality of a visionary is mainly indicated by her behaviour. The more virtuous the recipient, the higher the likelihood of the genuineness of the vision. The argument of negative capability derived from the quality of the divine instrument; it justified God's use of females, the unlettered, those who were feeble in mind or frail in body. However, negative capability was not an argument for moral incapacity; divine instruments could seem inappropriate but they could not be immoral. The rationale here differs significantly from that concerning the efficacy of the sacrament when administered by an immoral priest, a question which exercised most of the great theological minds of the Middle Ages. The majority of these arguments rest on the sanctity of the eucharistic elements themselves, a sanctity which cannot be contaminated by the celebrant.[47] The essential nature of the elements is already known, and is unalterable. With visions and visionaries, on the contrary, there is no inherent quality whose worth can be judged before the event, and which remains unaffected by its context. The virtue of the visionary, as exemplified by her behaviour, is therefore perceived as a crucial indication of the truth of the vision and consequently requires the most stringent scrutiny.

---

[47] For the teaching of Henry of Ghent on this issue see Minnis, 'The *Accessus*', pp. 291–304. See also the Virgin Mary's instruction to Bridget on this same issue. 'Go to him þat hase powere to asoile þe, for, be þe porter neuer so mesell or lepruse, and he haue þe keys he may als wele opyn þe ʒate as he þat is hole wythoute sekenes. On the same wyse it is of absolucion and of þe sacrament of þe awter' (*LC* IV: 41; *Revs.* IV: 41).

The most important indicator of a visionary's virtue was her submission to the guidance of her spiritual superiors. It is thus not surprising that a great deal of the *Epistola solitarii* is devoted to Bridget's relationship with her spiritual directors. Her willing submission to ecclesiastical observation and guidance is the principal component in Alfonso's claim for her virtue. There are somewhat token references to a conventional list of virtues: she embraces chastity both before and after the death of her husband; she imitates Christ's poverty; she is meek and devout; she is compassionate towards others, as exemplified by her offering her two sons as hostage to the king of Sweden so that he would not have to raise the taxes of his subjects.[48] However, these do not feature nearly as highly in establishing her quality as does her submission to her spiritual directors.

> ... whan she was reuertid to hir self [after an ecstatic trance] she told me on worthy thou I were and ye forseid hir ii confessores the visions the wheche sche had than and gret secret thinges of god.
>   (Appendix fol. 250r: 30 – 250v: 2)[49]

Alfonso gives the impression that she was constantly under the eyes of her spiritual fathers.

> And so sche came to Rome ... hauynge euer with hir ii old men sad and vertuos and verginis and expert spiritual fadris, the whech folwyd her til sche deyed. (Appendix fol. 249v: 14–17)[50]

In constructing Bridget as so consistently meek, and so accepting of the restrictions required by *discretio spirituum*, Alfonso helps to establish her as an exemplary visionary.

At one point, even, he compares Bridget to a 'meke monke' in her obedience to these clerics.[51] Obedience is thereby masculine – disobedience, after all, was Eve's sin – and Bridget the woman disappears inside the habit of an obedient monk. The effect of her submission is that Bridget vanishes behind an orthodox clerical screen, her body and behaviour under male control so that her voice will be amplified in the public sphere.

> This lady expounyd these visions mekely to examinacoun and doom of odir prelates and religious spiritual men ... After yat these perfite men in sciens and gostly in liff preuyd these visions and revelacouns shewid to ye seyd lady and gaff in sentens yat thei procedid fro ye sprith of treuye and not of an yllusor the sprith of falshed. (Appendix fol. 249v: 6–10)[52]

---

48 Lat. II: 4–32; Appendix fol. 249r: 25 – fol. 250r: 9.
49 Lat. IV: 11.
50 Lat. III: 13–15.
51 Lat. III: 20; Appendix fol. 249v: 26.
52 Lat. III: 9–11.

As well as demonstrating Bridget's submission, this passage also testifies to the qualifications of Bridget's confessors and spiritual directors. It is vital to establish the virtue of these clerics, for not only do these men authorize Bridget as a visionary and prophet, and license the distribution of her writings, but their impeccable virtue casts a reflected aura on Bridget. The more respected luminaries of the Church she can gather to her cause, the more light she can acquire. Margery Kempe's accumulation of clerical endorsements is motivated by similar considerations, but to much less effect, as will become evident in the next chapter.

Ancillary to Bridget's submission to spiritual guidance therefore is the approval given to her writings by these men. This approval attests that not only were Bridget's person and her visionary experiences under the scrutiny of learned and devout clerics, but that her communication of those experiences was also subject to the same wise and experienced judgement. The mantle of impeccable virtue and obedience which Alfonso casts over Bridget obscures the woman, but it certainly conforms impeccably to the requirements of *discretio spirituum*. The discourse of *discretio spirituum*, like the habits of monks and nuns, obliterates individuality. A good – a successful – visionary is a nobody speaking the words of God.[53]

Because the discourse of *discretio spirituum* has the effect of obliterating the body, the question of trance and ecstasy was a difficult one for ecclesiastical officials to judge. This is the second area of Bridget's behaviour on which the *Epistola* concentrates. The physical state in which a visionary experienced revelation inevitably drew attention to the body; a body in fits of ecstasy could obliterate the words of the visionary. On the one hand, there was sufficient precedent for holy figures being transported out of their senses. And surely, the sight or sound of God should render one oblivious to any other stimulus. On the other hand, there were equally numerous testimonies to demonic possession, and fits were thought to be manifestations of the devil's struggle for the soul. That these attitudes affected the perception – and the behaviour – of visionaries is demonstrated, for example, in a letter from Hildegard of Bingen to her younger contemporary, Elisabeth of Schönau. In it she urges Elisabeth to be temperate in her ecstasy.[54] Bridget's ecstatic behaviour would seem to be all that Hildegard could have wished. She is very decorous in her transports, usually being described in such terms as 'alyenat [*alienatam*] fro hir self rapt in hir sprith' (Appendix fol. 250r: 28–9).[55]

---

53 Just as Tolstoy, in *Anna Karenina*, claimed that all happy families are alike, so one could argue that all good visionaries resemble each other. It's the unsuccessful ones that stand out, as we shall see in the next chapter.

54 P. Dronke, *Women Writers of the Middle Ages* (Cambridge, 1984), p. 149; also K. Kerby-Fulton and D. Elliott, 'Self-Image and the Visionary Role', *Vox Benedictina* 2:3 (1985), 205.

55 Lat. IV: 10.

As with testimony to her virtue, the testimony of Bridget's spiritual directors in support of the manner in which she receives her visions is crucial. Alfonso himself attests to having seen Bridget in ecstasy on several occasions. This evidence is especially important in conveying an aura of respectability to one of Bridget's most dramatic moments. On this occasion she is described as rapt in prayer, her mind and spirit are suffused with the love of God.

> Once also this same person [Bridget], with an ineffable exultation of her spirit, perceptibly felt a wonderful bodily movement in her heart, as if a living infant was stirring there; this movement was visible from without.[56]

Not only is the experience itself dramatic, but the image used to convey it has very powerful connotations. Although there is a definite medieval tradition of mystical pregnancy, Bridget generally eschews such bodily manifestations of the divine presence.[57] This accords with her representation of herself as a disembodied voice. However, in the incident recounted above, the movement is seen by Alfonso, and one other of Bridget's advisors. The presence of outside witnesses, religious men, gives credibility and weight to an experience which could easily be discounted as *muliebria figmenta* – womanish fictions.[58] It is significant that Alfonso uses this incident as an example in his text; his authorizing of it at this point defuses the possibility of misinterpretation of the incident when Bridget herself recounts it in the *Revelaciones*.[59]

Describing the manner of Bridget's reception of visions provides Alfonso with further opportunities to demonstrate her submission, to translate her behaviour into the discourse of *discretio spirituum*. He says that she immedi-

---

[56] 'Aliquando quoque ipsa sensibiliter senciebat cum ineffabili exultacione spiritus quendam sensibilem corporalem motum mirabilem in corde suo, quasi si ibi esset infans viuus se reuoluens, qui motus ab extra videbatur' (Lat. IV: 14). This passage does not appear in the Middle English translation.

[57] Claire Sahlin examines the significance of this episode, and of pregnancy as a feature of Bridget's devotion, in ' "A Marvellous and Great Exultation of the Heart": Mystical Pregnancy and Marian Devotion in Bridget of Sweden's *Revelations*', in *Studies in St Birgitta and the Brigittine Order*, 2 vols., ed. J. Hogg (New York, 1993), I, 108–28. The tradition of mystical pregnancy is explored in relation to three fourteenth-century German nuns in R. Hale, '*Imitatio Mariae*: Motherhood Motifs in Devotional Memoirs', in *Medieval German Literature: Proceedings from the 23rd International Congress on Medieval Studies, Kalamazoo, Michigan, May 5–8, 1988* (Göppingen, 1989), pp. 129–45. See also C. Bynum, ' ". . . And Woman His Humanity": Female Imagery in the Religious Writing of the Later Middle Ages', in *Gender and Religion: On the Complexity of Symbols*, ed. Bynum et al. (Boston, 1986), pp. 257–88, and C. Bynum, 'Women Mystics' for passing references.

[58] This was the phrase used to describe the first of Elisabeth of Schönau's prophetic visions to be made public. See A. L. Clark, *Elisabeth of Schönau: A Twelfth-Century Visionary* (Philadelphia, 1992), p. 15.

[59] *Revs.* II: xviii and VI: lxxxviii; *LC* VI: lxxxvi.

ately reports her visions to her spiritual directors, often expressing doubts as to their meaning or origin; she defers to their authority, which then augments the authority of her visions.[60] The resultant testimony of the spiritual directors is vital then in locating Bridget's visions – they are usually received when she is 'vigilant in preyour' (Appendix fol. 250v: 16).[61] Visions experienced while the recipient was at prayer were more likely to be percieved as of divine origin than those experienced in less propitious circumstances – asleep, for example.

In constructing Bridget's behaviour so comprehensively within the discourse, Alfonso effectively obliterates her body. This obliteration creates the space for him to authorize her voice speaking God's words, to legitimize her private experience for utterance in the public sphere. He does this explicitly when he announces his intention to use her words in the *Epistola solitarii*.

> . . . I sey yat they may be certified of yat maner the whech sche sy ye visions not alonly be myn wordis but also be the wordis of hir self blissid Bregid.
>
> (Appendix fol. 250r: 21–3)[62]

Once again Alfonso involves Bridget in her own authorization; she is presented as co-author of her validation as a visionary.

Cloaking Bridget in the mantle of *discretio spirituum* amplifies her voice and ultimately empowers her. In the *Epistola solitarii* Alfonso establishes Bridget's authority, demonstrates her knowledge and describes her behaviour by employing the discourse of *discretio spirituum*. Bridget is constructed in terms which permit her to occupy space within the public sphere; her female body vanishes and her visionary voice emerges. The same pattern is followed in Bridget's construction in the *Revelaciones*. Her authority is established, her knowledge is demonstrated and her behaviour described in compliance with the restrictions imposed by the patriarchal discourse. This results in her empowerment as a visionary. This chapter will now consider how Bridget herself manifests knowledge of the criteria of *discretio spirituum* in the *Revelaciones*.

Sancta Birgitta Revelaciones[63]

The vexed question of agency is as pertinent to the writing of the *Revelaciones* of Bridget of Sweden as it is to *The Book of Margery Kempe*, and has generated a similar volume of scholarly speculation. However, more clues to its answer are

---

60 For example, Appendix fol. 249v: 6–10; Lat. III: 9–11.

61 Lat. IV: 25.

62 Lat. IV: 5.

63 Latin references for the *Revelaciones* are from *Sancta Birgitta Revelaciones*, Book I, ed. C. Undhagen, SSFS, ser. 2. Latinska skrifter 7:1 (Uppsala, 1978); *Sancta Birgitta Revela-*

available.[64] Whereas all the information which we have about the writing of *The Book of Margery Kempe* is given in the text itself, a variety of sources apart from the *Revelaciones* describe its composition and delineate Bridget's involvement. A certain observation of convention is probably inevitable in statements testifying to the unaltered recording of Bridget's words. However, to discount the significant collaboration of the visionary in the recounting of her experiences intimates, as my introduction to this study argues, a reading which disempowers her and utterly privileges the male voice.

Undoubtedly, editorial changes were made and Alfonso selected and organized much of the material for the *Revelaciones* after Bridget's death.[65] However, it is known that she actually wrote some of her visions herself; autograph fragments still survive.[66] It can be argued that one of the reasons she learned Latin in middle age was to maintain control over the translations made by the two Peters.[67] A number of sources testify to Bridget's checking of transcriptions and translations of her revelations; again, this is evidence of her desire for some control over the written revelations.[68] A distinct and forceful personality does emerge from her *vita*, and from other depictions of her life and work. Her history, her representations on her own behalf to the King of Sweden to acquire a home for her Order, her involvement in secular and ecclesiastical politics, her acquisition of Alfonso as a spiritual director and editor all argue that she was a woman actively involved in her own life. There can be little doubt that Bridget had a very strong sense of her mission, and a determination to accomplish it using all the skills at her disposal. It therefore seems

ciones, Book V, *Liber questionum*, ed. Birger Bergh, SSFS, ser. 2, Latinska skrifter 7:5 (Uppsala, 1971); *Sancta Birgitta Revelaciones*, Book VII, ed. B. Bergh, SSFS, ser. 2, Latinska skrifter 7:7 (Uppsala, 1967). For those books of revelations which have not yet been edited, the Latin references are from *Sancta Birgitta Revelationes* (Bartholomeus Ghotan: Lübeck, 1492); all are abbreviated as *Revs*. Middle English citations are from *The Liber Celestis of St Bridget of Sweden: A Middle English Version in British Library MS Claudius Bi*, ed. R. Ellis, EETS (Oxford, 1987), abbreviated as *LC*.

64 See for example: R. Ellis, 'The Visionary Universe of St Bridget of Sweden: A Revelation and its Editors: The *Epistola Solitarii* of Alphonse of Jaén, and Book VI, Chapter 52, of the *Liber Celestis* of St Bridget of Sweden', in *Interdisciplinary Research on Imagery and Sight (I.R.I.S.): Vision et Perception Fondamentales*, Actes du Colloque (Lyon, 20 and 21 June 1981), pp. 77–96; R. Ellis, 'The Divine Message and its Human Agents: St Birgitta and her Editors', in *Studies in St Birgitta and the Brigittine Order*, 2 vols., ed. J. Hogg (New York, 1993), I, 209–33; H. Aili, 'St Birgitta and the Text of the *Revelationes*: A Survey of Some Influences Traceable to Translators and Editors', in *The Editing of Theological and Philosophical Texts from the Middle Ages*, ed. M. Asztalos (Stockholm, 1986), pp. 75–91; B. Morris, 'Labyrinths', pp. 23–33.

65 *RE*, pp. 165–6.

66 Morris, 'Labyrinths', p. 24.

67 Colledge, '*Epistola*', 23–4.

68 See, for example, *A&P*, p. 84.

valid to assume that Bridget collaborated in her own construction,[69] and therefore to examine how the *Revelaciones* manifests her apparent internalization of the discourse of *discretio spirituum*. Consequently, in this chapter, recognition of Bridget's agency in her own construction is reflected in terminology such as 'self-portrayal' or 'self-fashioning'.

The *Revelaciones* is not only an account of Bridget's visions, but also a continual verification of her visionary experience, and sanction of her status as a divine instrument according to *discretio spirituum*.[70] Bridget constructs herself purely as a voice to articulate the word of God; she has no opinions, she is passive, she transmits the divine message without any glossing. She does not offer her own interpretation of any vision which is in the slightest degree allegorical or metaphorical – where interpretation is needed, it is offered by a celestial figure. In this Bridget contrasts vividly with Margery Kempe who, as will be seen, is portrayed as far from passive, frequently voicing opinions and negotiating the content of divine messages. Christ describes Bridget as a clean vessel for the wine that is his words.

> And þe vessell þat it [wine] is sent in is clene. Right so I sende mi wordes bi þe, whilke is a vessell accordinge, and þerefore speke þame boldeli where and when mi spirit biddis þe. (*LC* VI: lii)[71]

In other words, she is a disembodied voice, her only function to utter and to worship in words.

My exploration of the use of the discourse of *discretio spirituum* in the *Revelaciones* is organized under the same categories employed in the discussion of the *Epistola solitarii*: Authority, Knowledge and Behaviour. Under the heading Authority I consider Bridget's authorization as a visionary and the valorization of the words Bridget speaks, either by citing a divine or clerical interpretation, or by reference to some precedent. The category of Knowledge covers Bridget's own ability to discern the spirits, the justification of the type of visions that she has, and the manner in which she receives them. Behaviour includes Bridget's virtue, her way of life, and, most important, her submission

---

[69] As Roger Ellis writes in the introduction to his edition of the *Liber Celestis*: 'In principle the Alphonsine edition witnesses to the collaboration of three parties, and allows us to distinguish at least three hands, three voices, in the production of the *Liber*: those of the saint, of her translators the two Peters, and Alphonse, her editor-in-chief. The distinguishing of these voices from one another, however proves . . . difficult . . .' (*LC*, p. xiii).

[70] Roger Ellis writes that 'the *Liber* [*Celestis*] addresses itself almost obsessively to the question of its own status . . . it is not, and cannot be, a self-evident text, and the possibilities of misunderstanding are legion . . .' ('Visionary Universe', p. 78). To this I would add that the text also addresses itself almost obsessively to the question of Bridget's own status as a visionary.

[71] *Revs.* VI: lii.

to her spiritual directors. Sometimes one vision narrative will allude to all three categories; it is rare that there is no reference at all to the principles of *discretio spirituum*.

In examining the *Epistola solitarii* and the *Revelaciones* according to these categories, it becomes apparent that they reinforce each other. They work in concert to bring about Bridget's disappearance behind the restrictions of *discretio spirituum* in order that she can emerge, a disembodied voice, empowered in the public arena.

Authority

As I have already argued, the question of authority is a central concern of the doctrine of *discretio spirituum*. It is imperative that the visionary not appear to exercise her own power, to act in her own right, to assert her own interpretation of revelation or doctrine. She is the medium, not the message. While she may be the author, her authority must be presented as borrowed from other, higher, powers than those which reside in her womanly frame. To this end, she must appear powerless and passive in order that it can be believed that a higher power works through her. She must be authorized by both divine and ecclesiastical authorities. Whereas divine authorization is bestowed, ecclesiastical authorization must be earned. Earning this is, of course, the essential reason for the *Epistola solitarii*, and for Bridget's employment of the discourse of *discretio spirituum*. This section first investigates how Bridget's authority as a visionary rests on her construction as a channel for the divine word. It then examines the process whereby the words Bridget utters as a visionary are themselves also presented as validated by a higher power.

First, as mentioned above, Bridget acquires authority as a visionary by displacing that authority to a superior power. She accomplishes this through her self-fashioning as a passive, compliant vehicle for divine communication, and as an instrument of the divine will. She presents herself as without will, powerless, as one who follows directions, who avoids the limelight. This was the paradoxical way to power which lay before medieval women visionaries. By constructing themselves according to the discourse of *discretio spirituum* they could be effective and powerful, as God's instruments, in the public sphere that was normally prohibited to women. Bridget's construction according to this model is evident in the description of her first summons by God.[72] When she first hears a voice Bridget is terrified, and flees, fearing demonic illusion. This happens three times, until, the third time, the voice instructs her to consult her spiritual director, Magister Mathias, who is, says the voice, an expert in the discernment of spirits [*discretio spirituum*]. This episode is a masterstroke. It establishes Bridget's submission to her spiritual director. It introduces both the concept of *discretio spirituum*, and the fact that

---

[72] *A&P*, p. 80. This episode is quoted at the head of this chapter.

Bridget will be guided by someone who is divinely acknowledged to be an expert in the doctrine. And it also portrays Bridget as one who, in her humility, does not actually seek for communion with God. Finally, the episode establishes that Bridget has been chosen and sought out by God, that she is passive, that she initiated nothing, invited nothing. Although terror and disbelief at encountering the divine can be seen as a convention, here the convention is adapted to the discourse of *discretio spirituum*, personalized, in the sense of being used to establish Bridget's credentials as a visionary.

Bridget's presentation of herself as passive is reinforced by Christ's choice of her as his spouse. She is authorized as prophet and visionary by Christ.

> I haue chosen þe and taken þe to mi spouse, for it pleses me and likes me to do so, and for I will shewe to þe mi preuai secretis. (*LC* I: ii)[73]

Thus, not only is she presented as subject to the divine will, but also, as spouse of Christ, she acts under the authority and control of her divine husband. Uxorial submission is one variant of submission of women to men, including the submission of a visionary to her male spiritual director. Bridget's construction as divine spouse implies her location in a traditionally female role and subordinate position. Thus identifying Bridget's access to hidden knowledge with her position as spouse reflects the discourse of *discretio spirituum* in that she and the knowledge she acquires are subject to male control.

Yet another of Bridget's visions presents her as a passive, even unwilling, vehicle, at the same time as it addresses one of the concerns of *discretio spirituum*; the desire of a visionary for worldly fame.

> Crist apperid to þe spouse in hir praier and bad hir þat scho suld sai þat þat sho suld here and lett noght for drede of man, no tell it not for ani worldeli wirshipe: 'for þis reuelacion is noȝt for þi sake, bot for mi frendis þat are in Napils . . .' (*LC* VII: xxviii)[74]

Margery Kempe, in a similar situation which is examined in the next chapter, negotiates the content of a divine message to protect her own credibility.[75] In contrast, Bridget is portrayed in this passage as an exemplary visionary who is neither tempted nor deterred by earthly considerations in fulfilling her divinely ordained function; she is powerless in the power of God.

Bridget's construction of herself as powerless, submissive and invisible is also manifest in the role she takes in her visions, where she is inevitably a passive audience. Even when she witnesses the events of the Nativity and the Passion, she does not participate. In this she differs from other women vision-

---

[73] *Revs.* I: ii.
[74] *Revs.* VII: xxvii.
[75] See pp. 129–31 below.

aries who saw themselves playing a part in their visions.[76] The most Bridget ever does is ask a question, prompting a lesson from some heavenly figure. She is consistently presented as incapable of interpreting divine vision or locution without assistance. Her submission, willing to be taught yet not appearing to teach, is consistent with the discourse in its reflection of the belief that women should not teach in public.

The second way in which Bridget's authority is established is by presenting her visions as validated by a higher power. In the *Revelaciones*, Bridget portrays herself as able to understand straightforward, orthodox instruction, such as ways to pray to the Virgin, or how to worship Christ. However, whenever there is any material which calls for explication, a celestial interpretation is immediately forthcoming. For example, in one vision, the Virgin Mary describes Bridget as a lamb who puts her head in the lion's mouth. Christ says, 'Modir, tell what þis menys, þat þis spouse may vndirstande' (*LC* IV: xxxix).[77] Not only does Bridget's body seem to disappear through skilful use of the discourse of *discretio spirituum*, but also her autonomous intelligence is made to seem nonexistent. Every vision or revelation identified as such is interpreted for Bridget by some celestial figure. Every allegory is deciphered, most metaphors and symbols are translated. The effect of these celestial interpretations is that Bridget appears to convey messages which have been rendered free of ambiguity at the source, and is therefore released from suspicion of distorting – or even glossing – God's words. She is only a channel; all responsibility and authority for the words spoken rests with God. She is neither mind nor body, she is voice alone.

Presenting herself as powerless and passive, an instrument wielded by the hand of God, a voice speaking the words of God, was particularly vital for Bridget, given that many of the causes she espoused were controversial ones: the return of the papacy to Rome, an end to the war between France and England, and an end to clerical corruption.[78] It was her visions on these matters which made her particularly vulnerable; she risked alienating secular as well as ecclesiastical powers. Equally, it was these visions which provided her with opportunities to exercise power and to be effective in spheres traditionally closed to women. The care and skill with which she constructs herself

---

[76] For example, Margery Kempe makes spiced wine for the Virgin after the crucifixion (*BMK*, p. 195). Mechtild of Hackeborn offers the sacrament to the celestial hosts (*The Booke of Gostlye Grace of Mechtild of Hackeborn*, ed. T. A. Halligan (Toronto, 1979), p. 82).

[77] *Revs.* IV: xxxix.

[78] Colledge gives a detailed summary of Bridget's political activities in '*Epistola*', 19–49. Kathryn Kerby-Fulton argues that Bridget belongs to the tradition of apocalyptic prophets, such as Hildegard of Bingen and Robert of Uzès (d. 1296), who felt compelled to use their powers as visionaries to denounce ecclesiastical abuses (*Reformist*, pp. 196–7 and 102–11).

as a passive voice is particularly evident in those visions which imply an active agent, visions counselling specific action on matters of ecclesiastical or secular politics. It is obviously very useful for her to construct herself as a cipher, an empty channel through which God's words flow, when she is taking controversial stands. She scrupulously locates the source of the vision, providing the visionary utterance with a higher authority.

In one vision she is even represented rather like a secretary taking dictation. Christ tells her exactly what to write in a threatening letter to Pope Clement, commanding him to make peace between the kings of France and England.[79] In another vision, Bridget is commanded to reprove a certain deacon, and is told exactly what to say to him.[80] In a third, a message which condemns clerical corruption and urges the return of the papacy to Rome, a celestial voice explains the images of the vision and tells the Pope what he should do to purify the Church.[81] In these, and all similar directives, Bridget shelters behind the divine imperative; she is not responsible for what Christ says or does. She is, however, empowered by his saying it through her.[82]

Bridget's constant referral – and deferral – to the authority of others means that she frames her visionary representations in such a way that while the message may be controversial, the messenger is almost invisible. Constructed in this way, her visions, formulated within the discourse of *discretio spirituum*, constitute a testimony to her humility, her submissiveness, her lack of desire for worldly fame, power, or riches. Paradoxically, by embracing humility and abjuring power, she does, in fact, empower herself. Her invisibility in her visions cloaks her subsequent visibility in carrying out her divine mission. She utters God's words, but the voice which speaks is very much hers.

Knowledge

God's first command to Bridget is that she avail herself of expertise in *discretio spirituum*. However, Bridget's representations of her visions also demonstrate her independent knowledge of the doctrine. She displays her cognizance by referring continually to her instruction in the doctrine, to her ability to identify devils in disguise and to describe fiends, demons and angels. The source of her knowledge is always identified as divine, and her credentials are vouchsafed by celestial figures. She constructs herself as one whose ability to discern spirits is unerring, and therefore as one whose visions cannot be doubted. All

---

79 *LC* VI: lxiii; *Revs.* VI: lxiii.

80 *LC* VI: vii; *Revs.* VI: vii.

81 *LC* IV: xlix; *Revs.* VI: xlix.

82 Of course, such measures did not mean that Bridget generated no controversy. As I point out above, the disputed truth of her visions generated much discussion and a number of treatises. Dyan Elliott describes Bridget, with justification, as becoming 'something of a rallying point for resistance to female mysticism' ('Physiology', p. 164).

this is achieved through her understanding of the imperatives of *discretio spirituum*, and her facility with its discourse. Her understanding and discernment are constantly demonstrated and acclaimed in the *Revelaciones*, and focus on three main concerns. One is to establish that she can distinguish an angel from a demon. The second is that she is aware of the dangers presented by spiritual vision, but can also defend its function. The third is her knowledge of the appropriate manner and circumstances in which true visions are experienced.

The first of these strategies to be examined is the presentation of Bridget's learning as an immediate and constant feature of her intimacy with the divine. For example, as soon as Bridget has been chosen by Christ, he instructs her in *discretio spirituum*.

> I haue biden þe do thre þinges bi þe whilke þou mai knawe a gude spirit ...
> Right as bi þeere þou mai knawe a gude spirit, right so be thre, contrari to þere, þou mai knawe ane euell spirit. (*LC* 1: iv)[83]

Not only is Bridget thus instructed and reassured about her ability to tell a good spirit from an evil one, but readers – and the ecclesiastical authorities – can rest assured that Bridget has been taught by an unchallengeable authority. Nevertheless, even with the benefit of such impeccable instruction, Bridget is not encouraged to rely on her own judgement, but is told to submit her visions to her spiritual directors.[84] Submission and obedience to the spiritual director is, of course, the paramount principle of *discretio spirituum*, and in her willingness to conform to this requirement Bridget constructs herself within the discourse. Margery Kempe also subscribed to the notion of submission to a spiritual director, and like Bridget was often divinely directed to do so. However, whereas Bridget is always obedient to her spiritual superiors, Margery frequently evaded their control.

Instruction in *discretio spirituum* is given periodically throughout the *Revelaciones*. For example, on two occasions in addition to the one cited above, Christ tells Bridget the tokens of the good spirit and the evil spirit.[85] John the Evangelist teaches her to distinguish a good spirit from an evil one by the fruits of the visitation.[86] And on one occasion God himself teaches Bridget the same lesson, using Elizabeth of Hungary as an exemplar.[87] In this vision, an evil

---

[83] *Revs.* I: iv.

[84] *LC* I: iv; *Revs.* I: iv.

[85] *LC* IV: cx and VI: xxxviii; *Revs.* IV: cx and VI: xxxviii.

[86] *LC* IV: xxiii; *Revs.* IV: xxiii.

[87] *LC* IV: iv; *Revs.* IV: iv. Elizabeth (1207–31), daughter of the King of Hungary, was driven out of the court of Thuringia after the death of her husband, Ludwig IV, on the grounds that her charities were bankrupting the state. She placed herself under the spiritual direction of Conrad of Marburg, who deprived her of her children and imposed on her a regime of such extreme asceticism that it verged on the sadistic.

spirit is threatening a good spirit with tempting Elizabeth into lechery. God intervenes, with instructions to the good spirit as to how Elizabeth can protect herself. The implication is clear that Bridget would be afforded similar protection, that she is safe from demonic temptation, and that her visions can be trusted.

Bridget's familiarity with the doctrine of *discretio spirituum* is manifested in a second form; this is in her justification of the type of visions which she receives. As discussed earlier in relation to Alfonso's treatment of this subject, nearly all of Bridget's visions fall within the category of imaginative or spiritual visions. That is, she hears and sees things in bodily likeness, with her spiritual senses. This is generally deemed an inferior form of vision by patristic and scholastic theologians. That Bridget had internalized this assessment is demonstrated by her justifying the form of her transcendental experiences. A significant number of visions in the *Revelaciones* address the question specifically, often by invoking defences of spiritual vision by celestial figures. For example, in one vision, St Ambrose appears to her, and explains himself in these terms.

> I am Ambrose þe bishope þat aperis vnto þe, spekinge bi likenes, for þi hert mai noght take vndirstanding of gostli þinges withoute bodeli liknes.
>
> (*LC* III: vi)[88]

It is important to note that Ambrose here attests that it is the source, not the recipient, which is responsible for the form of a vision, and that the form chosen is that which is believed most likely to ensure understanding in the recipient.

God delivers perhaps the strongest argument in the text in favour of spiritual vision.

> . . . I send wordes to mi frendes, þe whilke ar noȝt so derke to vndirstand as is þe Apocalips þat I shewed to Jon, for I wald in mi time, of mi spirit, it should be plainli expounde; ne þai ar noȝt so derke as þe þinges þat Paule saw when he was ravishet, þe whilke wer not lefull to be spoken; bot þai are so opin þat all, both small and grete, mai knawe þaim and vndirstand þaime. (*LC* I: lvi)[89]

In this vision, God is portrayed declaring his desire for plain speaking, for

---

There is a clear parallel between Elizabeth of Hungary and Bridget, a parallel which serves to reinforce Bridget's place in the tradition of holy women. Both were nobly born, both gave up wealth and position when called by God, and both were submissive to their spiritual directors. Elizabeth was canonized in 1235, and was held in high esteem in fourteenth-century Europe (Bynum, *Holy Feast*, pp. 134–5). Being associated with her would have brought Bridget reflected glory.

[88] *Revs.* III: vi.

[89] *Revs.* I: lvi. The allusion to the Apocalypse suggests the approach of the latter days, a time traditionally signalled by a proliferation of prophets.

revelation using words and images which anyone – and everyone – can understand, and thus presenting a strong argument in favour of spiritual vision.
Again it is made clear that it is God, not the visionary, who determines the
form of vision. These arguments present an implicit challenge to the hierarchy
of vision which Bridget exploits without seeming to advocate. Her submission
to the wisdom of God and the saints contributes to her construction within the
discourse, at the same time that the argument they make enhances the
authority of her visions.

The central thread which runs through all the revealed defences of spiritual
vision in the *Revelaciones* is clarity of understanding. God sends visions in
bodily likeness so that the visionary will understand and be able to communicate what has been revealed.[90] The principal theological argument for the
privileging of intellectual over spiritual vision is that intellectual vision brings
about instant and unmistakeable knowing; the understanding of the recipient
is complete. The emphasis in the *Revelaciones* on a similarly complete understanding being conveyed by spiritual vision is an attempt to elevate it to the
level of intellectual vision.[91] It is also an attempt to eliminate the element of
doubt as to the provenance of the vision, a doubt which is always associated
with spiritual vision. This implied elevation of the form of Bridget's visions
would, of course, increase their authority.

Bridget is not content only to show divine figures instructing her in *discretio
spirituum*. Nor is she satisfied with defending the form of vision she receives.
She also demonstrates her facility in the discourse of *discretio spirituum* in a
third way, which is her description of the manner and circumstances in which
she receives visions. The physical state of the visionary was believed to be an
indication of the source of the vision. The less the physical body of the medium
intrudes, the more reliable the message is perceived to be. As Alfonso points
out in the *Epistola solitarii*, dreams, or visions experienced while sleeping, were
suspect. Visions which occur while praying, or during the mass acquire an
aura of respectability – the devil is less likely to intrude on sanctified pursuits.
Bridget often indicates that a certain vision occurred while she was awake. For
example, when she recounts a gruesome vision of two corrupted souls she
specifies,

---

[90] Implicit in the claim that visions are modified according to the capacity of the
visionary is, of course, the fact that Bridget, as a woman, was deemed incapable of
intellectual vision. Although this is never made explicit, nor is the form of vision
explicitly associated with the gender of the visionary, it does accord with the link
between women's perceived inferior capacity for intellection and their predilection
for spiritual vision.

[91] This is, of course, akin to Alfonso's 'redefinition' of some of Bridget's visions as intellectual.

And when I had sene þis, noght slepynge bot wakynge, I saide 'What is þis?'
(*LC* IV: lii)[92]

Similarly, a vision of St Denys occurs while Bridget is praying.[93] The whole of
Book V, the *Liber questionum*, she receives as a vision while she is praying.[94]

> It fell in a tyme, when sho . . . rydynge towarde a castell of her awn, had hir
> mynde in prayer lift vp to God almighti, on swhilke wise þat sho was rauysht
> in spirit, and in manere aliende fro bodily wittes, suspendid in exstasy of
> gostely contemplacion. (*LC* V: prologue)[95]

In these areas of waking and praying visions, Bridget does not deviate from
the criteria established by *discretio spirituum*. However, when she deals with
the question of ecstatic trances, Bridget presents an argument, which, while
not directly applicable to herself – her transports are quite decorous – does
suggest the irrelevance of physical states to the authenticity of revelation. This
is despite the fact that her own construction within the discourse has been
accomplished so as to effectively disembody her.

Ecstatic states presented ecclesiastical officials with some difficulties. In the
Revelaciones, Bridget describes Christ depreciating the importance of the
physical state of the visionary. In a vision in which Christ instructs Bridget in
the minutiae of *discretio spirituum*, he discusses ecstasy.

> . . . þare is som þat falsli and vntrewli sais of me þat þai, þe whilke are mi
> seruantes, of oure grete deuocion gase oute of þaire minde and are traueld
> with euell spirites . . . if sometime mi frendes seme oute of minde, þat is noȝt
> for þai suffir passion be pouere of þe fende, ne for þai serue me of birnand
> deuocion, bot owþir for defaute of brain or for mekinge of þaime or for som
> oþir cause knawen to me. (*LC* I: iv)[96]

Christ claims knowledge and understanding of aberrant behaviour in visionaries, and states that such behaviour is not a sign of demonic possession –
although neither should it be taken as a sign of great spiritual fervour. Physical
symptoms are just simply physical symptoms. By stating that the body does
not manifest the spiritual state of the individual, Christ is shifting the emphasis
from the body. Given the traditional ecclesiastical focus on women's bodies as
indicators of their spiritual insufficiency, implicit in Bridget's representation of
her vision is a divine directive to transcend the body – in quite a different

---

92 *Revs.* IV: lii.
93 *LC* IV: ciii; *Revs.* IV: ciii.
94 However, see also Alfonso's statement that Bridget experienced this as an intellec-
    tual vision, pp. 86–7, above.
95 *Revs.* V: *prologus.*
96 *Revs.* I: iv.

manner to that which Bridget herself accomplishes through conformity to *discretio spirituum*.

In addition to these explicit demonstrations of her knowledge of the doctrine of *discretio spirituum*, Bridget's knowledge is implicit in the construction of her behaviour within the discourse, which I examine in the next section.

Behaviour

The category of behaviour is the third, and final, category of manifestations of the discourse of *discretio spirituum* in the *Revelaciones* which I will discuss. As I have already argued, the behaviour of the visionary was of cardinal importance in *discretio spirituum*. The virtue of a woman visionary was largely deduced from her conformity to cultural expectations of holiness, and in the *Revelaciones* Bridget's behaviour exhibits that conformity. She is consistently depicted as meek, humble and obedient. She also addresses the question of her widowhood, and constructs it according to the discourse. And finally, she uses her relationship with her confessors and spiritual directors to exemplify her submission.

Her virtuous demeanour is demonstrated throughout the *Revelaciones*. Sometimes she is commended, sometimes she is instructed. For example, Christ tells her in a vision that she is coming to dwell in the house of the Holy Spirit, and must conform herself through meekness and devotion to the customs of that house, thereby suggesting that Bridget has demonstrated both her fitness to enter the house, and her ability to achieve the necessary meekness and devotion.[97] A number of other revelations are specific teachings on virtue, directed expressly to Bridget. So, for example, Christ tells Bridget to withstand the lure of worldly goods and honour;[98] he instructs her in meekness;[99] he teaches her to restrict both her material and spiritual desires;[100] and, likening her to a musical pipe on which the Holy Spirit plays, he tells her to keep herself clean and shining, wrapped in the love of God and stored in a case, safe from the depredations of the fiend.[101] St Agnes praises Bridget for being free from pride.[102]

This latter endorsement is significant because humility was a major preoccupation of the ecclesiastical authorities when assessing visionaries. The notoriety which some visionaries attracted, and the fear that they would use their influence to promulgate heretical teachings, and lead others astray meant that Church leaders needed reassurance that the visionary sought no earthly

---

[97] *LC* V: xiii; *Revs.* V: xiii.
[98] *LC* V: x; *Revs.* V: x.
[99] *LC* IV: xci; *Revs.* IV: xci.
[100] *LC* VI: xciii; *Revs.* VI: xciii.
[101] *LC* IV: c; *Revs.* IV: c.
[102] *LC* IV: xvii; *Revs.* IV: xvii.

renown. Far from seeking attention, Bridget strives to make herself invisible. She constructs herself to deflect attention from herself to her message.[103] By making herself invisible, she privileges her voice.

In addition to being taught herself, Bridget is audience to celestial conferences on virtue, on which occasions she demonstrates a good knowledge and a proper attitude. One such episode involves Christ, John the Baptist, the Virgin Mary and St Agnes condemning the life of an evil bishop, and describing the life he should lead.[104] Her conveyance of such intensive moral instruction also conveys the idea that she herself espouses and practises all that she preaches, and clearly demonstrates Bridget's virtue, devotion and submissiveness.

There are times, however, when Bridget is reproved for her behaviour. For example, Christ chastises her for her impatience, sharpness, lack of love for him, and for being a bad example to her fellow Christians.[105] Although recounting such episodes might seem a strange way for Bridget to assert her virtue, in actual fact this is what it accomplishes. These incidents serve to emphasize Bridget's ultimate humility. First, she is shown to be submissive – here, as submissive to her divine husband. She is humble, meekly accepting his reproof. She also presents herself as erring, as a sinner, thereby avoiding the accusations of spiritual arrogance which could arise from a portrayal of spiritual perfection. Presenting herself as learning from her errors – Christ inevitably instructs her how to do better in the future – she epitomises the soul which struggles and stumbles, but perseveres in its journey to God.

A second area in which Bridget's virtue is validated is in the gender-related issue of her widowhood. Alfonso deals with this matter in the *Epistola solitarii* by providing scriptural precedents for virtuous widows. Given the almost constant equation of virginity with spiritual purity in medieval theology, a non-virgin needed to justify her status. Bridget addresses the issue in two ways. One is an implicit challenge to received teaching on the three states of marriage – maidenhood, marriage and widowhood. In a vision resulting from Bridget's dedication of her daughter to him, Christ tells Bridget that maidenhood, wifehood and widowhood are immaterial to him, as long as the desire of the woman is for him alone.

It is bettir þat þe body be wythoute and þe saule wythin þan þe body closede and þe saule wauerynge abowte. (*LC* IV: lxxi)[106]

---

[103] Roger Ellis also notes Bridget's vanishing act. He writes 'She is present at the outset [of a revelation] to validate the extraordinary experiences that will follow, but their extraordinary character is speedily neutralised by the very explicit commentary, and by her disappearance except, so to speak, as a pair of eyes and ears taking everything in, and a mind blessed with total recall' ('Divine', p. 224).

[104] *LC* III: xi–xii; *Revs.* III: xi–xii.

[105] *LC* VI: vi; *Revs.* VI: vi.

[106] *Revs.* IV: lxxi.

As in the vision where Christ explains that bodily transports are no indicators of the state of the soul, here Bridget's representation argues that it is the integrity of the soul, not of the body, which is of concern to Christ. Margery Kempe also struggles over her lack of virginity, and, like Bridget, is reassured that she is as valuable to Christ as any maiden. For both Bridget and Margery, the health of the soul is privileged over the integrity of the body. It is particularly significant that this point should be made over the issue of virginity, which, although technically applicable to men as well, was in practice generally about women's bodies.[107]

The other strategy Bridget adopts in her effort to validate widowhood is to fashion herself in *imitatio Mariae*. She describes the Virgin Mary identifying herself as 'moder and maiden and, as it were, a wedow, for my son had none erthly fadir' (*LC* IV: liii).[108] Bridget's children are generally mentioned only when she is relinquishing them in some sense, just as Mary relinquished Christ. In the *Epistola solitarii*, Alfonso recounts how she offered her two sons as hostages to ease the tax burden on the people of Sweden.[109] She also dedicates her daughter, Katherine, to a religious life.[110]

This sanitized – and sanctified – presentation of her widowhood might have been prompted by a concern to mask the autonomy which she enjoyed as a widow. Bridget had comparative freedom, and she exercised it. She travelled, she left her native country and set up residence in Rome, she was active in both ecclesiastical and secular politics, she challenged popes and manipulated cardinals, she ran her own household and was involved in the editing of her revelations. She was a woman of considerable influence and power. To construct herself as a humble widow in the mould of the Virgin, as a second wife dutifully submissive to Christ, and as a meek, passive visionary seeking and following the guidance of spiritual men is to defuse the threat which her activities offered. Her self-fashioning according to the discourse of *discretio spirituum*, her evident acceptance of its restrictions in order to be empowered in the secular as well as the ecclesiastical arena, are demonstrated in her

---

107 In this argument for equality of souls, Bridget is in fact following the orthodox theological position that men and women were equal in soul, but unequal in body. Two excellent works explore this position, while demonstrating how this belief did little to change attitudes towards women, or to improve their lot. See Børreson, *Subordination*, and McLaughlin 'Equality'.

108 *Revs.* IV: liii. John Audelay, writing in the early fifteenth century, addresses a poem to Bridget part of which celebrates her chaste widowhood and identifies her as 'wyfe, wedow and may'. 'Hayle! fore þe loue of Ihesus Crist/ ȝe foresake ȝour fleschele lust, / Þer-fore be ȝe boþ e-blest/ In the name of swete Ihesus' (*The Poems of John Audelay*, ed. E. K. Whiting, EETS OS 184 (Oxford, 1971), p. 164: 6–9).

109 Lat. III: 31–2; Appendix fol. 250r: 5–9.

110 *LC* IV: lxxi; *Revs.* IV: lxxi.

narrative of a vision in which Christ commands her to be obedient to the great men of the world, because obedience is a condition of the Fall.[111]

> Criste said to þe spouse, 'On foure wise suld þou meke þe: firste, to þe grete men of þe werld, for, bycause þat man wald noȝt kepe þe obediens of God, þerfor he sall stand vndir þe obedience of man. (*LC* IV: xci)[112]

In this vision Bridget is instructed to obey secular rulers. However the most important submission for a woman visionary is submission to a spiritual director. In this way the control of the ecclesiastical authorities over the potentially disruptive pronouncements of prophets and visionaries can be assured. Christ's frequent injunctions to Bridget, to submit herself and her visions to 'some spirituall wise men'[113] provide opportunities for her to demonstrate her conformity to this vital principal. Such injunctions also constitute divine endorsement for ecclesiastical control of the visionary, thereby increasing the authority of the spiritual director and, of course, confirming the power of the Church. For example, St Francis appears to Bridget, and tells her that he always had with him a priest whom he obeyed, and that she should do likewise.[114] At one point she confesses to Christ her reluctance to obey her confessor gladly. Christ clearly outlines her duty.

> I ame in him þat þou art bunden to obey to, and ilke time and oure þat þou liues þine awen will, it sall be to þe clensinge of sin and encressinge of mede.
> (*LC* VI: xxxxiii)[115]

Since it is unthinkable that Bridget should disobey Christ, it is reasonable to assume that her submission to her confessor would thenceforward be impeccable, and certainly there is no record of less than perfect obedience. However, in presenting her error Bridget presents herself as reformed from that error, and possessing the understanding to avoid error in the future. Bridget ultimately always positions herself in the correct relationship to her spiritual director; she makes frequent mention of the involvement of her spiritual director in every aspect of her life, and of her continual submission to him. In doing so she epitomizes the ideal visionary.

---

111 Since God, according to Genesis 3. 16, allocates obedience specifically to Eve – and thereby to all women – as a punishment for her sin, the instruction here, to a woman, has added significance.

112 *Revs.* IV: xci.

113 *LC* I: iv; *Revs.* I: iv.

114 *LC* VII: iii; *Revs.* VII: iii.

115 *Revs.* VI: xxxxiii. Divine identification with the spiritual director is not uncommon in medieval visionary literature. Christ tells Margery Kempe, for example, that he will speak to her through the Dominican anchorite to whom he has directed her (*BMK*, p. 17: 31–4).

The *Epistola solitarii* outlines the criteria of *discretio spirituum* and constructs Bridget within the discourse as an ideal visionary, one who meets all the standards in authority, knowledge and behaviour. The effect is to make her body vanish, so that she is effective in the public sphere as a powerful voice, uttering the words of God. In the *Revelaciones*, Bridget's self-fashioning reinforces Alfonso's construction of her. Her facility with the discourse of *discretio spirituum* is demonstrated in relation to authority, knowledge and behaviour. She accepts the restrictions imposed by *discretio spirituum*, depicts herself as passive and compliant, and therefore is empowered as a divine instrument. The *Revelaciones* not only reveals the word of God, but also an exemplary visionary, Bridget of Sweden.

In marked contrast, *The Book of Margery Kempe* chronicles Margery's struggles with the restrictions of *discretio spirituum* and demonstrates an inconsistent employment of the discourse. She is an insistently physical presence, and though her voice is frequently raised, often it is perceived to be her own voice; consequently the words she speaks are doubted, derided or ignored. Far from being a vanishing visionary, Margery is the woman who will not go away.

CHAPTER FOUR

Margery Kempe:
The Woman Who would not Go Away

I bydde þe & comawnd þe, boldly clepe me Ihesus, þi loue, for I am þi loue wyth-owten ende . . . Thys is my wyl, dowtyr, þat þow receyue my body euery Sonday, and I schal flowe so mych grace in þe þat alle þe world xal meruelyn þerof. Þow xalt ben etyn & knawyn of þe pepul of þe world as any raton knawyth the stokfysh. Drede þe nowt, dowtyr, for þow schalt haue þe vyctory of al þin enmys. I schal ȝeue þe grace j-now to answer euery clerke in the loue of God . . . I schal ȝefe to þe hey medytacyon and very contemplacyon. & I byd þe gon to þe ankyr at þe Frer þrechowrys, & schew hym my preuytys & my cownselys whech I schewe to þe, and werk aftyr hys cownsel, for my spyrit xal speke in hym to þe. (*BMK*, p. 17: 4–34)

Conflict and controversy surrounded Margery Kempe during her lifetime. A similar storm has raged about *The Book of Margery Kempe* since the discovery of the only known extant manuscript of the work in 1934. While critics are generally in agreement that this, thought to be the first autobiography written in English, provides an intriguing glimpse of social life and devotional practices in England in the late fourteenth and early fifteenth centuries, opinions vary sharply on the question of Margery's spirituality and diverge even more radically on her status as a visionary. Critics all too readily assume the mantle of the Grand Inquisitor, and label her everything from an hysteric to a heretic to a heroine.[1] As Karma Lochrie writes in her study, *Margery Kempe and Translations of the Flesh*:

---

[1] The varieties and iniquities of modern critical responses to Margery Kempe have been well documented. See, for example, S. Beckwith, 'A Very Material Mysticism: The Medieval Mysticism of Margery Kempe', in *Medieval Literature: Criticism, Ideology, History*, ed. D. Aers (Brighton, 1986), pp. 37–41; C. Atkinson, *Mystic and Pilgrim: The Book and the World of Margery Kempe* (Ithaca, 1983), pp. 200–220; D. Aers, *Community, Gender, and Individual Identity: English Writing 1360–1430* (London, 1988), pp. 73–5; R. B. Bosse, 'Margery Kempe's Tarnished Reputation: A Reassessment', *Fourteenth-Century English Mystics Newsletter* 5:1 (1979), 9–19; E. Bremner, 'Margery Kempe and the Critics: Disempowerment and Deconstruction', in *Margery Kempe: A Book of Essays*, ed. S. J. McEntire (New York, 1992), pp. 117–35.

Mystical filiations tend still to be linked to issues of mystical legitimacy, in much the same way that Gerson attempts to measure mystical experience according to a code of legitimate signs of spiritual inspiration.[2]

This chapter will demonstrate that much of the controversy surrounding Margery, then and now, is rooted in the contradictory nature of her life as it is inscribed in her text. The quotation from the *Book* given above encapsulates this contradiction, a contradiction which arises from embedding Margery's visionary experiences in a life narrative of scorn and abuse deliberately sought, a life which placed her on the very edge of acceptable religious praxis. Bridget of Sweden is textually constructed in conformity with *discretio spirituum* and is empowered as a visionary. In contrast, *The Book of Margery Kempe* is a product of competing discourses, and presents Margery as inconsistently conforming to *discretio spirituum*. She does not appear to accept the restrictions of the doctrine, and her credibility as a visionary is consequently diminished.

This chapter first examines, under the subheading *The Tangled Text*, the writing of *The Book of Margery Kempe* and some of the critical problems that this unstable text presents. It then considers *The Woman Behind the Text* – surveying the biographical details which the text supplies for Margery Kempe. In *Margery's Mixed Blessing* the chapter presents the argument for Margery's construction according to two principal competing discourses, the discourse of *discretio spirituum* and a discourse of revilement, and examines the implications of this 'mixed blessing' for her success as a visionary. The chapter then focuses on the manifestation of *discretio spirituum* in *The Book of Margery Kempe*. My analysis is structured according to the same categories employed in Chapter Three for Bridget of Sweden: Authority, Knowledge and Behaviour. The final section of the chapter, *Exit the Woman*, traces the subsequent history of the *Book*, and considers the significance of the printed redaction by Wynkyn de Worde in relation to *discretio spirituum*.

The Tangled Text

One of the main topics of current academic debate over *The Book of Margery Kempe* is the author-subject-scribe issue. Margery Kempe was apparently illiterate; her book was written by two scribes, at her request and with her involvement. The first scribe wrote most of Book I before he died. This version the second scribe describes as 'neiþyr good Englysche ne Dewch, ne þe lettyr was not schapyn ne formyd as oþer letters ben' (4: 15–17). The second scribe reluctantly took up the task of deciphering the first scribe's effort and copying it out, and added Book II to complete the work. He also inserted some of his own comments into Book I, and added a new proem. The current debate centres

2   Philadelphia, 1991, p. 5.

around the question of who, in *The Book of Margery Kempe*, wrote what and, even more crucially, whose voice is being heard at any given point.[3]

This issue is one which surfaces in virtually all the writings of medieval women visionaries.[4] As Sarah Beckwith points out,

> The conventional vision narrative is only authorized on the basis of its being a revelation, so that the authority of the woman visionary is essentially always derivative and secondary and her task that of an amanuensis.[5]

In addition to the ambiguity concerning voice which divine dictation causes there is the ambiguity relating to the human voices – or hands – involved in recording this dictation. Nearly all women visionaries had scribes. Some of the women could not write, and even those who could write in the vernacular often did not do so. The composition of a work and the physical act of writing it were two distinct acts at this time, the latter usually being left to a skilled technician.[6] Beyond the ability to write at all lay the ability to write in Latin. As discussed in Chapter I, the credibility of a text was vastly enhanced by its presentation in Latin, and the likelihood of its wide dissemination was therefore increased. Very few women could write Latin, so the services of a translator were necessary at some point. How much either scribe or translator altered the dictated text is a moot point, and one which it is virtually impossible to resolve. Certainly, the convention, especially in the case of divine revelation, was that the words were recorded unaltered, because these were, after all, divine utterances.[7] Women's visionary texts nearly always record that they were read back

---

3 For some of the arguments which have been pursued in this debate see: J. Hirsh, 'Author and Scribe in *The Book of Margery Kempe*', *Medium Aevum* 44 (1975), 145–50; S. Holbrook, ' "About Her": Margery Kempe's Book of Feeling and Working', in *The Idea of Medieval Literature: New Essays on Chaucer and Medieval Culture in Honor of Donald R. Howard*, ed. J. M. Dean and C. K. Zacher (Newark, 1992), pp. 265–84; L. S. Johnson, 'The Trope of the Scribe: The Question of Literary Authority in the Works of Julian of Norwich and Margery Kempe', *Speculum* 66 (1991), 820–38. I am grateful to Dr Andrew Butcher for allowing me to read a draft of his forthcoming article, 'Reading *The Book of Margery Kempe*', which offers an extremely detailed analysis of all the possible stages in the composition of the *Book*, from oral narrative to final manuscript.

4 See my discussion of this issue in the Introduction to this study.

5 'Problems of Authority in Late Medieval English Mysticism: Language, Agency and Authority in *The Book of Margery Kempe*', *Exemplaria* 4:1 (1992), 180.

6 As an indication of the unremarkable nature of Margery's illiteracy, Julia Boffey discusses 'the easy acceptance, on the part of Margery's acquaintances, of her own inability to make a physical record of her experiences', and comments that no one suggested the practical solution that she should learn to write. See 'Women Authors and Women's Literacy in Fourteenth- and Fifteenth-Century England', in *Women and Literature in Britain, 1150–1500*, ed. C. M. Meale (Cambridge, 1993), pp. 163–5.

7 Some of the complex negotiations between visionary, scribe, translator, and divine

to the visionary, and approved by her.[8] How effective this exercise would have been is obviously dubious. In reality, changes were inevitable.[9]

Apart from either of these practical reasons for the involvement of others in the writing of a visionary text is, of course, the matter of control. As Gerson, and so many others, pointed out, the communications of women had to undergo close scrutiny. Scribes, editors and translators were the church's first line of defence in the battle against the promulgation of false revelations.[10]

Given then that the texts produced by most women visionaries were collaborative efforts, why has the role of the scribes in *The Book of Margery Kempe* excited such debate? The answer lies in the unruly, unconventional nature of the text. In general, hagiographic texts and books of revelations represented the visionary or saint according to well-established models. There was no ambivalence about the subject's virtue or about the authority of the text. In nearly all cases the editor and/or scribe is identified; he is often represented as chosen by God for the task; often he is the spiritual director or confessor of the woman. Although he does not intrude into the text, at least not obviously, his authority as an ordained cleric lends credence and weight to the words of the visionary; his presence facilitates her task. The *Revelaciones* of Bridget of Sweden is an obvious example of this model of composition.

The Book of Margery Kempe, in marked contrast, does not present a carefully edited seamless structure, conforming to a prototype of hagiography or visionary narrative.[11] It is almost a convention for a book of revelations to tell

source in the case of Bridget of Sweden are discussed by Bridget Morris in 'Labyrinths', pp. 23–33, esp. pp. 28–9. However, see also her statement that one at least of the visions (xlix) included in the *Reuelaciones extrauagantes* may have been omitted from the text of the *Revelaciones* because 'it admits to the licence given to the confessors as editors' (p. 28).

8 For example, see *BMK*, p. 5. See also my discussion in the Introduction, p. 2.

9 In translation from the vernacular to Latin, for example, a more sophisticated vocabulary would often be used, which would subtly change the effect of the text. The Old Swedish and Latin renderings of some of Bridget's visions are discussed by Hans Aili. He argues that alterations in the Latin translations (e.g. an image of the brewing of beer being replaced by one of fermenting wine) represent an attempt to move the subject matter of the visions into an international context ('St Birgitta', pp. 76–80).

10 For, example, the editorial licence granted to Alfonso of Jaén is noted by Carl-Gustaf Undhagen. 'Briefly, Alfonso's task consisted in examining all the visions with regard to both form and content; in doing this, special attention was to be paid to clarity and orthodoxy' (Undhagen, 13).

11 That such a drastic editing of the material is not impossible is evident from the de Worde redaction. See pp. 147–51 below. Attempts by modern scholars to determine organizational principles in the structure of the *Book* often seem contrived and so complex that one wonders how medieval readers – let alone listeners – might have been expected to recognize the principles. See, for example, S. Holbrook, 'Order and

the story of the writing of the book, including, often, some kind of divine mandate to the scribe.[12] This story serves to further authorize and authenticate the revelations. However, in *The Book of Margery Kempe* the story of the book perpetuates the ambiguities and inconsistencies of the whole narrative.[13] The second scribe makes no secret of his mixed feelings about Margery. It is suggestive that he is never identified, and that his qualifications, beyond the fact that he is a priest, are never given (4–5).[14] Arguably, his status and identity would not have been advantageous to Margery's cause. If the lack of cited qualifications does indeed indicate a lack of qualifications, this could also explain the inconsistencies, the seemingly indiscriminate choice of material, the haphazard quality of the text and the flawed construction of Margery as a visionary or holy woman.[15] It is obvious that at least three people are writing this book, and none of them is particularly good at it. This lack of skill raises questions about the nature of the collaboration between visionary and scribes, and doubts about the authenticity of the memories recorded in the *Book*.

Phillipe Lejeune, in *On Autobiography*, discusses the autobiographies of those who do not write. Of the relative functions of the model – that is, the subject of the autobiography – and the writer, he says:

> The function of the model is to tell what he knows, to answer questions; he is momentarily relieved of responsibility. By the mere fact that the other listens, notes, questions, and must later take on the composition of the text, the model is reduced to the state of source. Being free of the restraints related to written communication, he can let his memory take over.

Coherence in *The Book of Margery Kempe*', in *The Worlds of Medieval Women: Creativity, Influence, Imagination*, ed. C. Berman et al. (Morgantown, 1985), pp. 97–110.

12 Women visionaries nearly always include an account of a 'call-to-write' vision in their narratives, whereby they are divinely commanded to write their visions down for the benefit of others. The function and significance of this vision is examined in my article 'God's Almighty Hand: Women Co-Writing the Book', in *Women, the Book, and the Godly*, ed. L. Smith and J. Taylor (Cambridge, 1994), pp. 55–66.

13 After considering scribal involvement in the texts of other women visionaries, David Lawton remarks 'there is simply no account of textual mediation as complex and as circumstantial, almost wantonly obscure, as that provided in *The Book of Margery Kempe*'. He continues by declaring that the writing is dependent 'on Kempe's dictation and memory – literally, on her voice' ('Voice, Authority and Blasphemy in *The Book of Margery Kempe*', in *Margery Kempe: A Book of Essays*, ed. S. J. McEntire (New York, 1992), pp. 100–101).

14 This is especially significant given that when learned or high-ranking clerics support Margery's cause their qualifications are always cited.

15 Felicity Riddy has suggested to me that the scribe might have been a clerk in an ecclesiastical court; the training and practice he would then have received, recording every detail of cases heard by the court, would explain the apparent lack of discrimination or privileging of the material he records in the *Book*.

The writer, on the other hand, is entrusted with all the duties of structuring, of control, of communication with the outside.[16]

If *The Book of Margery Kempe* is considered according to this model, then Margery is the source and the scribes are the writer.[17] The scribes' role then becomes clearer and comparable to the role played, for example, by Bridget's various scribes, and finally by Alfonso of Jaén. The fact of the scribes' contribution to the construction of Margery is therefore acknowledged, although the extent of that contribution will always be unknown.[18]

It is also necessary to acknowledge that, even though the scribe states that 'sche dede no þing wryten but þat sche knew rygth wel for very trewth' (p. 5: 17–18), he also explains that 'it was so long er it was wretyn þat sche had for-getyn þe tyme & þe ordyr whan thyngys befellyn' (p. 5: 15–16). This caution that the source's memory was less than infallible is also a reminder that *The Book of Margery Kempe* is a deliberate creation, a literary construction – however flawed – which should not be taken for historical truth.[19] *The Book of Margery Kempe* is a text, a set of spoken or written discourses which undertakes to tell a succession of events.[20] The text features a protagonist – who is here the source of the autobiographical material – that is, Margery, and a narrator, that is, the scribe. Both of these 'personae' are constructed within the framework of the text, and to serve its purposes.[21]

This being so, the ostensible 'facts of life' of Margery Kempe of Lynn, as given in the *Book*, must be recognized as elements of the text.[22] In this, Margery

---

16 *On Autobiography*, trans. K. Leary, ed. P. J. Eakin (Minneapolis, 1989), pp. 188–9.

17 This is except for those interjections from his own experience, where he becomes both source and writer.

18 The role of the scribes in the *Book of Margery Kempe* has been explored by a number of scholars in far greater detail than can be considered here. See J. C. Hirsh, 'Author', pp. 145–50; L. S. Johnson, 'Trope', pp. 833–8; R. Ellis, 'Margery Kempe's Scribe and the Miraculous Books', in *Langland, the Mystics and the Medieval English Religious Tradition*, ed. H. Phillips (Cambridge, 1990), pp. 161–75.

19 This is forcibly brought home by the obviously fictional nature of the incident involving the 'lystere' and his mother (*BMK*, p. 143: 15–20). Their conversation is narrated in direct speech, and, since it is specifically located 'whan sche [Margery] was gon', it is not possible that either Margery or the scribe heard the actual words given in the text, although, of course, the gist of the conversation could have been reported to either of them. Although this is the only incident of this kind in the text, it does serve to indicate narrative licence.

20 S. Rimmon-Kenan, *Narrative Fiction: Contemporary Poetics* (London, 1983), p. 3.

21 Lynn Staley Johnson discusses the place of the scribe in *BMK* in a tradition of scribes to religious women, and points out that scribes, as well as holy women, are constructed according to conventions ('Trope', pp. 837–8). See also Voaden, 'God's Hand', pp. 62–4.

22 An extract from the Account Roll of the Trinity Guild of Lynn for 1438 which

is different from Bridget of Sweden, for example, whose existence is recorded in historical sources independent of her own *Revelaciones*. All that is known of Margery *The Book of Margery Kempe* tells us. There are no corroborating sources to testify to the truth of even the most basic of details given in the text, such as the number of her children. However, the text does supply a context for Margery which is of value in imparting a sense of her subjectivity.

The Woman behind the Text

According to the *Book*, Margery Kempe was born around 1373 in Lynn, Norfolk, daughter of John Brunham, who was to be five times mayor of Lynn. No information is given about her mother, or siblings, but it is known that John Brunham was a public figure of considerable status in Lynn, and it is implied that the family enjoyed comfortable means.[23] When she was twenty, Margery married John Kempe, son of a skinner of Lynn, a man of similar social standing to her father – John Kempe also became an alderman – but probably less financially successful.[24] After the birth of her first child she experienced what would now be identified as a severe post-natal depression, exacerbated, perhaps precipitated, by her confessor's brusque reaction when she, fearing for her life, wished to confess a long-concealed sin and receive absolution.[25] His response

mentions Margery Kempe is cited by Sanford Meech, but, as he acknowledges, there is no proof that she was the Margery Kempe of the *Book* (*BMK* 358–9).

[23] *BMK*, p. 9: 18–25. For historical records of John Brunham's family and career, see *BMK* 363–68. For a discussion of the possible effect of the relative success of Margery's father and her husband on Margery's life and vocation, see A. E. Goodman, 'The Piety of John Brunham's Daughter of Lynn', in *Medieval Women*, ed. D. Baker (Oxford, 1978), pp. 351–3. See also Atkinson, *Mystic*, pp. 67–101.

For information on events contemporaneous with those reported in the *Book*, and a tentative chronology for Margery's life, see *BMK*, pp. vii–xi; xlviii–li.

[24] See *BMK* 9 for evidence of Margery's material ambitions and her husband's failure to live up to her father, in her eyes. Nancy Partner suggests that Margery's father had a profound psychological effect on the nature of Margery's spirituality. See ' "And Most of All for Inordinate Love": Desire and Denial in *The Book of Margery Kempe*', *Thought: Fordham University Quarterly* 64 (1989), 255–6 and 263.

[25] *BMK* 7. The nature of this sin has excited considerable critical speculation. Possibilities range from some unthinkable sexual perversion to dabbling in Lollardy under the influence of her parish priest, William Sawtry, who was later burnt as a heretic. For the latter possibility, see S. Medcalf, *The Later Middle Ages* (London, 1981), p. 117. This seems to be one of the few secrets which Margery kept; it isn't used to augment her self-fashioning as a miserable sinner, or to incite her neighbours to greater scorn. Neither of the scribes ever mentions this sin again, nor is it mentioned in conjunction with any of her confessors, to whom she supposedly told her whole life. Given that

intimidated her, she did not confess the sin, and the immediate effect was to drive her 'owt of hir mende'.

> þerof sche bot hir owen hand so vyolently þat it was seen al hir lyfe aftyr. And also sche roof hir skyn on hir body a-ȝen hir hert wyth hir nayles spetowsly . . . (p. 8: 1–5)

This state lasted for more than eight months (p. 7: 22). Then, Christ appeared in the likeness of a man, sitting on her bedside. He asked her 'Dowtyr, why hast þow forsakyn me, when I forsoke neuyr þe?' (p. 8: 20–21), then floated up into the air until he vanished from her sight. Immediately, she was restored to her senses, and resumed her normal way of life. This was Margery's conversion experience. Not that she immediately changed her ways; the text recounts her continuing vanity, her desire – which was not fulfilled – to succeed in business, even her agreement to an adulterous liaison, which was similarly not fulfilled. But eventually, all her time and energy came to be devoted to prayer, contemplation and emulation of Christ.

In 1413, by which time she had borne fourteen children, her husband agreed to a chaste marriage. After this she undertook a number of pilgrimages, to Jerusalem, to Rome, to Compostella in Spain, and to certain holy sites in Germany and Scandinavia, as well as in England. It was close to twenty years later, around 1432, that, according to the text, Margery finally consented to having her experiences written down, and found a scribe who would do this for her.[26]

The Book of Margery Kempe gives the story of her life, but nowhere is there the story of her death. Given the importance of the foreknowledge of death, the deathbed scene and posthumous signs in finally establishing the credibility of a visionary, let alone the sanctity of a saint, their absence from the text is significant. There is no indication in the text that the scribe anticipated a sequel. It is possible that his belief in Margery, or his support for her, did not extend beyond doing what he had promised to do – copying the first book and writing the second. But of course, he may have predeceased her. In her old age, Margery may have lacked the energy to find another scribe who would bring the book of her life to its final conclusion. There are many possibilities, but it

she recounts accusations of a variety of sins – even having and abandoning an illegitimate child – but is remarkably defensive about any which she may have actually committed, it is probable that this sin was one for which no convincing defense suggested itself. I doubt if it was a sexual sin; she freely tells of succumbing to the temptation posed by a fellow parishioner, and later, she testifies before the Abbot of Leicester 'þat I neuyr had part of mannys body in this worlde in actual dede be way of synne, but of myn husbondys body . . .' (p. 115: 28–30).

26 Throughout her life, various clerics had apparently urged her to write her visions and experiences, but she always insisted that she would do so when God willed (*BMK*, p. 3: 20–30; p. 6: 5–12).

remains that Margery's life does not seem to have attracted either the clerical or popular support which would have ensured its last chapter being written.

Margery exists nowhere but in the text, and all that is known of her is written there. There is no shrine, no monument, no religious order or record of a local cult.[27] All that remains of 'þe creatur' is a single extant manuscript and two brief printed extracts.[28]

Margery's Mixed Blessing

One Friday in Advent, while praying in the Church of St Margaret's in Norwich, we are told that Margery Kempe was ravished in spirit. She had a divine revelation, in the course of which Christ described for her the life that she was to lead, and promised her full remission for her sins.[29] As with nearly all of Margery's visions, it is difficult to locate the incident precisely in time. It may have occurred as early as two years after her childbed conversion (1396), or as late as the year before her pilgrimage to Jerusalem (1412). Although it is written as a single incident, it is more likely that it is an amalgamation of several revelations.[30] However, it is highly significant that the text represents it as a single incident, and that it is placed close to the beginning, since it functions as a comprehensive *apologia* for the life which that text is about to recount.

This vision narrative encapsulates the paradoxical elements of the text's fashioning of Margery as a holy woman; it contains both those elements which authorize Margery as a visionary and those elements which subvert that authority. In the particular enactment of a holy life to which Margery is represented as being called, she is to be the intimate and instrument of the divine as well as despised and rejected of men. Here is an inherently unstable interpretation of her calling which dooms her to a life on the mystical margins. Being offered as an object of scorn and abuse undermines the construction of her as a visionary. To elicit abuse she must be nonconforming, suspect, outcast; yet to be credible as a visionary she must conform to the doctrine of *discretio spirituum*, be beyond suspicion, be obedient to the power of the church. Margery is constructed in conflicting discourses – the discourse of *discretio spirituum* and the discourse of revilement. The text consists of continual negotiation of the conflict – negotiation which never achieves resolution. The

---

27 Richard Kieckhefer attributes the lack of any cult to two possible causes: Margery's personality, and the failure of any of her clerical associates to promote her cause (*Unquiet Souls*, pp. 188–9).

28 For the subsequent history of the manuscript and the printed extracts, see below, pp. 147–54.

29 This incident is quoted at the head of this chapter.

30 Hope Emily Allen's notes discuss the possibilities: *BMK*, p. 261 n. 16/27sq.

following analysis of the vision cited at the beginning of the chapter reveals the genesis of this contradictory construction.

The text's articulation of Margery's vision clearly demonstrates awareness of the doctrine of *discretio spirituum*. This vision is carefully located, in time and place. It occurs in church, while Margery is engaged in penitential prayer, an activity appropriate to the advent season.[31] Parts of it are almost identical to the account which Bridget of Sweden gives of her initial divine call, and, like Bridget's vision, are couched within the discourse of *discretio spirituum*.[32] Margery is identified as the beloved of Christ; she is promised 'hey medytacyon and very contemplacyon' through which she will gain secret knowledge; and, most importantly, she is provided with a spiritual director, a man who is specifically identified, someone who will validate her visions for her, and whose advice she is told to follow, since he is Christ's agent on earth. This is all highly orthodox. It upholds the authority of the church hierarchy as custodian of the divine word, whatever the medium, and identifies the clergy as the proper channel for communication between earth and heaven. It creates space for Margery's divine inspiration while simultaneously restricting that space by providing for Margery's submission to 'sum spiritual fadir vertuos and expert in spiritual lyff'.[33]

However, this same revelation also demonstrates the contradiction implicit in the way of life she is reputedly called to follow, and contains within it the foundation of Margery's unsatisfactory relationship with ecclesiastical authority. Christ tells her:

> Þow xalt ben etyn & knawyn of þe pepul of þe world as any raton knawyth the stokfysh. Drede þe nowt, dowtyr, for þow schalt haue þe vyctory of al þin enmys. I schal ȝeue þe grace j-now to answer euery clerke in the loue of God.
>
> (p. 17: 16–20)

In this manner her adversarial position is authorized by Christ. While on the one hand she is located in a traditionally submissive position to the clergy, on the other the text also explicitly locates her where she can be reviled, a position which is identified as imitative of Christ.

> For sche wyst rygth wel sche . . . was worthy mor schame & sorwe þan ony man cowd don to hir, & dyspite of the werld was þe rygth way to-Heuynward sythen Cryst hym-self ches þat way. (p. 13: 5–9)[34]

---

31 *BMK*, p. 261 n. 16/27sq.

32 See *Sancta Birgitta Revelaciones*, pp. 96–7 above.

33 Appendix fol. 252v: 9.

34 For the scriptural basis for this particular version of *imitatio Christi* see Matthew 27. 29–45; Mark 15. 17–32. For Christ's blessing of the reviled and persecuted, see Matthew 5. 10–12: 'Blessed are ye, when men shall revile you, and persecute you, and shall say all manner of evil against you for my sake./ Rejoice and be exceeding

But Margery is not to suffer the abuse meekly. In the vision narrative, the conjunction of the promise of scorn with the promise of victory suggests a somewhat different resolution from the usual heavenly reward. It implies that Margery's victory will be here on earth, in the form of verbal triumph over those who scorn her, among whom *all* clerics are specifically included and identified with the enemy. Margery is promised the grace to 'answer' them, to defend herself and her way of life. She is, then, endowed with a voice to answer 'euery clerke', a blanket dispensation which accords ill with the principles of *discretio spirituum*. Although this voice is represented as deriving from divine grace, it is not represented as Christ's voice speaking through Margery, as, for example, his voice will speak through the Dominican anchorite whom he has appointed as Margery's spiritual director.[35] Herein lies one of the chief paradoxes of the way in which Margery Kempe is constructed: she is divinely commanded to be submissive to her spiritual director, while at the same time being given the means to answer clerks. This is part of the continual negotiation which makes up her text: seeking yet challenging clerical authorization.

The previous chapter argues that the effect, for women visionaries, of conformity to *discretio spirituum* is to privilege the voice of God by disembodying the visionary. Bridget's troublesome female body is written out of the visionary narrative, and she is constructed as voice alone, uttering the unmediated words of God. Margery Kempe's *Book*, attempting to reconcile conflicting discourses, mapping her visionary experiences on to a geography of abusive attention, fails to achieve this effect. Her successful construction as a visionary is fatally compromised by her simultaneous construction as an object of abuse. Her perceived failure as a visionary in turn becomes a stimulus for further abuse and criticism. A visionary formulated within the discourse of *discretio spirituum* should not be seen, neither should her voice be heard, except speaking God's words. However, to be scorned means that Margery must be both seen and heard. She cannot vanish; it is the sight and sound of her which elicits abuse.

The extremely public nature of Margery's *imitatio Christi*,[36] as well as the attention which this construction directs to her bodily presence, is exemplified in the following passage.

And I wolde, Lorde, for þi lofe be leyd nakyd on an hyrdil, alle men to wonderyn on me for þi loue, so it wer no perel to her sowlys, þei to castyn

glad: for great is your reward in heaven: for so persecuted they the prophets which were before you.' These verses from the Beatitudes supply a paradigm by means of which Margery can interpret her ambivalent reception as prophet, as well as the revilement she elicits.

35 *BMK*, p. 17: 34.
36 This term is defined and discussed in Chapter One, Mystics and Visionaries.

slory & slugge on me, & be drawyn fro town to town euery day my lyfe-tyme
... (p. 184: 19–23)[37]

That this wish is symptomatic of the desire for attention which permeates the text is indicated by the use of the phrase 'alle men to wonderyn at me'. This phrase, or variations of it, appears frequently throughout the text.[38]

Significantly, the passage cited above concludes an instance of negotiation between Margery and Christ about public and private devotion (pp. 181: 16 – 184: 25). The sequence begins with Margery asking to be allowed to suffer her loud crying in private, because she has heard that 'þe pepil wondryth' at her, and are caused to sin by her, presumably because they are so angry or annoyed. Christ refuses her request – one of the few times when he does so – saying that her loud cries and roarings in public are designed to stir others to devotion. Margery then responds with an extravagant affirmation that if she were slain a hundred times a day she could never recompense Christ's goodness. Christ, who has just confirmed the need for her to demonstrate her devotion publicly, then says, 'I prey þe dowtyr, зeue me not ellys but lofe' (p. 184: 5–6). Margery's response is the passage quoted above. She wishes for the most public demonstration imaginable, in which her love for Christ would be literally embodied, and laid bare to the gaze of all men – as long as it did not imperil their souls. In this one short sequence, Margery moves from requesting private, rather than public manifestations of Christ, because she fears causing others to sin, to offering a public demonstration of abject devotion, which she

---

37 Margery is not alone in this desire. Angela of Foligno (1248–1309) wished to be led naked through the town, hung around with pieces of meat and fish, with a rope around her neck while people jeered, although in her case this desire was a manifestation of her alienation from God (Angela of Foligno, *Works*, p. 219).

Angela and Margery are also similar in their loud weeping. 'Afterward, this fire of the love of God in my heart became so intense that if I heard anyone speak about God I would scream. Even if someone stood over me with an axe ready to kill me, this would not have stopped my screaming' (Angela of Foligno, *Works*, p. 131). Controversy apparently surrounded the dissemination of Angela's *Liber de vere fidelium experientia* partly because of its fiery emotionalism, and partly because of her perceived connection with the Spiritual Franciscans, and her status as a Franciscan tertiary (Angela of Foligno, *Works*, pp. 24–36 and 111–13). Although there is no direct evidence that Margery or her priests might have known of Angela, three extant manuscripts of the *Liber*, dated 1409, 1413 and 1424, circulated in Belgium, possibly among the Beguines. It is therefore possible that something might have percolated through to Margery (Angela of Foligno, *Works*, pp. 112–13). Hope Emily Allen briefly mentions Angela (*BMK*, p. lv), and speculates that Margery might have been told of her by Franciscans in the Holy Land (*BMK*, p. 295 n. 73/28). Karma Lochrie compares the bodily nature of devotion in the writings of Angela and Margery (*Margery*, pp. 42–6).

38 See, for example: pp. 61: 7; 76: 15; 114: 36; 181: 19; 174: 24; 184: 24; 17: 15; 121: 20.

seems to trust would not be an occasion of sin for others.[39] Christ makes corresponding moves, so that by the end of the sequence they have changed places: Margery offering public demonstration, Christ requesting private devotion. This is characteristic of the negotiation between the conflicting discourses which occurs throughout the text. The interchange clearly indicates the impossibility of Margery's successful construction within the discourse of *discretio spirituum*; the vanishing visionary cannot also be the object of everyone's attention, laid bare to the wondering gaze of all eyes.

The desired effect of *discretio spirituum* is to make the visionary disappear, as Bridget disappears behind the screen of her revelations. In sharp contrast, to be abused and reviled, to imitate Christ's suffering in the particular manner Margery feels called to do, requires that she invite attention – hostile attention, certainly, but attention nonetheless.

> Than thys creatur þowt it was ful mery to be reprevyd for Goddys lofe: it was to hir gret solas & cowmfort whan sche was chedyn & fletyn for þe lofe of Ihesu for repreuyng of synne, for spekyng of vertu, for comowning in Scriptur whech sche lernyd in sermownys & be comownyng wyth clerkys.
>
> (p. 29: 27–32)

Such attention asserts Margery's presence – she is insistently there; she is often unwelcome, unwanted and inappropriate. 'What, woman, art þu come a-ȝen? I wolde fayn be delyueryd of þe' (p. 131: 28–9). As the Archbishop of York discovered to his annoyance and chagrin, she is the woman who will not go away.[40]

Although Margery's 'mixed blessing' militates against her successful construction as a visionary, the discourse of *discretio spirituum* is nonetheless one of the two primary discourses of the text. This chapter now considers the manifestation of *discretio spirituum* in *The Book of Margery Kempe*. It will also examine how the discourse is at times undermined, with deleterious consequences for Margery's construction as a visionary. This investigation will be structured according to the same categories I employed in the study of Bridget of Sweden: Authority, Knowledge, and Behaviour.[41] In the section entitled Authority, I consider the valorization of Margery's life and visions, either through divine or clerical endorsement, or by reference to some precedent. The section on Knowledge covers the presentation of Margery's scriptural knowledge, references to her own ability to discern the spirits, the justification of the type of visions that she has, and the manner in which she receives them.

---

[39] It is difficult to comprehend how throwing sludge and slurry at a naked Margery would imperil men's souls any less than whatever sin they had been drawn to commit by the sound of her roaring and crying.

[40] In a wonderfully evocative phrase, H. Leith Spencer describes Margery Kempe as 'some medieval Ancient Mariner' (*English Preaching in the Late Middle Ages* (Oxford, 1993), p. 52).

[41] For the medieval foundation for these categories see Chapter Three, p. 81 n. 26 above.

Behaviour encompasses Margery's virtue, her way of life, and, most important – and most problematical – her perceived preaching and her relationship with her spiritual directors.

Discretio spirituum in *The Book of Margery Kempe*

Authority

To be credible, a visionary must be presented as authorized by both divine and ecclesiastical powers. Bridget of Sweden acquires clerical sanction by her construction as a passive channel for the voice of God, an instrument of a higher authority. Much of *The Book of Margery Kempe* is a record of Margery's overt pursuit of ecclesiastical authorization of her visions and way of life, a pursuit rewarded with indifferent success. Like Bridget, Margery is presented as divinely chosen, and like Bridget, she seeks to substantiate her mission by gaining clerical endorsement. However, unlike Bridget, Margery is not consistently constructed as a compliant divine instrument. Although there are episodes in the text where Margery conforms impeccably to the doctrine of *discretio spirituum*, and where the influence of the discourse on her construction is evident, she also often negotiates her authority with higher powers – divine and ecclesiastical. The resultant sense of agency, of Margery's vivid and demanding presence, undermines her presentation as a compliant channel for the voice of God. In order to examine this unstable aspect of the representation of Margery, this section considers her quest for authority in three parts. First is her search for clerical endorsement of her way of life and visions. The second part examines the problematic area of Margery's negotiation for authority. The third part then explores her divine authorization as chosen intimate of Christ and the way in which it complicates her search for clerical approval.

A considerable part of *The Book of Margery Kempe*, as stated above, is occupied with recounting Margery's continual battle for ecclesiastical authorization, a battle which seems never to be won. There is no sense of the issue having been successfully resolved and Margery winning acceptance as a visionary and holy woman. Instead, the narrative ends on the same note as it started, with Margery at odds with her confessor.[42] This is despite the great number of clerical endorsements recorded by the text, a number which is certainly noteworthy, and most unusual when compared with visionary

---

[42] The first encounter between Margery and a cleric that the text describes is with the confessor to whom she fails to confess before the birth of her first child. The last encounter is with her confessor on her return from pilgrimage to Germany. Both are 'sharp' with her, and in both cases, though in different ways, she evades their authority. In the former case, she doesn't confess, so she performs no penance and receives no absolution; in the latter, she simply disobeys her confessor by going on pilgrimage.

narratives of other late-medieval women. Hildegard of Bingen had her visionary status authenticated by Bernard of Clairvaux, and later by the pope.[43] Mechtild of Hackeborn and Gertrude the Great do not specifically mention clerical approval, although their status as enclosed nuns perhaps meant that their submission and obedience could be assumed. However, a testimonial by Franciscan and Dominican theologians who had known Gertrude – author of part of both visionary texts – did become part of the manuscript tradition.[44] Bridget of Sweden identifies the four priests attached to her household at various times in her life as providing clerical authentication of her visions. Julian of Norwich does not write of authorization by specific clerics, although, as with Mechtild and Gertrude, her status as anchoress perhaps meant that her obedience to clerical authority could be assumed.

No other medieval woman visionary marshals so many clerics to her cause as does Margery. The sheer number of citations of clerical approval is testimony to the sense her *Book* conveys of the precariousness of her position as a divine channel whose way of life invites scorn and derision.[45] It is as if Margery seeks safety in numbers; this applies both to her general quest for clerical approval and to her specific need for reassurance as to the provenance of her visions.

Like Bridget of Sweden, Margery first recounts her visions to a confessor, here the Dominican anchorite, because Christ tells her to; here she conforms perfectly to the conventions of *discretio spirituum*. In this case, she is shown to secure ecclesiastical sanction by giving evidence of divine authorization.

> Þan þis creatur went forth to þe ankyr, as sche was comawnded, & schewyd hym þe reuelacyons swech as wer schewyd to hir. Þan þe ankyr wyth gret reuerens & wepyng, thankyng God, seyd, 'Dowtyr, ȝe sowkyn euyn on Crystys brest, and ȝe han an ernest peny of Heuyn. I charge ȝow receyueth swech thowtys whan God wyl ȝeue hem as mekely and deuowtly as ȝe kan & comyth to me and telleth me what þei be, & and I schal, wyth þe leue of ower

---

[43] Newman, *Sister*, pp. 8–9.

[44] Gertrude the Great, *Revelationes Gertrudianae ac Mechtildianae*, 2 vols., ed. Benedictines of Solesmes (Paris, 1875), I, 424–5.

[45] Sarah Beckwith argues that 'Margery Kempe averts the potential threat in her position by drastically pluralizing the authorities she seeks' (*Christ's Body*, p. 97). Although this is certainly true, it is only one factor in her compulsive quest. She is equally motivated by fear of deception, by a desire for attention, and by an apparently insatiable thirst for clerical conversation.

Margery identifies at least nineteen individual clerics or holy men who commend her way of life and validate her visions, in addition to several clusters of holy men and women whom she cites as having approved of her. For example, she speaks of 'many worshipful clerkys, bothe archebysshopys & bisshoppys, doctowrs of dyuynyte & bachelers also' (p. 3: 10–12).

Lord Ihesu Cryst, telle ʒow wheþyr þei ben of þe Holy Gost, or ellys of ʒowr
enmy þe Deuyl. (p. 18: 2–8)

In this episode, Margery is impeccably constructed. She does as Christ
commands her: she presents her vision to the specified spiritual director for
verification. The anchorite identifies himself as an expert in *discretio spirituum*,
knowledge which he is prepared to share with her.[46] She is thus definitely
located within that particular tradition: she has a spiritual director to whom it
is implied she will be submissive, she is meek and obedient to God, and her
visions will undergo clerical scrutiny.[47]

Following her initial meeting with the anchorite, the first episodes in the
book concerned with ecclesiastical authorization are her visits to the Bishop of
Lincoln and to the Archbishop of Canterbury. The placement of these episodes
so early in the text is probably not accidental, despite the chronological
confusion of the entire text. In the text's quest for clerical approbation of
Margery it seems the more powerful the cleric, the better. Often, when
describing a positive encounter with a cleric, she will cite his qualifications,
title, degree of learning or depth of virtue. For example, when the conflict
which Margery's crying caused among the clergy of Lynn is described, her
supporters are listed as including the prior of St Margaret's Church, who was a
Doctor of Divinity, the Bishop of Norwich, a White Friar, who was also a
Doctor of Divinity, and another cleric who was a Bachelor of Canon Law (p.
167: 16 – 168:3). On the other hand, her major opponent, the friar who refused
to allow her to hear his sermons, is pointedly identified as being 'at þat tyme
neyþyr bacheler ne doctowr of diuinyte' (p. 152: 9–10). The more high and
learned the cleric, the more glory and authority are reflected onto Margery – or
so the text appears to hope.

Margery's meeting with Thomas Arundel, the Archbishop of Canterbury, is
an excellent example of this reflected glory contributing to Margery's construction within the discourse. Not only does Arundel approve her way of life, and
find no fault with her visionary experiences, but he also gives her permission
to choose her own confessor, and to receive the sacrament every Sunday (p. 36:
21–2). The Fourth Lateran Council (1215) established mandatory yearly
confession and communion.[48] Communion on the three major festivals of

---

46 The credentials of the anchorite as an expert in *discretio spirituum* are further established by the assertion later in the text that he has the gift of prophecy (pp. 43: 35 – 36:
18; see also p. 278 n. 43/35sq.). Jean Gerson and Alfonso of Jaén both state that to
have had mystical experience themselves is a most desirable qualification for
spiritual directors of mystics. See p. 58 above.

47 It is typical of the paradoxical fashioning of Margery that it is this same vision which
also lays the foundation for her construction within the revilement discourse, a
construction which undermines her successful presentation as a visionary.

48 Rubin, *Corpus*, p. 64.

Christmas, Easter and Pentecost was often recommended,[49] but more frequent reception of the host – a common feature of the devotional praxis of many holy women – was viewed with suspicion and could require special dispensation.[50] Confession was usually to the parish priest,[51] and special dispensation from the bishop was needed to choose another confessor. However, this does not seem to have been unusual, or particularly difficult to obtain.[52] Medieval holy women frequently appear to have had some say in the choice of their confessor.[53] The positive endorsement which Margery acquires from Arundel is particularly significant given that he was a noted enemy of Lollardy, and responsible for the anti-Lollard Constitutions of 1409.[54] Margery's request for more frequent communion and her concern with confession, as well as other features of her devotion, would have averted any suspicions Arundel may have had that she was infected by Lollardy – although, of course, these same features did not prevent her being accused of it several times during her adventures.[55]

Following, in the text if not in time, her authorization by the highest ecclesiastical power in England, Chapters Seventeen and Eighteen recount Margery's ecclesiastical authorization at a local level, and with greater detail as to the nature of her holy life and visionary experiences. Chronologically, the events in these two chapters occurred earlier than her visits to Repingdon and Arundel, which took place in the summer or autumn of 1413.[56] Their placement in the text after Arundel's authorization of her choosing her own confessor implies that Margery had ecclesiastical authority for her procession from priest to priest, surely indicating awareness of the need to represent her as submissive to ecclesiastical authority, as required by *discretio spirituum*.

[49] Rubin, *Corpus*, pp. 147–8.

[50] Bynum, *Holy Feast*, pp. 57–8. This important study explores the complex relationship of medieval women with the host in great depth. See esp. pp. 57–69 and 228–36.

[51] T. N. Tentler, *Sin and Confession on the Eve of the Reformation* (Princeton, 1977), p. 22.

[52] 'Bishops' registers of the later Middle Ages record numerous concessions to lay petitioners of the right to resort to a confessor of their own choosing' (C. H. Lawrence, *The Friars: The Impact of the Early Mendicant Movement on Western Society* (London, 1994), p. 125).

[53] Bridget of Sweden was certainly involved in choosing both Mathias and Alfonso as her spiritual directors, even if this was ostensibly divinely ordained. It should be noted that, with Margery, Christ later takes responsibility for having chosen her spiritual director (pp. 216: 34 – 217: 30).

[54] A. Hudson, *The Premature Reformation: Wycliffite Texts and Lollard History* (Oxford, 1988), pp. 12–15 and 23. Arundel also presided over the trial of William Sawtry, the first Lollard to be executed, in 1401, under the newly-passed statute, *De heretico comburendo*. Previous to 1399, Sawtry was Margery's parish priest (*BMK*, p. 274 n. 35/28–9; Hudson, *Premature*, p. 435).

[55] Hudson, *Premature*, p. 435.

[56] *BMK*, pp. xlix; 273 n. 33/24–5; 274 n. 35/28–9.

These chapters recount her visits to Richard Caister, vicar of St Stephen's Church in Norwich, to William Southfield, a White Friar of Norwich, and to the anchoress Julian of Norwich.[57] During these visits Margery is acknowledged as a mouthpiece of the Holy Spirit.[58]

Her authorization by Caister is given added weight by the presentation of his credentials as a spiritual director. As I argue in Chapter Two, it was of great importance that the spiritual director of a visionary, the man who would exercise the discernment of spirits, should be of impeccable training and judgement. When Margery first encounters Richard Caister, he is conversing with his own spiritual director, a testimony to his virtue and an implication of his expertise. He is described as a man whose holiness God has amply demonstrated. He is initially sceptical of her, because she is a woman. 'Benedicite. What cowde a woman occupyn an owyr er tweyn owyrs in þe lofe of owyr Lord?' (p. 38: 25–6). He is the very model of a medieval spiritual director. Jean Gerson warned of the dangers in too readily accepting women's visions, but also affirmed the need to test all visions. Richard Caister's acceptance of Margery, his belief in her 'felyngs' and his subsequent support of her are enhanced by his initial doubts.

After receiving Caister's approval, Margery is divinely commanded to go to the Carmelite, William Southfield, who is described as 'a good man and an holy leuar'.[59] Southfield in turn endorses her visions, which he identifies as the Holy Spirit working within her and sanctions her way of life. He and Caister both employ the traditional argument of negative capability to explain Margery's gifts. This is the same argument which Alfonso uses to locate Bridget in the tradition of female prophecy. Here, Margery's very inappropriateness as a divine instrument helps to validate her as a visionary.

> And þerfor, syster, I cownsel ȝow ... put non obstakyl ne obieccyon a-ȝen þe goodnes of þe Holy Gost, for he may ȝevyn hys ȝyftys wher he wyl, of vnworthy he makyth worthy, of synful he makyth rygtful. (p. 41: 22–7)

In his instruction to her, Southfield counsels her to be passive and receptive, that is, to embrace the qualities prescribed by *discretio spirituum*. He also reassures her that she is not deceived in her visions, which is a constant fear of hers.

When Margery visits Julian of Norwich however, she is taught to discern

57 For historical information about Caister, see *BMK*, p. 276 n. 38/12. For Southfield see *BMK*, p. 278 n. 41/2–3; 14/2sq. For Julian see Showings, I, 33–5.
58 *BMK*, pp. 40: 15–20; 41: 13 – 42: 5; 42: 17–22.
59 Hope Emily Allen, citing John Bale, says that Southfield had visions himself (p. 278 n. 41/2). It is curious that Margery did not mention this, since this fact could have added to the weight of his authorization of her in the same way as the reported prophetic powers of the Dominican anchorite (see above). However, since Bale is not always reliable, perhaps Margery knew more than Bale.

the spirits on her own behalf. Margery's meeting with Julian has important implications in that it chronicles the teaching of the doctrine of *discretio spirituum* by a woman to a woman. The text actually identifies Julian as an expert in *discretio spirituum* who could give good advice (42: 16–17). As noted in Chapter Two, although the charism of *discretio spirituum* was not restricted to men, and although there is no explicit scriptural proscription against women discerning the spirits, in practice this function had been gradually appropriated by the learned male clerical establishment. It is therefore significant that Julian is the only one of all the spiritual advisors whom Margery consults who is represented as actually telling Margery how to recognize the provenance of her visions, how to read the signs for herself. Julian is acting within the limits of the injunction whereby women, though prohibited from teaching men, were permitted to teach other women and children.[60] That the text shows none of Margery's many male advisors teaching her the principles of *discretio spirituum* could indicate either male reservation of this knowledge to themselves, or the text's recognition of the greater potency of clerical discernment in the authorizing of Margery.

What Julian actually tells Margery is that a true vision will not be against charity, the worship of God, or the merit of her fellow-Christians. A true visionary will be moved to live chastely, will not doubt, and will steadfastly believe that the Holy Spirit resides in her soul. Tears, says Julian, are a definite sign of grace, since they torment the devil, and are tokens which he cannot bestow. All of this advice is a conventional rendering of features of the doctrine.

> Ther may non euyl spyrit ȝeuyn þes tokenys, for Ierom seyth þat terys turmentyn mor þe Devylle þan don þe peynes of Helle. (p. 43: 6–8)[61]

---

60 For a discussion of late-medieval attitudes towards women teaching, see Minnis, '*Accessus*', pp. 311–14.

61 For further endorsement of Margery's weeping see also pp. 51: 12; 64: 8–9; 82: 1–9; 89: 37; 99: 19–24 (when Jerome himself appears to her and authenticates her tears as a divine gift); 152: 8 – 154: 29 (where the scribe compares her tears to those of Marie d'Oignies, and cites other precedents for this phenomenon); 165: 12–19; 166: 11 – 167: 15; 205: 4–32 (where Christ tells her that tears cannot be counterfeit as can other forms of devotion). Hope Emily Allen discusses the tradition of religious tears in relation to Margery in her notes (pp. 256 n. 2/20sq; 272 n. 31/3). In *The Booke of Gostlye Grace of Mechtild of Hackeborn* (an early fifteenth-century Middle English translation of the work of the late-thirteenth-century visionary) Christ describes tears shed for love of him as a great treasure to which he assigns a special place in his heart (Halligan, *Booke*, p. 214). That tears were recognized as a desirable aspect of affective piety is demonstrated in a late-fifteenth-century poem, *De Arte Lacrimandi*, in which the Virgin Mary offers to teach sinners to weep by reflecting on the Passion of Christ. 'Who can not wepe come lerne att me' (R. M. Garrett, '*De Arte Lacrimandi*', *Anglia Zeitschrift* 32 (1909), 269–94 (p. 270)).

However, what is most interesting is what isn't mentioned: Julian apparently omits any instruction to be under the guidance of a spiritual director. Whether this reflects Julian's own experience as an anchoress, or the focus of their conversation on the gift of tears, or whether the text deliberately excluded it, is impossible to say. Its absence, though, is suggestive, given that Margery never has a stable, continuing, submissive relationship with a spiritual director and given that submission to a spiritual director is a fundamental requisite of *discretio spirituum*. Instead the text represents Margery as moving from one ecclesiastical authority to another, searching for those who will affirm her visions and her way of life.

Margery's visit to Julian of Norwich does achieve a kind of authorization by association. Julian was acknowledged as a holy woman, she was an anchoress, she had all the external trappings which Margery lacked.[62] By describing the two of them in 'holy dalyawns' for many days, and recounting Julian's enthusiastic endorsement of her revelations, and her tears, Margery is constructed as sharing some of Julian's characteristics. By this means she shelters under the mantle of Julian's established spirituality.[63]

In all these episodes cited above, the text presents Margery in accordance with the discourse of *discretio spirituum*. She does not appear to act in her own right, and she is externally authorized and directed. She is constructed as passive, obedient and submissive. Her own will and desire are absent. She is a channel for the divine word, an instrument of the divine will. However, the text by no means offers a consistent construction of Margery, as the second part of this section demonstrates. Frequently, Margery is shown encountering clerical censure and criticism of her way of life. When this occurs, she often challenges ecclesiastical authority, either implicitly or explicitly, and negoti-

---

[62] The scribe of the short text of Julian's revelations, writing in 1413, describes her as 'A deuote Woman and her Name is Iulyan that is recluse atte Norwyche and ȝitt on lyfe.' Cited in Julian of Norwich, *A Revelation of Love*, ed. Marion Glasscoe, rev. ed. (Exeter, 1986), p. vii. Felicity Riddy notes: 'Unlike Margery Kempe, [Julian] occupies without strain a marginal cultural space, embracing its confines rather than struggling against them' (' "Women talking about the things of God": A Late Medieval Sub-culture', in *Women and Literature in Britain, 1150–1500*, ed. C. M. Meale (Cambridge, 1993), p. 111).

[63] In a recent densely argued essay challenging many received ideas about Julian of Norwich, Nicholas Watson discusses the minimal tradition of women's visions in England, as compared with the Continent, and notes Julian's apparent ambivalence about her own visionary experience. See 'The Composition of Julian of Norwich's *Revelation of Love*', *Speculum* 68:3 (1993), 649. However, Julian's status as a holy woman was acknowledged, and it is as an anchoress and spiritual counsellor, expert in *discretio spirituum*, rather than as a fellow visionary that Margery initially seeks her out. And it is Julian's *gender*, in relation to her acknowledged expertise in *discretio spirituum*, which make her stand out in the list of clerics and spiritual advisors from whom Margery sought authorization and reassurance.

ates for power, clearly contravening the principles of *discretio spirituum*, and undermining her construction as a visionary.

Her implicit challenges usually take the form of dismissing a disapproving cleric as a bad priest. She then sets out in search of a good one who will praise her.[64] This pattern of behaviour is reinforced by divine approval. A particularly all-encompassing example of this strategy occurs when Christ makes a self-fulfilling prophecy to Margery.

> Ther is no clerk can spekyn a-ȝens þe lyfe whech I teche þe, &, ȝyf he do, he is not Goddys clerk, he is þe Deuelys clerk. (p. 158: 12–14)

This teaching enables Margery to evade any responsibility for clerical hostility; in fact, it confirms her in whatever action she chooses to take, including outright defiance of the clergy.

Often, Margery is shown mounting explicit challenges, by arguing for what she wants and appealing to divine authority to overrule the Church. For example, when she first visits the Bishop of Lincoln, Philip Repingdon, he denies her permission to wear white clothing (p. 35: 8–12). She then seeks advice from God, who gives her a message for the bishop which criticizes him for caring more for the things of the world than for the love of God. This is obviously not the meek and submissive behaviour mandated by *discretio spirituum*. The protracted subsequent struggle over Margery wearing white clothes embodies a struggle for power between Margery and her spiritual superiors. Ultimately, the white clothes become not a symbol of meekness but a sign of Margery's victory over Church authority.

This negotiating for authority imparts, throughout the *Book of Margery Kempe*, a strong sense of agency. Margery is presented as instrumental in establishing her own authority. She mediates not only with priests and with laypeople but also with Christ. She is rarely completely and unquestioningly obedient to any of the higher authorities she encounters. She is very much there; she does not go away and become a disembodied voice, as Bridget does. Although Margery wins the occasional battle, gaining permission to wear white clothes, or refuting charges of heresy, for example, ultimately her transgression of the boundaries of behaviour deemed appropriate for holy women severely diminishes her credibility as a visionary.

A striking example of Margery's negotiation for authority, which deserves

---

64 There seems to have been a varied enough response to Margery amongst the clerical establishment that she could always find a supporter – even in foreign lands. David Aers notes that 'among the diverse and complex contexts in which Margery's version of herself was formed, combative interactions with clerics played a notable part. In this connection, it is also noticeable that we get an image of a clerical community whose responses to her were so far from homogenous that they could range from the most intimate and reverential support to the most aggressive dismissal' (Aers, *Community*, p. 109).

detailed analysis, occurs when a monk who is suspicious of her powers asks her whether he will be saved, and how he has sinned.

> Damsel, I her seyn God spekyth on-to þe. I pray þe telle me wheþyr I schal be sauyd or nowt and in what synnes I haue most dysplesyd God, for I wyl not leuyn þe but þow con telle me my synne. (p. 26: 9–12)

Margery tells him to go to Mass, and proceeds to weep for his sins. She then asks Christ what answer she should give.

> 'My derworthy dowtyr, sey in þe name of Ihesu þat he hath synned in letthery, in dyspeyr, & in wordly goodys kepyng.'
> 'A, gracyous Lord þis is hard for me to sey. He schal do me meche schame ȝyf I telle hym any lesynge.'
> 'Drede þe not but speke boldly in the name of Ihesus, for þei arn no lesyngs.'
> And þan sche seyd a-ȝen to owyr Lord Ihesu Crist, 'Good Lord, schal he be savyd?'
> 'ȝa,' seyd owyr Lord Ihesu, 'ȝyf he wyl forsaken hys synne & don aftyr þi cownsel.' (p. 26: 18–27)

There are several levels of arbitration revealed in this incident. First, the monk, by threatening not to believe Margery without proof, refutes the divine authority which is implicitly vested in her as a visionary. He tests her powers by requesting a specific revelation, just as her scribe did before agreeing to write the book (p. 55: 6–21). Margery responds to the monk by asserting a temporal authority of a sort, and telling him to go to mass. The negotiation now shifts to a celestial level. Christ tells Margery what to say, only to encounter resistance from Margery herself.

Far from Margery being a conduit for the divine message, here she involves herself in its composition. The grounds for her temporizing are, astoundingly, fear for her own reputation should what she says be untrue. In this incident, it is clear that Margery is not just clarifying her understanding of Christ's words; she is questioning their truth, just as the monk had questioned the truth of her words. To suggest that Christ should be lying to her, should be giving her a false prophecy to communicate, is to question the authority of the divine word, on which she tacitly acknowledges her own authority is based. This incident is on a different level from her customary 'drede for illusyons'; here she expresses no doubt that her revelation is of divine provenance, just concern that it is true and will redound to her credit.

In response, Christ affirms the authority of his word, and invests her with that authority, by telling her to speak boldly in his name and to prescribe a course of action whereby the monk can achieve salvation. When the monk returns from mass Margery continues to modify the divine word, and to negotiate for a position of authority. She delivers only part of the divine message, and tells the monk that he shall be saved. She has been commanded to 'sey in the name of Ihesu þat he has synned in letthery, in dyspeyr, & in wordly goodys kepyng'. So, even after reassurance by Christ as to the truth of his words, she evades the command, begging the monk not to force her to reveal his sins. Here she grants to the monk the power which she resists in Christ; it is the monk's threat of disbelief of her which finally prompts her to enumerate his sins. The accuracy of her prophecy provokes a final shift in the balance of power, with Margery promising the monk salvation if he follows her advice, and reassuring him that 'God schal ȝeue ȝow grace for my lofe' (27: 7–8). This last promise asserts her favoured relationship with the divine and her God-given authority. This final shift is marked by a temporal representation of her position of power when the monk 'led hir into a fair hows of offyce, made hir a gret dyner, & sythen ȝaf hyr gold to prey for hym' (p. 27: 8–10).

This incident contradicts many of the tenets of *discretio spirituum*. Margery is not humble or meek, she is engaged in demonstrating and asserting her power in relation to both God and man. She is shown as an agent in her own construction as prophet, not just a mouthpiece of God. And her status is recognized, in an elaborate dinner and payment for prayers, in a manner which contravenes *discretio spirituum*, but to which Margery clearly responds.[65]

It is true, as this episode demonstrates, that divine sanction is never withheld from Margery. On the contrary it is freely bestowed and continuously replenished. However, this divine approval generates tension in relation to Margery's quest for clerical validation. Virtually everything that Margery is, says or does is presented as pleasing to Christ, and is endorsed by him. For example, in one lengthy vision, Christ details Margery's devotional and contemplative practices and thanks her for her great devotion.

> . . . þu xalt ben receyuyd in-to þe blys of Heuyn, þer to be rewardyd for euery good thowt, for euery good word, & for euery good dede, & for euery day of comtemplacyon, and for alle good desyrs þat þu hast had her in þis world wyth me euyrlestyngly as my derworthy derlyng, as my blissyd spowse, & as myn holy wife. (p. 213: 6–11)

She is granted plenary remission of her sins early in the text, during the Advent vision which charts the course of her life.

> I, þe same God, forȝefe þe þi synnes to the vtterest poynt. And þow schalt neuyr com in Helle ne in Purgatorye, but, whan þow schalt passyn owt of þis world, wyth-in þe twynkelyng of an eye þow schalt haue þe blysse of Heuyn . . . And I grawnt þe contrysyon in-to þi lyues ende. (pp. 16: 36 – 17: 3)

However, as noted above, this total divine endorsement is problematical in that Margery seems to interpret such divine assurance of her place in Heaven

---

[65] In the *Epistola solitarii* Alfonso includes as part of the first sign whereby a true vision is discerned '. . . the persone yat seis presumys not on him self nen is not left vp with pride nen desires no mannys praysinges . . .' (Appendix fol. 252v: 10).

as investing her with power to challenge ecclesiastical authority. Far from presenting Margery as meek and submissive to her spiritual superiors, the text chronicles her dissent and her assertion of her own will. She appears to seek from clerical powers the same kind of total dispensation she is shown receiving from Christ. What she pursues is not spiritual guidance from learned holy men, expert in discerning the spirits, but official endorsement of the idio-syncratic path she feels herself called to follow.

Ideally, in the eyes of the Church a visionary derives her authority from two sources: divine and ecclesiastical. She has no authority of her own, and speaks only those words given to her by God. To this end, the visionary is constructed, as Bridget is so effectively constructed, in the mode endorsed by *discretio spirituum*. The ideal visionary is meek and submissive, a channel, an instru-ment of God's will. She speaks the words she has been divinely taught, and utters them under the aegis of the church.

As this section demonstrates, the process whereby Margery seeks authority is much more complex and problematic. It involves a continual process of negotiation between God and the clergy, between Margery and the clergy, between Margery and God, between clerical power and secular power. Margery's authority is always in flux, never stable, always open to question. Her construction as a visionary according to the discourse of *discretio spirituum* is undermined by her apparent agency in her negotiation for authority. In a similar manner, which is examined in the next section of this chapter, Margery's knowledge is sometimes represented as being deliberately sought, and used to assert her power, a representation which militates against her credibility as a passive recipient of divine wisdom.

Knowledge

There are two principal areas to examine in relation to Margery Kempe under the rubric of Knowledge. The first is the source of her knowledge: is it natural, that is, learned, or supernatural, that is, revealed? The second area is her autonomous knowledge of *discretio spirituum* as manifested in the *Book*. The discussion of Bridget of Sweden's knowledge focused on her demonstrated knowledge of *discretio spirituum*, much of which she is shown to have acquired through divine instruction. I argued that this presentation of her knowledge contributed to Bridget's credibility as a visionary. In contrast, *The Book of Margery Kempe* presents Margery as comparatively unlearned in *discretio spirituum* although at the same time it cites evidence of her knowledge of other religious matters, and of her employment of that knowledge in ways which deviate from the meek behaviour endorsed by *discretio spirituum*.

First, this section considers the sources of Margery's knowledge, and how these affect her construction within the discourse. When her knowledge is attributed to a celestial source, as befits a passive receptacle of the divine word, Margery's presentation as a visionary is enhanced. More frequently, however, she is portrayed as actively seeking learning, and using it to establish authority on her own behalf, a portrayal which obviously detracts from her construction as a compliant vessel.

The text depicts Margery's knowledge as obtained from two sources: divine instruction, and the earthly teaching she encounters in sermons, devotional texts and preaching. As with the derivation of her authority, there is a continual tension between these two sources of knowledge, with divine teaching being consistently privileged over earthly. This tension is not quite so problematical as the adversarial position Margery adopts with regard to her authorization, because, for the most part, there is no conflict between what Christ teaches her and what men teach. Generally, they complement each other. As the following passage indicates, her exposure to sermons and devotional reading is sometimes depicted as increasing her receptivity to Christ's teaching. Constructed in this manner, Margery's love of learning conforms to *discretio spirituum* in that she is concerned only with greater compliance with the will of Christ.

> Thus, thorw heryng of holy bokys & thorw heryng of holy sermownys, sche euyr encresyd in contemplacyon & holy meditacyon. It wer in maner vn-possibyl to writyn al þe holy thowtys, holy spechys, and þe hy reuela-cyons whech owr Lord schewyd vn-to hir . . . (p. 144: 5–9)

The more Margery's understanding is represented as divinely given, as it is here, the greater her credibility both as a religious figure and as a visionary.

As an unlearned woman, Margery taps into the traditional opposition between natural and supernatural knowledge which often manifests itself in the perceived complementarity of holy women who are mystically inspired, and ordained priests, whose knowledge and understanding are achieved largely through their own efforts.[66] Women were traditionally depicted, and depicted themselves, as unlettered and ignorant, a reflection of the reigning perception that women were less capable of intellection than men. For example, Julian of Norwich declares her own lack of learning while asserting her supernatural knowledge.

> . . . I am a woman, leued, febille and freylle. Botte I wate wele, this that I saye, I hafe it of the schewynge of hym that es souerayne techare.[67]

Of course, this is also a convention, a form of the modesty topos, which could be invoked to protect women from charges of usurping the male territory of learning while reinforcing their claim to inspired knowledge. However, it is a

---

[66] Paul Strohm examines the idea that women were encouraged to cultivate an other-wordly spirituality, which would not compete with male, clerical domination of lay religious life, but which would also 'supply a male lack' (*Hochon*, p. 103). The complementarity of priest and visionary is also explored in Coakley, 'Friars', p. 225.

[67] *Showings* I, 222.

convention to which many women visionaries resort, and which serves to protect and empower them in their articulation of that inspired knowledge.[68] When Margery conforms to this behaviour, and is fashioned as unlettered but divinely inspired, she is generally accepted.

For example, at York, because Christ has given Margery 'not lettryd witte & wisdom to answeryn so many lernyd men . . .' (p. 128: 29–30), he is praised, and clergy and laity are both shown to be receptive to her. This dynamic is further exemplified in the episode at Lincoln when she defends herself 'wysly & discretly' against detractors.

> Þer wer men of lawe seyd vn-to hir, 'We han gon to scole many ʒerys, & ʒet arn we not sufficient to answeryn as þu dost. Of whom hast þu þis cunnyng?' & sche seyd, 'Of þe Holy Gost . . . owr Lord Ihesu Crist seyd to hys disciplys, "Stody not what ʒe schal sey, for it schal not be ʒowr spiryt þat schal spekyn in ʒow, but it schal be þe spiryt of þe Holy Gost." (p. 135: 25–35)

Here Margery is constructing herself as a channel of the Holy Spirit in the best tradition of *discretio spirituum*. She takes no responsibility, or credit for the words she speaks, or, to return to the original question of the men of law, for the knowledge she has. Both words and knowledge, are, however, attributed to a divine source, an attribution which is reinforced, in a very sophisticated manner, by scriptural citation. Not only does Margery know that her understanding is from the Holy Spirit, but she knows it because she knows the Scriptures.

However, this knowledge of the Scriptures points to an area where Margery's learning is troublesome. This is when it is perceived or presented as knowledge that she has acquired, rather than knowledge divinely imparted. The traditional construction of the visionary women is as a passive channel, whose every attribute is either divinely or ecclesiastically bestowed.[69] Even Bridget of Sweden's learning of Latin is represented as divinely assisted.[70] With the majority of women visionaries, learning does not feature in their

---

68 This use of this convention in relation to Hildegard of Bingen is discussed by Barbara Newman (*Sister*, p. 2). See also Kathryn Kerby-Fulton, who argues that Hildegard 'exploits the modesty topos persistently, both in her insistence that she is unlearned and incapable of eloquence, and in the assertion that she writes under divine compulsion' (*Reformist*, p. 65). Margery, in contrast, tends to assert her own learning at times, which, as I have already noted, militates against her empowerment as a visionary.

69 For example, of Hildegard of Bingen, Kathryn Kerby-Fulton writes, 'Hildegard must have possessed no small amount of bookish learning, yet she never, or rarely ever, mentions a source or cites an authority outside of the Bible. In everything she wrote . . . she was at pains to credit her vision with all the knowledge she had acquired, always minimizing anything learned from earthly teachers' (*Reformist*, p. 68).

70 See Undhagen, pp. 7–8; Colledge, '*Epistola*', p. 23.

writing; all that they need to know they acquire through divine intervention or the instruction of their spiritual director. Although some of Margery's knowledge is presented in this manner, as in the above incidents, her acquisition of knowledge through natural, rather than supernatural, means serves to alienate some of the clergy and works against her acceptance as a visionary.

This ambivalent reception of her as knowledgeable is evident when she is at York. Some clerics praise her learning; her exegesis of *Crescite et multiplicamini* is well received and the Archbishop likes her *exemplum* of the priest, the pear tree and the bear, although another cleric first describes it as an evil tale told against priests (pp. 121: 2–10; 126: 22 – 127: 38).[71] On the other hand, when she demonstrates her knowledge of the gospels, ' "A, ser," seyd þe clerkys, "her wot we wel þat sche hath a deuyl wyth-inne hir, for sche spekyth of þe Gospel" ' (p. 126: 13–15). The problem lies not so much with Margery's learning as with the use she makes of it. When she challenges clerical authority, and cites scripture in the process, Margery is often perceived to be usurping priestly functions and is accused of preaching. In this case, however, her ability to cite Scripture signals to the clergy that she is possessed by devils. As I have argued at length, it was commonly believed that spiritual visions could be appropriated by the devil, and that women were also susceptible to the devil's blandishments. Hence, for Margery, a woman who claimed to have visions, to be accused of harbouring devils was a very serious charge. Even so, Margery continues to present herself to clerics as a relatively learned woman.

Despite the quite insistent demonstration in the text of Margery's learning and knowledge, surprisingly little of it is specifically concerned with her instruction in, or understanding of, *discretio spirituum*. Her comprehension of this doctrine is the second aspect of Margery's knowledge which I examine in this chapter. Unlike Bridget's experience of celestial instruction, divine figures never teach Margery how to tell a true vision from a false one. It is true that Christ guides her to spiritual directors who are expert in the doctrine; however, Margery is not represented as acquiring or exercising knowledge of *discretio spirituum* herself. As noted earlier, her confessors do not instruct her in discerning the spirits, and, although Julian of Norwich does teach her four signs of *discretio spirituum*, Margery is never shown actually applying this knowledge to her own visions.

Yet it is certain that Margery fears demonic illusion, and that she rarely feels confident of the provenance of her revelations.[72]

---

71 H. Leith Spencer suggests that exegesis of biblical passages such as *crescite et multiplicamini* was part of a catechetical type of teaching of which devout lay folk could avail themselves. She further suggests that this is what is intended when the 'enuyows person' complains that Alan of Lynn 'enformyd hir in qwestyons of Scriptur' (*English Preaching*, pp. 44–5).

72 Hope Emily Allen, in her notes to the text, suggests that 'Margery's "dread for illusions" was a motive which trained her in an accuracy of expression (as to external

Sche had leuar a sufferyd any bodily penawns þan þes felyngs & sche mygth a put hem a-wey for þe dred þat sche had of illusyons & deceytys of hir gostly enmys. (p. 54: 35–8)[73]

Such doubts and fears are expressed by virtually all visionaries, and can betoken humility and a willingness to be guided, either by divine or clerical wisdom.[74] In other words, they provide an opportunity to demonstrate the submission to spiritual authority which *discretio spirituum* demands. However, despite her apparent lack of ability, or unwillingness to discern the spirits for herself, neither is Margery always willing to accept either divine or clerical authentication of her visions. The entire process of validation of Margery's visions does not inspire confidence; her own doubt is contagious, and her continual negotiation of authority with both divine and clerical figures interposes her own voice and body between divine source and human mouthpiece.

The chief criterion by which she judges her visions is result. If a prophecy comes true, then it was from God.[75] Although this is indubitably one of the approved tests of a vision, the way in which the *Book* represents these incidents

events) quite exceptional in the Middle Ages' (257 n. 3/8). While it may have done so – although scholars are continually discovering how difficult and frustrating it is to test the accuracy of Margery's expression – her detailed location and description of visions is far from exceptional. In fact, it could well be argued that scrupulous location and description of both the circumstances and the content of visions was mandatory in establishing the credibility of visions and satisfying ecclesiastical authorities. Kathryn Kerby-Fulton contends that such attention to detail was a convention which helped in establishing the veracity of many medieval apocalyptic prophecies (*Reformist*, pp. 117–18).

73 It is worth noting that this passage is part of one which argues that Margery is not writing her visions and holy deeds in order to accrue commendation to herself, and that her visions were a source of great pain and suffering to her. This construction is in accord with the principle of *discretio spirituum* whereby a true visionary seeks no profit from, and exhibits no pride in her visions. See also p. 173: 14–24. However, see also pp. 130–31 above for Margery's encounter with the lecherous monk, where she arguably manifests some pride in her achievements.

74 Angela of Foligno spends most of a journey to Assisi engaged in a debate with the Holy Spirit as to whether it really *is* the Holy Spirit speaking with her. Unlike Margery's periods of doubt, this episode provides an opportunity for the Holy Spirit to teach Angela the signs whereby its presence can be recognised. Cited in Petroff, *Medieval Women*, pp. 261–3.

75 Although this was generally believed to be so, it should be noted that there was also an awareness that the devil could send true prophecies, in order to lull his victims into security. Isidore of Seville states that demons are knowledgeable partly because of the subtlety of their sense, partly because they have lived a long time, and partly because God has allowed them to retain some of their angelic powers of revelation. Cited in A. J. Minnis, *Chaucer and Pagan Antiquity* (Cambridge, 1982), p. 34.

fails to reassure the reader. The only means Margery has to judge the truth of her visions is experience, rather than knowledge.

> ... þe drede þat sche had of hir felyngys ... made hir ful meke for sche had no joye in þe felyng tyl sche knew be experiens wheþyr it was trewe er not.
>
> (p. 220: 11–15)

There is inevitably a period of high anxiety while Margery awaits the fulfil-ment of her prophecy, and then a sense almost of surprised relief when the prophecy comes true. On one occasion, a priest asks Margery to find out from God whether his prior would go overseas. God tells her that he will not, but the prior continues to make his preparations to travel. It seems clear that Margery is not sure of the truth of her prophecy until, almost miraculously

> in þe mene-tyme þe Kyng deyid, & þe Priowr bood at hom. & so hir felyng was trewe wythowten any deceyte. (p. 172: 2–4)

Margery's growing uncertainty and subsequent surge of confidence are almost palpable.

In some cases of supremely confused reasoning, she even asks God to fulfil a prophecy so that she will know that her original revelation was true, and from God. For example, when she and Master Alan of Lynn are forbidden to see each other, Christ assures her that she will be able to talk with him again (p. 169: 7). Then Margery hears that Alan is ill, and becomes very upset, not so much because he might die, but 'ʒyf he had deyd of þis sekenes, hir felyng had not ben trewe' (p. 169: 24–5). She prays 'late þis worthy clerk neuyr deyin tyl I may spekyn wyth hym as þu hast behite me þat I xulde do' (p. 169: 29). She seems to remind Christ of his promise and his prophecy in order to ensure its fulfilment.

It appears at times as if even Christ is exasperated by her continuing doubts. When he tells her of the forthcoming death of the prior of Lynne, and the identity of the new prior, he does so every day for a week until the prophecy is fulfilled and she can comfortably believe.

> 'Dowtyr, as loth as þu art to leuyn my steryngs, ʒet schal þu se hym of whom I schewyd þe be-forn Priowr of Lynne er þis day seuenyth.' & so owr Lord rehersyd þis mater ech day þe seue-nyth tyl sche sey it was so indede, þan was sche ful glad & joyful þat hir felyng was trew. (p. 171: 23–6)

Although Margery is driven by fear of illusion to submit her 'felyngs' to her spiritual directors, confessors and various clerics, the text does not show her as emerging from these encounters any more capable of distinguishing illusion for herself. Despite this, she does not always bow to the judgement of her superiors; at times she disobeys them, or questions their interpretation, insisting that she must obey the will of God rather than the commands of the Church. Her apparent lack of confidence in her own visions is, therefore, paradoxically coupled with reliance on her own judgement, a judgement not demonstrably based on knowledge of *discretio spirituum*. The effect of this is, once again, to convey a sense of Margery's active, wilful involvement in the composition and interpretation of her visions, rather than her obedient articulation of the word of God according to the guidance of the Church.

Although Margery is never shown to test her own visions against the criteria of *discretio spirituum*, the text shows an awareness of the hierarchy of vision by specifying the involvement of Margery's 'gostly', as opposed to bodily senses in her 'felyngys'. It is characteristic for the text to state, for example, that Christ speaks to her 'thowt', and that she speaks to him in her mind (pp. 226: 38 – 227: 4). It also describes how God the Father 'dalyd to hir sowle as pleynly and as veryly as on frend spekyth to a-noþer be bodyly spech' (p. 39: 16–18). In her meditations on the Passion she distinguishes between ghostly and bodily sights, and it is clear that her visions, like Bridget's, are spiritual (imaginative), not intellectual.

> . . . sche sey swech gostly sy3tys in hir sowle as freschly and as verily as 3yf it had ben don in dede in hir bodily syght . . . (p. 190: 27–9)[76]

There seems to be a belief in the text that the hierarchy of vision is linked to the different persons of the Trinity. Margery describes a profound shift in the quality of her spiritual experience, an increased intensity, which the text attributes to her increased devotion to the Godhead, as opposed to the manhood of Christ.

> . . . owr Lord of hys hy mercy drow hir affeccyon in-to hys Godhed, & þat was mor feruent in lofe & desyr & mor sotyl in vndirstondyng þan was þe Manhod . . . hir vndirstandyng was mor illumynyd & hir deuocyon mor feruent þan it was be-for whyl sche had hir meditacyon & hir contemplacyon only in hys manhod . . . (p. 209: 5–11)

Such an understanding of meditation and contemplation as rungs on the ladder leading to mystical union with the Godhead is very much in the spirit of pseudo-Dionysian mysticism.[77]

This sense of spiritual development is expressed at another point, when Margery says that her visions stimulated her devotion to the manhood of

---

76 See also, for example, pp. 184: 30; 192: 17; 198: 5–7.

77 *The Book of Privy Counselling*, for example, indicates that the progression towards mystical union leads away from imaginative meditation on the form and quality of God. '. . . 3yf þou felest þat þou hast trewe experience of one or of two [tokens of grace], prouid by trewe examynacion of Scripture & of counseil & of concyence: þan it is speedful to þee sumtyme for to cees of þees queinte meditacions & þees sotyle ymaginacions of þe qualitees of þi beyng & of Goddes . . . & for to lerne how þou schalt be ocupied goostly in felyng of þi-self & of God . . .' (Hodgson, *Cloud*, p. 170: 13–22).

Christ 'vnto þat tyme þat it plesyd owr Lord to ȝeuyn hir vndirstondyng of hys invndirstondabyl Godhed' (p. 208: 25–9). This passage manifests awareness of some of the basic concepts of apophatic mysticism, and of the teaching which privileges apophatic mysticism over affective piety. However, it is clear throughout the *Book* that Margery's spiritual inclination is to devotion to the manhood of Christ, and that this accords with her level of understanding. This is obvious in her fear on the occasion of her marriage to the Godhead (p. 86: 9 – 87: 31), and the manner in which, in the 'consummation' of the mystical marriage, the Godhead acquires a mouth, head, and feet (p. 90: 25–6), and is generally indistinguishable from the incarnate Christ.[78] It is worth noting that this shift to a 'higher' form of devotion is linked in the text with Margery's embarking on a chaste life, and having 'suffyrd mech despite & repref for hir wepyng & hir crying . . .' (p. 209: 1–5). The more holy her life, the greater her spiritual reward, here as well as hereafter.

The text's presentation of Margery's knowledge is in many ways as inconsistent and problematic as its presentation of her authority. Although her revealed knowledge complements rather than competes with her acquired knowledge, the overt manner in which that acquired knowledge is employed puts her in conflict with the tradition of unlearned women serving as vessels for inspiration, and consequently in conflict with Church authorities. Generally, when Margery is depicted as troubled and fearful over her visions and her way of life, her presentation conforms most closely to the discourse of *discretio spirituum*. When she is buoyed up by conviction, or challenged in her beliefs, then her behaviour tends to deviate from that which *discretio spirituum* mandates, as the next section demonstrates. Then she challenges authority, demands a hearing, invites attention. She alienates spiritual superiors, fellow pilgrims and secular officials and is perceived as a dissident presence rather than as a benign absence.

Behaviour

It is in her behaviour that Margery Kempe most obviously contravenes the strictures of *discretio spirituum*, and manages by various means, to cause 'alle men to wonderyn' at her. In other words, the revilement discourse, which was described earlier in this chapter, is most evident in the text's presentation of Margery's behaviour, competing with, and frequently undermining, her construction as a credible visionary. As noted before, in many ways *discretio spirituum* served as a kind of conduct code for medieval women visionaries.

---

78 In her fear of mystical union compared with union with Christ through the spiritual senses which might be termed visionary union, Margery is not alone among women visionaries. Total absorption into the Godhead – the spark into the fire, the water into the wine – while fervently desired was also feared. After Mechtild of Hackeborn, for example, 'was rauyschede alle hoole into God . . . þat es to saye, felte noght of hereselfe', God comforts her and soothes her fears (Halligan, *Booke*, p. 357).

Not only did the doctrine prescribe the manner of reception of a vision, and its content, but it also imposed a code of behaviour and style of living. Although there are times when Margery's behaviour does conform to the doctrine, and is constructed within the discourse, this is not consistent. Unlike that offered by the *Revelaciones* of Bridget of Sweden, the *Book's* presentation of Margery's behaviour is rarely an uncomplicated presentation of an exemplary visionary.

The following section examines this presentation in four parts. First is the manner in which the text deals with Margery's status as a married women, and with her childbearing. Second is one of the most contentious issues surrounding Margery: her perceived preaching. Third is her relationship with, and submission to, her spiritual superiors, an area which was touched on in both the discussion of her authority and of her knowledge, but which is dealt with more fully here. Fourth is the representation of Margery's virtue and piety.

The first issue to be considered is that of Margery's married state. The question of chastity and children was problematic for all married women visionaries. In many cases, the solution was to evoke the model of the Virgin Mary as mother, and sometimes as widow. Women visionaries such as Bridget of Sweden, Elizabeth of Hungary, Angela of Foligno or Dorothea of Montau generally constructed themselves as if chastity were their natural state, to which marriage and motherhood were interruptions.[79] Margery deals with the issue somewhat differently. Although she also presents a model of the Virgin Mary as mother, for the most part she defuses the issue by involving Christ, often at a very practical level, in both her childbearing and her struggle for chastity. On one occasion, Christ tells her that she is with child, and promises to 'ordeyn for an kepar' for it (p. 48: 29). When Margery expresses her shame, Christ valorizes her childbearing by telling her:

> Þerfor is it no synne to þe, dowtyr, for it is to þe raþar mede & meryte, and þow xalt haue neuyr þe lesse grace, for I wyl þat þow bryng me forth mor frwte. (p. 48: 31–4)

Nevertheless, even divinely endorsed childbearing is evidence of sexual activity. To demonstrate conformity to *discretio spirituum*, the text needs to reconstruct Margery as chaste. This is accomplished by locating her vow of chastity and the cessation of her childbearing at the same point in the text as her initial acknowledgement by ecclesiastical authorities as a vessel of the Holy Spirit. While she is still weak from the birth of the child mentioned above, Christ informs her that she shall bear no more children. He then instructs her to go to Norwich, to the Vicar of St Stephens, Master Richard Caister, to tell him

---

[79] The issue of chastity in association with the mysticism of married saints is examined in D. Elliott, *Spiritual Marriage: Sexual Abstinence in Medieval Wedlock* (Princeton, 1993), pp. 234–45.

of her revelations.[80] This episode, the first in Margery's procession from devout cleric to worthy friar to holy woman collecting ecclesiastical *imprimatur*, therefore apparently occurs at a watershed in her life, where the reproductive business of a woman's life is represented as over for Margery. She can now devote herself body and soul to Christ.[81]

This construction of Margery conforms to the discourse of *discretio spirituum*. Her woman's body is relegated to the past, her role as voice of the Holy Spirit is privileged. Caister's approval of her is, as noted earlier, grounded in the traditional justification of negative capability.

> . . . he trustly beleuyd þat sche was well lernyd in þe law of God & indued with grace of the Holy Gost, to whom it longyth to enspyr wher he wyl.
>
> (p. 40: 15–18)

Margery may be a laywoman, married and the mother of fourteen children; none of these factors disqualify her as a divine channel.

While Margery's motherhood is presented within the discourse of *discretio spirituum*, her construction as a wife is much more troublesome. Her efforts to be perceived as chaste incur censure for neglect of her husband. When he falls down stairs, she is held to blame for living apart from him (179: 6–31). She is a married woman, yet she travels alone, exciting suspicion and attracting attention. In Leicester the mayor charges Margery with coming to 'han a-wey owr wyuys fro us' (p. 116: 13–14); she is accused of encouraging Lady Greystokke to leave her husband (p. 133: 27–8); her fellow pilgrims say that they would never tolerate what her husband puts up with (p. 61: 20–23).[82] She is obviously seen

---

80 This location of her initial encounter with Caister as following the birth of her last child may help to establish the dating a little more precisely than Meech has done. Caister was appointed to the parish of St Stephen's on 20 May 1402 (p. 276 n. 38/12), and Margery and her husband took their vow of chastity on 23 June 1413 (p. 269 n. 23/9). Meech suggests that this first meeting with Caister therefore took place between these two dates (p. 276 n. 38/12). However, if this meeting followed the birth of Margery's last child, if she married in 1393 or 94 (p. xlix), and had an average of a child a year for fourteen years, the earliest date possible would be 1407, unless she had several pairs of twins. Given that she and John did not live chastely until 1413, it seems unlikely that she would not have become pregnant during the course of six years of normal married life, when she was between thirty-five and forty, and presumably still fertile. I would therefore be inclined to suggest a date for this encounter much closer to 1413 – perhaps 1411.

81 From a psychological point of view, it is of interest that Margery, looking back, would identify her real embarkation on a visionary life with what was probably her menopause. It is also noteworthy that Margery's conversion experience occurs after the post-natal depression following the birth of her first child. The birth of her final child is succeeded by her full commitment to Christ.

82 It should be noted that John, Margery's husband, is depicted as almost unfailingly supportive of her and concerned with her welfare. The chaste marriage is the only

as a bad example to wives, and a threat to male domination in the home as well as in the church. Chastity, more usually associated with meekness and submission, in *The Book of Margery Kempe* signals freedom from her husband's control, and contributes to her presentation as deviant and subversive.

The most obvious threat to male domination which Margery offers is, of course, her engagement in a kind of theological 'communycacyon' which is seen to be perilously close to preaching. This is the second aspect of her behaviour to be examined. Her ability to cite *exempla* she may have heard in sermons, or to give orthodox exegeses to standard questions, could be deemed appropriate for a devout woman. As discussed earlier, sometimes her knowledge is well received. However, more frequently, the manner in which she deploys her 'communycacyon'[83] and knowledge of the scriptures is perceived as infringing on clerical preserves.[84] Aware of this, she often cites the somewhat sophistic defence that she offers communication, not preaching.[85]

'I preche not, ser, I come in no pulpytt. I vse but comownycacyon & good words, & þat wil I do whil I leue.' (p. 126: 18–20)[86]

At York she asserts her intention to speak of God, in the face of the Archbishop's forbidding her to do so (pp. 125: 37 – 126: 13). In her support she cites

issue on which he holds out. There are obvious similarities between Margery's relationship with her husband and with Christ. I intend to pursue these in a future paper entitled 'An Ideal Husband: The Case for John Kempe'.

83 The Middle English Dictionary defines 'communicacyon' as 'conversation, a conversing', citing *BMK*, pp. 37: 17; 93: 9; 119: 22; 126: 19 as examples. 'Conversacyon' is defined as 'manner of living, conduct, behaviour'. The example given is *BMK*, p. 167: 33 '. . . tweyn good clerkys þe whech longe & many ȝerys had knowyn hir conuersacyon and al hir perfeccyon . . .'.

84 H. Leith Spencer suggests that 'it is very likely that [Margery's] "good words" were coloured by her familiarity with preachers and their sermons. Certainly, her godly conversation, larded with *exempla*, could seem remarkably like preaching to her contemporaries . . .' (*English Preaching*, p. 54).

85 Chapter One examines the late-medieval controversy over who could preach, paying particular attention to the arguments against women preaching. I am grateful to Alastair Minnis for suggesting that the *Book* exploits the medieval binary of *praedicatio* and *conversatio*. While *praedicatio* is reserved to preachers, *conversatio* can be exercised by all devout Christians. John of Wales recommends that the evangelical preacher should exercise both arts, according to the age, station and level of understanding of his audience. See J. Swanson, *John of Wales: A Study of the Works and Ideas of a Thirteenth-Century Friar* (Cambridge, 1989), p. 63.

86 Margery may come in no pulpit, but at Beverley she stands ..t a high window telling good tales to those who will listen – all of whom seem to be women (pp. 130: 34 – 131: 9). The minor female conspiracy which ensues perhaps lends credence to the fears of the mayor of Leicester that Margery might lead away the wives.

the gospel verse 'Blessed is the womb that bore thee and the paps that gave thee suck' (Luke 11. 27). She then interprets this herself as giving her permission to speak of God. 'And þerfor, sir, *me thynketh* þat þe Gospel ʒeuyth me leue to spekyn of God' (p. 126: 12–13).[87] Margery here cites her own interpretation of scripture in an attempt to establish her authority; in so doing she defies the authority of the Church and appropriates the Gospel to her cause. Not only is her construction as a visionary thereby undermined, but evidence is offered to those who view her as a Lollard.

The reasons Margery is accused of Lollardy are fairly obvious, and are found in those aspects of her behaviour which deviate from *discretio spirituum*. These include her apparent lack of submission to clerical authority, her flaunted knowledge and her persistent presence. Margery's actual religious praxis – frequent communion and confession, pilgrimage, devotion to the saints and to the Virgin Mary – testifies to her orthodoxy and undoubtedly helps her refute charges of Lollardy. However, it was believed that Lollard women were unnaturally learned, read scripture and preached to both men and women.[88] Despite repeated official clearance of Margery, the association with Lollardy remained and the accusations were reiterated.[89] Her failure to conform clearly and consistently to the behaviour encoded in *discretio spirituum* means that those activities she feels compelled to undertake as a visionary and prophet become identified in the eyes of some of her contemporaries with a dissenting ideology rather than a visionary calling.

The apparently unstable nature of Margery's affiliation with her various spiritual directors and confessors undoubtedly contributes to her lack of credibility as a visionary. This relationship constitutes the third area of her behaviour to be explored. The importance of a woman visionary's submission to a spiritual director has been noted several times; the spiritual director's role was both to guide and to control the visionary. Margery does have a series of

---

[87] My emphasis.

[88] M. Aston, *Lollards and Reformers: Images and Literacy in Late Medieval Religion* (London, 1984), pp. 49–50; C. Cross, ' "Great Reasoners in Scripture": The Activities of Women Lollards 1380–1530', in *Medieval Women*, ed. D. Baker (Oxford, 1978), pp. 359–80. Walter Brut was arrested and tried for heresy in a trial which lasted from 1391–3. One of his claims was that 'women have power and authority to preach and make the body of Christ, and they have the power of the keys of the church, of binding and loosing'. Alcuin Blamires and C. W. Marx point out that his examination became something of a show trial, which actually functioned to ensure the wide dissemination of his ideas. ('Woman Not to Preach: A Disputation in British Library MS Harley 31', *The Journal of Medieval Latin* 3 (1993), 34–5). Interestingly, in a vision experienced by Gertrude the Great of Helfta, Christ confers on her the powers of binding and loosing. For a discussion of this and related visions, see Bynum, *Jesus*, pp. 205–7.

[89] For a stimulating study which explores some of the issues raised by the 1413 trial of Sir John Oldcastle, with whom Margery was accused of being involved, see Beckwith, *Christ's Body*, pp. 70–76.

spiritual directors – the Dominican anchorite, Alan of Lynn, Richard Caister and Robert Spryngolde, as well as Wenceslaus in Rome and other unnamed clerics – who play an important role in her life. Nevertheless, the text does not highlight these very significant associations, or present them as central to Margery's life as a holy woman and visionary. Margery values these men, and is distressed when the anchorite dies, and when she is prevented from seeing Alan of Lynn (pp. 142: 25; 168: 28–38). However, what she appears to value most is their spiritual comfort, and their support. They are rarely depicted as guiding, let alone controlling, her, and Margery is rarely submissive to them. As discussed earlier, Margery sometimes disputes their judgement of her visions, usually with divine support. She also evades their control and asserts her own – or divine – will, as when she goes on her German pilgrimage against Spryngolde's explicit direction: 'ȝe may not gon' (p. 226: 20).

The importance of the spiritual director is forcibly demonstrated in the incident when Thomas Netter, Provincial of the Carmelites, forbids Alan of Lynn to see Margery.[90] The text states that this was the result of a complaint that Alan was 'to conuersawnt' with Margery, a fear of a kind which was often expressed about the relationship between holy women and their confessors, or spiritual directors. The imposed separation has the effect of silencing Margery, restricting her access to both clerical authorization and scriptural knowledge: '. . . sche xulde no mor gon to þe frerys, ne spekyn wyth þe sayd doctowr, ne askyn hym no qwestyons . . .' (p. 168: 17–20).[91]

In attempting to control Margery in this way, Netter was acting in conformity with the position he expresses in his anti-Wycliffite treatise, *Doctrinale antiquitatum fidei catholicae ecclesiae*. In this work he strongly refutes the heretical claim that lay preaching by women is an obligation, and fiercely attacks public preaching and teaching by women.[92] His attitude was clearly informed by the discourse of *discretio spirituum*. Netter was apparently something of a champion of holy women, as long as they knew their place – presumably within the walls. He is recorded as having accepted as anchor-

---

90 Thomas Netter of Walden (*c.* 1372–1430) was elected Provincial Prior of the English Carmelites in 1414, and held this post until his death. He was confessor to Henry V and spiritual advisor to Henry VI. For further information about his life and work see D. J. Dubois, 'Thomas Netter of Walden OC (*c.* 1372–1430)' (unpublished B.Lit. thesis, Oxford, 1978). See also Hudson, *Premature*, pp. 50–55.

91 Alan of Lynn was a man of considerable learning, a Doctor of Divinity; among many other works, he had compiled indices to the *Revelationes Brigittae* and to the *Prophetiae Brigittae*. Hope Emily Allen describes him as 'the most illustrious of Margery's friends at Lynn' (p. 268 n. 22/11–12). His expertise and influence increase the significance of his separation from Margery; such a separation would inevitably diminish her credibility.

92 *Doctrinale antiquitatem fidei catholicae ecclesiae*, 2 vols., ed. F. B. Blanciotti (Venice, 1757–9), I, 636; II, 71–2.

esses five women who are named, as well as others who are not.[93] One of these women, Emma Stapleton, had *five* Carmelites assigned by Netter to be her spiritual directors.[94] Clearly, Netter conformed to both the letter of *discretio spirituum* and to its spirit, both of which decreed the containment of holy women.[95] Margery, with her dramatic, performative spirituality, unenclosed and unruly, would have posed an obvious threat to the virtue of any man.[96] Cutting off her access to Alan of Lynn would have been tantamount to an official declaration of doubt as to her status as a visionary and holy woman, which would have adversely influenced the way in which others saw her. It certainly seems to have had that effect. Margery obviously feels abandoned. Rather than her more customary list of clerical supporters, she recites their absence – even Robert Spryngolde hardly dares speak to her (pp. 168: 36 – 169: 1). This episode clearly demonstrates the unhappy outcome of Margery's inconsistent conformity to the principles of *discretio spirituum*.

Underlying and informing these more specific facets of the text's construction of Margery's behaviour – her married state, her preaching and her submission to spiritual advisors – is the overall presentation of her virtue and piety. This is the fourth aspect of her behaviour which I consider. Margery's devotional exercise is extravagant, idiosyncratic, and overt enough to elicit frequent censure. Additionally, her observance of some conventional religious practices is inconsistent, and contributes to her ambivalent reception.

During the course of her life Margery, with divine encouragement, alters her devotional practices, often abandoning many of the visible manifestations of holiness for their internal and hence invisible, equivalents. For example, she wears a hair shirt for some time; then Christ tells her that he will replace it with 'an hayr in þin hert' (p. 17: 6–8).[97] Christ encourages her to spend less time

---

93 Dubois, 'Thomas Netter', p. 38.

94 N. P. Tanner, *The Church in Late Medieval Norwich 1370–1532* (Toronto, 1984), p. 63.

95 Netter started to write his *Doctrinale* just after the Council of Constance, which he may have attended, though evidence for this is sparse (Dubois, 'Thomas Netter', pp. 25–7, but see also Hudson, *Premature*, p. 51). It was after the Council of Constance, with the trial of Hus, the focus on heresy, and debate over the canonization of Bridget of Sweden, that Jean Gerson was moved to write his *De probatione spirituum* (pp. 55–6 above). Clearly, the issue of visionary veracity was a topical one, with particular relevance for women visionaries.

96 The threat Margery offered to male domination of preaching may also have motivated Netter. The *Book* implicitly associates Netter's move against Margery with the matter of the Grey Friar's refusal to preach if she was in church (p. 167: 28–30). Perhaps Margery's punishment was to fit her perceived crime – her crying drowns out the friar's words, and so she is forcibly silenced.

97 This may not be the best example of a visible sign transmuted to an invisible one. Margery wore her hair shirt while she was still intimate with her husband, and he never noticed it – which is suggestive about the range of John's lovemaking. For

praying and more time meditating. He tells her to abstain from meat, then tells her to start eating it again (p. 161: 24–7). She fasts one day a week for many years, until the Virgin Mary discharges her of her vow, so that she can keep her strength up to perform her spiritual labours (p. 162: 11–17). Even her chastity is not discernible; it is something not done, rather than something done and demonstrable. Lacking outward and visible sign, her professed chastity is a myth as far as most of her contemporaries are concerned, and she and her husband are accused of sneaking off 'to woodys, grouys, er valeys to vsyn þe lust of her bodijs' (p. 180: 5–6). Finally, and most crucially, after ten years Margery's crying is taken away (p. 155: 27–31). As discussed earlier, she had previously begged Christ to allow her to weep in private, and he refused; this is one of the few times when he gets the better of her (p. 182: 5–11). After ten years, although she still weeps, the loud cryings which commenced at the Holy Sepulchre, and which drew such attention to her, cease.

The predictable result of these shifts in devotional praxis is accusations of hypocrisy. Margery seems to have an acute sensitivity for the degree of devotional deviance which will engender the most derision. Certain of her practices tend to be ostentatious, inviting comment and often censure. After some time, her persistence in a particular exercise reassures her critics of her sincerity, or perhaps familiarity simply breeds indifference, and hostility diminishes. Yet at this point, Margery often changes her practice, which generates new accusations, aimed either at the new practice, at her abandonment of the old one, or at her perceived hypocrisy. The revilement elicited is interpreted by the text within the paradigmatic *imitatio Christi*. She is persecuted and so her spiritual merit is increased.

> &, as summe spoke euyl of hir aforn for sche cryed, so sum spoke now euyl of hir for sche cryid not. & so slawndir & bodily angwisch fel to hir on euery syde, & al was encresyng of hir gostly comfort. (p. 156: 4–8)

As discussed above under Margery's Mixed Blessing, the text constructs Margery within two competing discourses – *discretio spirituum* and the revilement discourse. The effect of her presentation within the rival discourses is that she appears to challenge the behavioural expectations of a visionary produced by *discretio spirituum*. She seems unruly, uncontrolled, fleshly, noisy, indubitably present, persistent, lusty, perverse. She embodies – quite literally – much of what the Church feared and dreaded about women. She is the woman who will not go away, and hence her credibility and effectiveness as a visionary is undermined.

---

similar invisible signs of holiness, see Gertrude the Great's invisible stigmata (Bynum, *Jesus*, p. 192), and the cross imprinted on the heart of Claire of Montefalco (Lochrie, *Margery*, p. 13).

There exists, however, one text in which Margery does conform, and thus offers a credible version of a visionary and holy woman. This text and its presentation of Margery is examined in the next section of the chapter.

Exit the Woman

A truly discreet Margery does emerge in one variant of her *Book*, a variant in which the text itself has all but vanished, and Margery has almost completely disappeared. This is the redaction printed by Wynkyn de Worde in London around 1501. It consists of seven pages in a quarto pamphlet, entitled 'A shorte treatise of contemplacyon taught by our lorde Ihesu cryste, or taken out of the boke of Margerie kempe of Lynn'.[98] The Margery who features in this treatise is completely unexceptionable as a holy woman. However as Sanford Meech states,

> The extractor . . . chose passages . . . which in their total effect give a very imperfect and one-sided impression of Margery's character, and a rather flavourless one of the *Book*. (pp. xlvi–xlvii)[99]

Insipid though the printed redaction may be in relation to the original *Book*, its very existence supports the argument that this chapter has made. As already demonstrated at some length, the text of the *Book* encompasses competing discourses; the revilement discourse undermines the credibility of Margery's construction within the discourse of *discretio spirituum*. The virtual elimination of the revilement discourse in the treatise resolves the conflict of

---

[98] For the sake of clarity, the redaction in any of its editions will henceforward be referred to as 'the treatise', while *The Book of Margery Kempe* will be referred to as the *Book*.

The printed extracts are reproduced in the Appendix of *BMK* (pp. 353–7). Full information on the printed extracts is given in the Introduction (pp. xlvi–xlviii). De Worde's printed treatise has the Short Title Catalogue number 14924. A useful analysis of the redaction, which supplies valuable information on de Worde and the trade in devotional literature in the early sixteenth century, is found in S. E. Holbrook, 'Margery Kempe and Wynken de Worde', in *The Medieval Mystical Tradition in England IV*, ed. M. Glasscoe (Cambridge, 1987), pp. 27–46. George Keiser considers the possible readership for the treatise, and speculates about de Worde's reasons for printing it in 'The Mystics and the Early English Printers: The Economics of Devotionalism', in *The Medieval Mystical Tradition in England IV*, ed. M. Glasscoe (Cambridge, 1987), pp. 9–26. Karma Lochrie examines the implications of the transformation of the *Book* into a devotional handbook (*Margery*, pp. 201–28).

[99] See also Atkinson, *Mystic*, p. 19. 'The selections were taken largely from the quieter (less eccentric) colloquies of Margery with Christ or the Virgin; none of them concerns her life in the world, and they offer a rather colorless and misleading impression of author and book.'

discourses and results in the consistent construction of Margery as a holy woman.[100] In the de Worde treatise, Margery is reconstructed as a model for devotion who conforms to the doctrine of *discretio spirituum*. Here she is meek and obedient, conventionally devout, affectively pious, her roarings moderated to compassionate weeping. Although there is no mention of her submission to a spiritual director in the treatise, she is obedient and submissive to Christ. The tone throughout is humble, she is presented as passive, she reacts rather than initiates; there is none of the negotiation for authority which characterizes so much of the *Book*. The complex of familial relationships used to describe her bond with Christ in the *Book* is reduced in the treatise to that epitome of patriarchy, the father-daughter relationship. Christ always addresses her as daughter; she always refers to him, or addresses him, as lord. Her name is given only in the title.[101]

There is little danger of the protagonist of the treatise being accused of seeking attention, power or gain. Even the notorious passage where Margery offers herself to be dragged naked on a hurdle (p. 356: 23–7) acquires a different coloration in this moderated context. The emphasis throughout the treatise is on contemplation, and Christ repeatedly promises her the same reward for the thought as for the deed. Consequently the text presents this offer as a response to Christ's promising her full reward in Heaven for all her 'good wylles and desyres' (p. 356: 19–20). It is to be read as an expression of devotion rather than of actual ambition. In the treatise, the revelations accord with received teaching and scriptural knowledge, and there is no conflict with the authority of the institutional church or its officers. The fruits of her visions are increased devotion, compassion, patience and charity resulting in her finding 'þe ryght way to heuen' (p. 357: 18).

Sue Ellen Holbrook, who has analyzed the structure of the de Worde treatise, concludes that:

> . . . eighteen percent of the words come from the woman as direct or indirect speech; twenty-two percent are in the voice of the narrator; and sixty percent are uttered directly by Christ.[102]

---

[100] A few remnants of the revilement discourse do remain, but in the new context they acquire a more conventional tone. In the *Book*, of course, the actual revilement of Margery is narrated in minute and lurid detail. In the treatise the conditional nature of Margery's desire for revilement is apparent: for example, 'thou woldest be hacked' (p. 356: 17); 'I wolde be layde naked' (p. 356: 23); 'it is more plesure to me þat thou suffre . . . than yf thyne hed were stryken' (p. 357: 11–13). The effect of this is to create a sense of a ritualistic exchange of courtesies between Margery and Christ.

[101] Although her full name – Margery Kempe – is only given once in the *Book* (p. 243: 19), she is addressed sixteen times as 'Margery', and certainly enough contextualizing information is given in the text to convey a sense of her subjectivity.

[102] Holbrook, 'Margery', p. 29.

Although no such analysis has yet been done of the *Book*, it is evident that there Margery dominates the entire text in a variety of ways, whereas in the treatise Margery is simply a vehicle for divine teaching. The title – 'A shorte treatyse of contemplacyon taught by our lorde Ihesu cryste, or taken out of the boke of Margerie kempe of lynn' – conveys this privileging, and is ambiguous about the authorship of the treatise. There is nothing to indicate that Margery had anything to do with the actual writing of the book from which the extracts are taken, whereas in the *Book* itself her involvement in its creation is declared by the end of the first folio.

> Sum [clerics] proferyd hir to wryten hyr felyngs wyth her owen handys, & sche wold not consentyn in no wey, for sche was comawndyd in hir sowle þat sche schuld not wrytyn so soone. & so it was xx 3er mor fro þat tym þis creatur had fyrst felyngys & reuelacyons er þan sche dede any wryten.
>
> (p. 3: 25–30)

Although the Margery of the treatise is quite unexceptionable, it is worth noting that she is promised graces denied to 'relygyous men & to prestes' because of their unwillingness to suffer for Christ (p. 357: 23–9). Criticism of ecclesiastical and clerical corruption was part of the acknowledged mandate of female visionaries and prophets – provided, of course, that they were genuine. It was a role performed, for example, by Bridget of Sweden, with great determination, and some considerable success. However, it was always of the greatest importance that such criticisms be represented as divine, issuing from the mouth not the mind of the visionary. The redactor therefore chose a passage in which it is Christ, speaking to Margery, who condemns the clerics for whom Margery is urging compassion.

> O my dere worthy lorde: these graces sholdest þu shewe to relygyous men & to prestes.
> Our lorde sayd to her . . . they shall not haue this grace, for doughter he that dredeth þe shames of this worlde may not parfyghtly loue god. (p. 357: 23–9)

This is in striking contrast to the *Book*, where time and again, it is Margery, speaking her mind in her own voice, who attacks various clerics.[103]

In the treatise, Margery the troublesome woman of the *Book* has found an editor who reads the text selectively and rewrites her unambiguously as holy.[104] The excess has been excised: not only the extremes of her inscribed life,

---

[103] See, for example, p. 125: 4–7 and 19–21.

[104] The separation of disorderly woman from divine word in relation to *The Book of Margery Kempe* is not limited to the medieval and early modern period. The first translations of the *Book* by William Butler Bowden continued the tradition. 'The English version placed all the chapters having to do with Kempe's revelations in an appendix; the American translation . . . found this placement awkward and, while retaining the original order, "had all the chapters entirely devoted to mystical

but also the more spectacular aspects of her performative spirituality have been written out. What remains is a passive, receptive, anonymous channel for Christ's teaching constructed within the discourse of *discretio spirituum*. What remains is a vanishing visionary.

The circumstances surrounding the writing of the treatise are not known. Most scholars speculate that it existed in manuscript form before de Worde printed it in 1501.[105] This surmise is based on de Worde's usual practice with the devotional material he produced, which was not to edit work extensively.[106] However, nothing is known about this possible manuscript version, and apparently no copies of it exist. All that is certain is that the second part of *The Book of Margery Kempe* was begun on 28 April 1438;[107] that at least one copy of the original text, the extant copy, was made by a scribe named Salthows, in Norfolk, around 1450;[108] and that at some point between the completion of the original manuscript[109] and 1501, material was extracted from the original to form the treatise which de Worde printed.[110]

Sue Ellen Holbrook speculates that Margery's confessor, Robert Spryngolde, might have been responsible for the redaction, although she acknowledges that there is no direct evidence for this.[111] Basing her argument on the *Book's* presentation of Spryngolde, Holbrook suggests that he respected Margery's spiritual integrity, cared about her safety, and could see the virtue of a less controversial version of *The Book of Margery Kempe*.

> . . . given controversies over modes of devotion and the piety of unenclosed women, and also given Lollard activity in Lynn, Springold [*sic*] might well

---

matters set in a smaller type to keep them distinct from the narrative text" ' (S. J. McEntire, 'Introduction', in *Margery Kempe: A Book of Essays* (New York, 1992), p. ix).

[105] For the dating of the printed extracts see *BMK*, p. xlvi n. 1; Holbrook, 'Margery', p. 50.

[106] Holbrook, 'Margery', p. 40; Lochrie, *Margery*, p. 222; Keiser, 'Mystics', p. 10. However, see also S. Dickman, 'Margery Kempe and the English Devotional Tradition', in *The Medieval Mystical Tradition in England I*, ed. Marion Glasscoe (Exeter, 1980), p. 157, who 'assumes' that de Worde borrowed a copy of *BMK* from the library at Syon (which she assumes had one) to make the extracts.

[107] *BMK*, p. 341 n. 221/7–9.

[108] *BMK*, p. xxxiv. See also R. Beadle, 'A Handlist of Later Middle English Manuscripts Copied by Norfolk Scribes', in *Regionalism in Late Medieval Manuscripts and Texts: Essays Celebrating the Publication of A Linguistic Atlas of Late Mediaeval English*, ed. F. Riddy (Cambridge, 1991), p. 104.

[109] Of course, the original manuscript may not have been made available on completion. It is worth noting that Margery reportedly asked the scribe she paid (who wrote only a leaf) not to reveal her book as long as she lived (4: 36). However, the second scribe doesn't mention a similar request being made of him.

[110] For information on the location of copies of the de Worde print, see Holbrook, 'Margery', p. 43 n. 2.

[111] Holbrook, 'Margery', pp. 38–40.

have preferred a version of Kempe less likely to excite trouble than the full *Book of Margery Kempe's* vivid accounts of sacred and profane events in which a merchant-class wife and mother survives persecution for heresy, reads the mystical extremists and feels like one of them, had a mystical marriage to God, and triumphs in writing in her own words a book of her revelations.[112]

If this were indeed so, it would certainly place Spryngolde in the tradition of confessor-editors like Alfonso of Jaén who ensured that the woman visionaries under their pastoral care were textually constructed according to the doctrine of *discretio spirituum*.

However, Holbrook's speculation fails to consider the fate of the original *Book*. If the excerpted version was created soon after the original was completed, then it must be assumed that both the full text and the excerpts could have been in circulation simultaneously, and quite possibly in the same area. In this case, the clamorous, controversial Margery would have coexisted with her devout, submissive alter-ego. This would tend to invalidate the rationale which Holbrook offers for Spryngolde's putative role as redactor. Just as in the original text the life-narrative undermines Margery's construction as visionary, so the continued circulation of the full-blooded text would have undermined the devotional treatise.

This is, of course, purely speculative, since we have no evidence that the treatise did exist before de Worde's publication. However, there is some evidence which could suggest a severely restricted circulation of the *Book*. It is significant that the only extant manuscript of the *Book* belonged to an enclosed monastic order, the Carthusians of Mount Grace. It is also suggestive that there are apparently no contemporaneous references to either Margery Kempe or her book. Neither have excerpts from it been found in any devotional compendia of the period. *The Book of Margery Kempe* would seem to have been intended for a lay audience, considering that Margery is presented as a model whereby other sinful wretches and caitiffs can come into the love of Christ (1–6). However, it would also seem possible that it did not reach this audience. Perhaps its perceived associations with Lollardy were too strong for wide acceptance. It originated in Norfolk, one of the hot-beds of Lollardy, and recounted the adventures of a woman several times accused of Lollardy, even of being 'Cobham's daughter', a woman who was known to cite scripture, was perceived to preach, and who reproached members of the clergy. It may have been known that Margery belonged to the parish of the priest William Sawtry, first Lollard to be burnt, in 1401, under the newly-passed statute *De heretico comburendo*.[113] The fact that the only surviving copy ended up in a monastic library could suggest that the circulation of the *Book* might have been somehow restricted to an informed readership, a readership which could

---

[112] Holbrook, 'Margery', p. 40.

[113] *BMK*, p. xlix; Atkinson, *Mystic*, pp. 103–4; Hudson, *Premature*, pp. 435–6.

winnow the wheat of spiritual illumination from the chaff of an unruly, unconventional life.[114] Evidence of the reception of the *Book* by some monastic readers is supplied by the marginal glosses in red ink in the manuscript of *The Book of Margery Kempe*.[115] These may have been made by a monk at Mount Grace in the early sixteenth century.[116] The notations reveal an affirmative response to the visionary aspects of the text, often categorizing them as recognized spiritual phenomena: for example, 'amor impaciens' (p. 107 n. 3), 'Non est in hominis potestate prohibere spiritum s[anctum]' (p. 149 n. 4).

The annotator remarks on Margery's 'discretion' in three places.[117] The first such gloss, '*nota* dyscrescion' (p. 25 n. 4), is in the margin beside an account of Margery's travels to visit 'Goddys seruawntys, boþen ankrys, reclusys & many oþer of owyr Lordys louerys' to whom she revealed 'hir felyngys & hyr contemplacyons, as sche was comawnded for to don, to wetyn yf any dysseyt were in hir felyngys'. Clearly the annotator is identifying Margery's conformity to the requirement of *discretio spirituum* that the visionary should submit her visions to one learned in the spiritual life.

The second marginal comment on Margery's 'dyscresion' (p. 36 n. 3) accompanies a similar incident when Margery is visiting Archbishop Arundel at

---

[114] There is a parallel in the possible limited circulation of *BMK* with the circulation of copies of *The Mirror of Simple Souls* by Marguerite Porete. The Middle English translation of this work by M.N. records his concern that some aspects of the work in an earlier translation 'haue be mystake', and that a work of such mystical profundity and difficulty could lead to misinterpretation by the devout souls for whom it was intended. To prevent this, M.N. provides explanatory glosses for passages he considers obscure or open to misunderstanding. (Marguerite Porete, '*The Mirror of Simple Souls*: A Middle English Translation', ed. M. Doiron, *Archivo italiano per la storia della pietà* 5 (1968), 247–8. See also E. Colledge and R. Guarnieri, 'The Glosses by "M.N." and Richard Methley to *The Mirror of Simple Souls*', *Archivo italiano per la storia della pietà* 5 (1968), 357–82.) It is of interest, given the association of Mount Grace Charterhouse with Margery Kempe, that M.N.'s Middle English text of *The Mirror of Simple Souls* was rendered into Latin in 1491 by Richard Methley, prior of Mount Grace (Colledge and Guarnieri, 'Glosses', 357). On Methley and Margery, see below p. 153.

[115] Sanford Meech writes in his Introduction, 'The interest and value of the bulk of these [red ink] annotations . . . are in their revelation of the interests and enthusiasms of the annotator, who was probably a Carthusian of Mount Grace' (*BMK*, pp. xlii–xliii).

[116] *BMK*, p. xxxvi; Lochrie, *Margery*, p. 209; Holbrook, 'Margery', p. 36. Since this discussion of the marginal glosses does not include those earlier ones made in brown ink, the writer of the red ink glosses will be referred to simply as 'the annotator'. The brown ink glosses, in three different hands and earlier than the red ink ones, mainly draw attention to certain parts of the text, alter spelling, or, in one instance, provide a translation into Latin (*BMK*, pp. xliii–xliv).

[117] Although the glosses use the basic term 'discretion', it is clear from the context that the annotator is referring to the doctrine of *discretio spirituum*.

Lambeth. '. . . sche schewyd þis worshepful lord hir maner of leuyng & swech grace as God wrowt in hyr mende & in hir sowle to wetyn . . . ʒyf he fond any defawte eyþyr in hyre contemplacyon er in hir wepyng'. Here the annotator is noting as a sign of Margery's discretion her submission of her visionary experiences to the expertise of the highest ecclesiastical authority.

The third and final marginal comment specifically directed to Margery's discretion is in response to a different situation. It is located in the margin next to Margery's request that Christ send her cryings in private. The gloss is '*nota dyscretion*' (p. 181 n. 1). The passage referred to reads: 'Lord, why wilt þu ʒyf me swech crying þat þe pepil wondryth on me þerfor?' The annotator here recognizes as conformity to the doctrine of *discretio spirituum* Margery's apparent desire not to be the focus of attention (p. 181 n. 1).

The annotator also makes a significant comparison of Margery in some of her more extreme bodily transports with Richard Methley (*c.* 1451–1528), prior of Mount Grace, and with John Norton, who became prior on Methley's death. Both were ecstatic mystics, who left accounts of, and reflections on, their experiences.[118] To place Margery in the same category as these learned and respected monastic mystics is to valorize precisely those experiences which caused discomfort and hostility in some of her contemporaries.

Karma Lochrie states that the annotator 'clearly found Kempe's roaring to be a legitimate expression of religious devotion, and one with which he was familiar'.[119] This could be so, but it is important to remember that the annotator was an informed reader, who was able to isolate Margery's spiritual experiences and map them onto an appropriate devotional tradition using, a matter of considerable significance, enclosed, male mystics as points of comparison.

The red-ink glosses delineate a construction of Margery which conforms much more consistently to *discretio spirituum*. In much the same manner, the

---

118 *BMK*, pp. 291 n. 68/31 and 271 n. 29/n. 3. For information on Methley see J. Hogg, 'Richard Methley: To Hew Heremyte, A Pystyl of Solytary Lyfe Nowadayes', *Analecta Cartusiana* 31 (1977), 91–119, and 'A Mystical Diary: The *Refectorium Salutatis* of Richard Methley of Mount Grace Charterhouse', *Analecta Cartusiana* 55:1 (1981), 208–38. Methley apparently wrote several treatises on mysticism and on contemplation, few of which have survived. A work on the discernment of spirits entitled '*Experimentum Veritatis*' survives only in part in Public Record Office MS SP 1/239. This treatise has been edited by M. Sargent, 'Self-Verification of Visionary Phenomena: Richard Methley's *Experimentum Veritatis*', *Analecta Cartusiana* 55:2 (1981), 121–37. In the treatise Methley argues for an intuitive knowledge of the truth of visionary phenomena. Methley also translated *The Cloud of Unknowing* into Latin, and translated into Latin and glossed Marguerite Porete's then anonymous work, *A Mirror of Simple Souls* (Hogg, 'Mystical Diary', p. 209). For John Norton, as well as Methley, see J. Hogg, 'Mount Grace Charterhouse and Late Medieval English Spirituality', *Analecta Cartusiana* 82:3 (1980), 1–43.

119 Lochrie, *Margery*, p. 211.

redaction offers a sanitized – even sanctified – version of *The Book of Margery Kempe* which was evidently seen as a useful devotional text, first by Wynkyn de Worde, and then by Henry Pepwell in 1521. It is surely ironic that Pepwell identified Margery, whose text is a testimony to her geographical as well as her spiritual journeys, and whose orthodox devotion was frequently challenged, as 'a deuote ancres' (p. 357 n. 11). Furthermore, he included the redaction in an anthology of six mystical treatises, two of which, *Epistle of Discretion of Stirrings in the Soul* and the *Treatise of Discerning of Spirits*, instruct the reader in ways to identify false visions, counselling moderation in devotional praxis and a close, humble association with a spiritual counsellor.[120] As has been demonstrated, neither of these features figure large in *The Book of Margery Kempe*.

Had the original text heeded the lessons promulgated by these treatises, and fashioned Margery in the image which they offer, then Margery might have been the woman who went away, instead of the problematic presence who intrigues and troubles her medieval contemporaries and modern readers alike. Then she would have exemplified the qualities enshrined in the discourse of *discretio spirituum* and, like her model, Bridget of Sweden, she would have been a vanishing – and successful – visionary.

---

[120] For full texts of these two treatises, see Hodgson, *Deonise*, pp. 62–93. These texts are included in my discussion of popular knowledge of *discretio spirituum*, pp. 61–6 above. A modern version of Pepwell's anthology is J. Griffiths, ed., *The Cell of Self-Knowledge* (Goldenbridge, 1981).

CONCLUSION

Belief in direct access to the divine is a central tenet of Christianity. It is a powerful stimulus to faith and, simultaneously, a serious threat to ecclesiastical authority. Those who claim to have experienced an intense and unmediated contact with God may be led to question traditional religious paradigms and controls. Indeed, a 'mystic may substitute his own opinion for that prescribed by authority, precisely because his opinion seems to stem from the very same authority'.[1] Consequently institutional religions have historically been wary of those claiming new revelations, fearful of a challenge to reigning orthodoxy and to established authority.

Organised religions have, as a result, often evolved ways to control those inclined to trust their own transcendental experience more than established religious authority. In the Catholic Church, with its long tradition and highly developed institutional life, an elaborate system was evolved to control and channel visionaries, a system designed to contain their revelations within the approved frameworks of prescribed Church teachings and institutions. This system is embedded in the doctrine of *discretio spirituum*, the discernment of spirits.

As I have argued in this book, the combination of women, traditionally believed to be susceptible to demonic deception, with spiritual visions, also perceived as potential vehicles for satanic illusion, made the Church particularly hesitant to accept women's claims to divine inspiration. As a result of this ecclesiastical scepticism, the doctrine of *discretio spirituum* was interpreted with particular stringency and rigour in regard to women visionaries. It functioned as a kind of code of conduct, prescribed the way for visionaries to articulate their revelations, dictated their relationship with their spiritual directors, and established the appropriate demeanour for women visionaries.

Nevertheless, despite its function as a mechanism of control, *discretio spirituum* gave rise to a significant paradox. Those women visionaries who accepted the restrictions, who conformed to the terms of the doctrine, that is, those who were constructed as meek, submissive to their spiritual directors, and as compliant, transparent instruments of the divine, could achieve great influence.

By conforming, medieval women visionaries not only gained acceptance for their divinely ordained vocation and influenced subsequent generations,

---

[1] G. Scholem, *On the Kabbalah and Its Symbolism*, trans. R. Mannheim (New York, 1969), p. 9.

they were able in some cases to wield real power; they left the narrow space of home and family, or of convent, to which medieval life confined them, and entered the public arena. Bridget of Sweden, well-born, educated, sophisticated, in alliance with Alfonso of Jaén, her skilled spiritual director and editor, was successfully presented as a model visionary according to the precepts of *discretio spirituum*. Her reward was the attainment of status and authority, enabling her to advise kings, popes and emperors, to establish her own religious order, and eventually to be canonized.

Margery Kempe lacked Bridget's advantages and, perhaps, her shrewdness as well. A laywoman of the merchant class, she seemed to be fired by the intensity of her visionary encounters in a way that apparently encouraged her to believe that she could challenge religious authority, while simultaneously seeking its endorsement of her visions and her way of life. In place of the required humility, modesty and submissiveness, Margery was difficult, defiant and disputatious. Unlike Bridget, who offered herself as a clear channel for God's message, Margery was obtrusive, and loudly and insistently *there*. Her adversarial stance in relation to certain clerics, and her ambivalent reception by her fellow Christians made her, according to the text, a controversial figure, even to the point of being accused of Lollardy. Had Margery been better versed in *discretio spirituum*, or better served by her amanuensis, we might now have Saint Margery, and pilgrimages to her tomb, instead of an unknown burial place, a single extant manuscript and a remarkable amount of critical hostility.[2]

Yet both Bridget and Margery were part of the remarkable flowering of women visionaries in the late Middle Ages. As women they lent new richness of meaning and new depth to the religious traditions of which they were a part. As women, they gave new life to old forms, forms which were always in danger of ossifying. And as women they brought new voices, new dimensions, to a tradition which was historically suspicious of women and distrustful of visions and doubly sceptical when there was a conjunction of the two.

In the Middle Ages, vision and prophecy represented one of the very few spaces in the patriarchal institution of the Church within which women could be empowered. Such empowerment, however, depended on access to the discourses of authority embodied in formal knowledge and organized religion, in institutions entirely dominated by men. Women who were educated, women who were part of the religious establishment, women who could form useful alliances within the ecclesiastical hierarchy had a great advantage over their illiterate sisters in translating their feminine experience of the divine into the language of men. Those women who were most effective in fulfilling their divine mandate to communicate the word of God were those

---

2   What a skilled editor could have done with Margery is illustrated by the treatise excerpted from her *Book*, and published by Wynken de Worde. See above, pp. 147–51.

women who could articulate the ineffable according to the discourse of *discretio spirituum.*

I began this study with a quotation from Jean Gerson in which he warns that the words and works of women must be viewed with suspicion. I would like to end it with some of those women's words, words in which Bridget of Sweden claimed the authority with which she believed God had invested her. In the last months of her life, still trying to persuade Pope Gregory XI to return to Rome from Avignon, she sent him a message through her spiritual director Alfonso of Jaén. The message begins, 'God has spoken wonderful words through a woman.'[3]

3   Harris, *Birgitta*, p. 12.

The Middle English *Epistola solitarii ad reges* of Alfonso of Jaén: An Edition of the Text in London, British Library, MS Cotton Julius Fii

Introduction

Shortly after the death of Bridget of Sweden in 1373, her spiritual director and editor, Alfonso of Jaén (1329/30–1389; also known as Alphonse of Pecha), added an eighth book, the *Liber celestis imperatoris ad reges*, to the collection of her visions and revelations, the *Sancta Birgitta Revelaciones*, which he had been largely responsible for organizing and editing. Alfonso was concerned at this time to amass all the documentation which he could so that a comprehensive account of Bridget's life and visions could be published in time for the opening of Bridget's canonization process. Some of the material in this eighth book was excerpted from the first seven; the remainder appeared here for the first time. All of the visions and revelations which it contains are concerned, as the name implies, with temporal rulers. To serve as a preface to this book, Alfonso wrote the *Epistola solitarii ad reges*, in which he defends Bridget's status as visionary and prophet by outlining how she conforms to the principles of *discretio spirituum*, the doctrine which establishes the criteria for distinguishing true visions and visionaries from those inspired by the devil. Demonstrated adherence to *discretio spirituum* was a very important factor in the successful journey toward sainthood. The *Epistola* was divided into eight chapters, the last serving as the true introduction to the *Liber celestis imperatoris ad reges*.

Copies of the *Revelaciones* circulated in various forms; sometimes Book VIII was lacking in its entirety; sometimes all or part of the *Epistola* served as a kind of epilogue to the first seven books of revelations. In England there are six Latin manuscripts of the complete *Revelaciones*, which were executed in England. All these manuscripts are in one group; copies of fragments from later in the century reveal the influence of continental manuscript groupings.[1] There are two extant Middle English translations of substantially complete versions of the *Revelaciones*, entitled the *Liber celestis*: one is found in London,

---

1   Roger Ellis, '*Flores ad fabricandam . . . coronam*: An Investigation into the Uses of the Revelations of St Bridget of Sweden in Fifteenth-Century England', *Medium Aevum* 52 (1983), 165–6.

British Library, MS Cotton Claudius Bi, the other in London, British Library, MS Cotton Julius Fii. MS Claudius Bi ends part way through Book VII and Julius ends after the seventh chapter of the *Epistola*. MS Cotton Julius Fii, even though it lacks the last chapter,[2] is thus the only extant Middle English version of the *Epistola solitarii ad reges* of Alfonso of Jaén.

The Manuscript: London, British Library, MS Cotton Julius Fii

'The Revelations of S. Bridget, princess of Nerike in Sweden', Bks. I–VII, translated into English; with the Prologue of Matthias, canon of Linkoping. Book VII is complete, and ends with chapter 31 on fol. 246v. It is followed immediately by the *Epistola solitarii ad reges*, beginning: 'O ȝe clere and bright kynges and wold to god . . .'. The *Epistola* includes Chapter VII, the Recapitulation, which ends on fol. 254r with the words: 'And the seyinges of al doctours and holy fadris vpon this mateer diffusely and manyfold wise speking.' It is followed by an epilogue giving a brief account of Bridget's death and canonization. The last page of the manuscript – fol. 254v – contains two Latin prayers to St Bridget.

Paper: fols. 254. 12 inches x 8.5 inches.

Date: Dr Ian Doyle has suggested a date for the manuscript in the late 1430s or early 1440s.

Provenance: Norfolk.[3]

Editorial Method

Editorial emendations have been kept to an absolute minimum and are indicated by [square brackets].[4] Scribal errors are reproduced in {braces}. When the letters are legible, they are given, otherwise they are indicated by one period for each letter. Interlineations are enclosed in <angle brackets>.

---

2   In this respect it was faithfully following what looks to have been the pattern in the ancestor of the English MSS of the Latin text.

3   R. Beadle, 'Prologomena to a Literary Geography of Later Medieval Norfolk', in *Regionalism in Late Medieval Manuscripts and Texts: Essays Celebrating the Publication of A Linguistic Atlas of Late Medieval English*, ed. F. Riddy (Cambridge, 1991), p. 104.

4   Any corrections that have been made are based on the critical edition of the Latin text of the *Epistola* in A. Jönsson, *Alfonso of Jaen: His Life and Works with Critical Editions of the Epistola Solitarii, the Informaciones and the Epistola serui Christi* (Lund, 1989), pp. 115–71. Hereafter this version of the text will be abbreviated to Lat. Although the Middle English version is an abridged one, material has been excised in sections; outside of these sections, the Middle English is a very faithful translation of the Latin.

Abbreviations and suspensions have been expanded in *italics*. An apostrophe'
indicates an unexplained flourish. Where possible, expansions have been
made consistent with the scribe's own expanded spelling; however, the scribe
him- or her- self is rarely consistent. In these cases, the expansion takes the
most common form. Punctuation and capitalization have been maintained as
far as possible as they are in the manuscript, as have word divisions. *i, j, u,* and
v are as they appear in the manuscript. Yogh (3) and thorn (þ) are reproduced.
The scribe rarely uses thorn, preferring *y*, which is formed quite differently.
S/He sometimes draws a stroke across the stem of *h* and *l*; this seems to be
simply an otiose flourish. Obliques / and / / reproduce the same symbols in
the manuscript. Their purpose is not clearly apparent, although they are
sometimes used in conjunction with hyphens to indicate the end of a chapter.
Hyphens of varying length -- and --- also reproduce marks in the manuscript,
which, again have no consistently discernible purpose, and may just be otiose.
The suffixes for the ordinal numbers have been placed on the line and itali-
cized, but have not been expanded. In the manuscript, rubrics are in red ink,
and set off from the body of the text on lines of their own. Half-bracketed
Arabic numbers indicate lines in the manuscript. Note that these numbers do
not appear in the manuscript itself, but have been inserted to convey the layout
of the manuscript. In the manuscript, a two-line space has been left at the
beginning of each chapter for an illuminated capital. After Book I: 2, the
chapters are not numbered. For ease and clarity of reference, in this edition a
line space has been inserted between each chapter. This space is not in the
manuscript, where chapter breaks are, of course, indicated by rubrics. The
same clearly legible hand is used throughout the *Epistola*, indeed, throughout
the entire manuscript of Julius Fii, for both text, corrections, and marginal
glosses.

Comparative Study

The Middle English translation of the *Epistola* is a considerably abridged
version of the Latin text. MS Cotton Julius Fii is the only extant Middle English
version of the *Epistola*; none of the Latin manuscripts executed in England is an
ancestor of MS Cotton Julius Fii. With the manuscript information available at
present, it is impossible to tell whether Julius Fii was an original abridgement
made directly, or at a remove, from a copy of the Latin text or from a Middle
English text; whether it was the only abridged version; and whether any
Middle English versions were complete translations of the Latin.[5]

The method I have followed in the comparative study is to place in
footnotes all material in the Latin edition which has no correspondence in

---

[5] I am grateful to Dr Roger Ellis for confirming that the abridgement almost certainly
originated with the translator, rather than with a Latin source.

Julius Fii. Chapter and line numbers are keyed to A. Jönsson, ed., *Epistola solitarii ad reges*, in *Alfonso of Jaén: His Life and Works* (Lund, 1989), pp. 115–71. Excised passages of less than a line I have quoted fully, in Latin. When the passage omitted is more than a line, I have provided a précis, in English.

A comparison between the most nearly complete version of the Latin *Epistola* that we have and the abridged Middle English translation is valuable in that the excised material could suggest a motivation for the abridgement; this in turn could indicate factors influencing the translator/scribe, and thereby enhance our understanding of the reception of treatises such as the *Epistola*.[6]

References to Bridget's *Sermo angelicus* and to its creation are excised in the translation because the *Sermo* is not part of the *Revelaciones* proper, and does not appear in the manuscript of the *Liber celestis*. Apart from this, an initial survey of the excised passages suggests four possible motivations: (1) the obvious – to shorten and simplify the material, understandable after 250 folios of exhaustive detail; (2) to suppress material giving practical advice about conformity to *discretio spirituum*; (3) to suppress details of ecstatic behaviour; (4) to suppress material dealing with Bridget's authorization to write. The last three possibilities excite conjecture that perhaps the manuscript was destined for a female audience; in this case the suppression of material could result from a fear of women's alleged suggestibility in the area of visions, and a desire not to stimulate *imitatio Brigittae*.

---

6 My article 'Rewriting the Letter: Variations in the Middle English Translation of the *epistola solitarii ad reges* of Alfonso of Jaén', in *The Translation of St Birgitta of Sweden's Works into the European Vernaculars*, ed. B. Morris and V. O'Mara (Turnhout, forth-coming), addresses this issue, particularly as it arises in *The Chastising of God's Children*. In a future project I intend to probe further the implications of the abridge-ment, and investigate the relationship between the *Epistola* and the text of the *Liber celestis* as it appears in MS Cotton Julius Fii.

The Text

[fol. 246v] 16) In this booke yat followis here. yei are repreuyd the whech on warys with 17) ought examynacoun preuys or repreuys. personys seying them self to have 18) godly. visions and revelacouns, / the ferst chappetre/ 19) o ȝe cler and bright kynges and wold to god ye were very kinges in god 20) myn deer lordis derly be fore louyd with sympil and meke recomendacouns 21) before sent on to ye feet of ȝoure regal maieste. ffor it is the maner of kinges 22) to wil discus {curuosly}<curiously>. and in discussinge to know the qualiteys of personys to 23) them writynge / ony onwont secretes of goddis wyl. And for yat now inyese 24) late dayes cloudid with a thik derkenes / Aserteyne nobil woman of body and soule 25) has resin[7] callid. lady brigid[8] the bewty of all women The whech as a bright 26) sterre. diffudis and yetes forth his shinyng bemys of holynes be diuers clymes 27) of the wyde word. The whech writes now to vs be ye precept of most hy and[9] [fol. 247r] 1) heuenly empror this present boke. withyn wretyn godly reuelat to hir as a bright merour 2) and a regal adornamente / and corepcoun or blamyng of oure maneris and sogettis 3) of the kingedom ʌ to be exsercisid ʌ[10] holy gouernans Therfore my lordes les yat no sodeyn 4) or on avisid indiscrete iugement of ony indiscret men./ inducyng you to mys 5) beleue or incredulite. and the hardnes of Kinge pharao / as a whirle wynde. shuld 6) drawe ought fro youre hertis the seed of beleue and feith./ mekely taking and beleuyng 7) this glorious boke wretyn / in ye herte of the forseid lady / with the fynger of all 8) m[i]ghty god. Therfore I haue decreyd yat ȝe be not illudyd soche wyse . brefly and 9) plenarly. to schewe you the condicouns and the qualite of the blissid soule of 10) the forseid lady. Brigid / and ye maner of wise yat she had the visions of god. 11) Also I intende to write and in writyng to teche boþe ȝou and odir a breff maner 12) of discernyng godly. visions fro the cursid illusiouns of sathan the deule./ Therfore 13) myn lordis I sey brefly. yat yer be many and diuers kendis of visiouns And for yis 14) mateer is on knouyn as apilgrim {.} a mong men / for ye ignorauns and on cunnyng 15) of holy scripture. and experiens of[11] mental prayour and contemplacoun And of gostly 16) lyff/ Therfore I have desirid oftyn sethis to eke with wordes {..} oon breff tretyse / the 17) wheche shuld be as <a> wenewyng scotyl to discerne visions for the gret perelis 18) the whech has happenyd to many personys in myn tyme. for the onknoulache of 19) this so secrete and on vsid mateer And for yis blissid lady. to whom this present 20)

---

7 I:3. *de regno Suecie*

8 I:3. *de regno Suecie*

9 Catchword: heuenly empror

10 In the manuscript, this phrase is written on the line within carets, as it appears here.

11 I:8. *sentimentorum*

booke godlich was reuelat in vision / sche seis in the be gynnyng of yt / yat 21) sche sy. in Vision agret paleyce incompr*e*hensibil for gretnes / like the cler heue*n* 22) *et cetera* / Therfore now I haue decreyd the forseid tretysse & compile here be ye man*er* 23) wise of a epistyl/ yat good and godly visions. shuld be excussid and dep*a*rtid fro 24) the deulys and wikkid visions as corn fro the chaff / And yat it may be pure 25) and clene corn./ <and>in ye berne or lathe of sp*i*ritual[12] holy me*n* may be leyd and wor 26) schepid.,. And the chaff of the deulys illusions be cast on the myddinge[13] .. fer fro 27) the winde of goddis scripture blouyn' / Therfore <at ye> beginny*n*g in the name of crist 28) puttyng vndir alwey. ye thing*es* the whech I sey to ye correccou*n* of holy[14] chirch **[fol. 247v]** 1) and sad counsel./ I sey. yat he yat wyl iuge discerne discusse or rightuosly to ex 2) amyn. the kendis of visiou*n*s or reuelacou*n*s / it be houys yat he haue the forseid holy 3) theorike of holy scripture/ in and on the mateer of visiou*n*s the whech holy fadris 4) and doctor*es* clerly. has describid. And the practike of exp*e*riens of sp*i*ritual liff[15] and 5) mental visiou*n*s sp*i*ritually or intellectually. godly infudid to them. And for 6) this theorike and pra{va}ctyke in fewe p*e*rsonys this day of discernyng the forseyd 7) thing*es*. or demynge visiou*n*s and sprit*es* are foundin/ Therfore many <me*n*> erringe 8) as blinde men in this mateer {..} ar turned to contempne sempyl and holy 9) p*e*rsonys knet to god. The whech to discerne p*e*rfitly and to p*r*eue or rep*r*eue tho -- 10) thing*es* the whech suld be p*r*euyd or repreuyd / legginge no thinge resonabil 11) in yer on wysse iugement*es* and sodeyn seying*es* or rader detraccou*n*s / but that the 12) aungil of the deule oftyn tymes tr*a*nsfoormys him vnd*er* the spice and kende 13) of the aungil of light / and bringis foorth exsamplis of odyr sp*i*ritual p*e*rsonys 14) the whech in tymis past {we}<was> deludid of the deule in yer visions not thinking 15) on the*m* yat where illumynid of god be visiou*n*s . And be tho thei have lightned 16) the chirch of god and odir men condempny*n*g namly simpil sp*i*ritual p*e*rsonys 17) ydiot*es* and the kende of a woma*n* as ignorau*n*t / and of <a> light capacite a*n*d reputacou*n* 18) and y*er*fore to be taken on worthy. on to godly . visions or profecyes / nat {.} 19) attendinge y*a*t almighty god as weel in the old testame*n*t as in ye newe. 20) to shew his gret might has chosin to him as wel in woma*n*kende as 21) man kende . to confounde wisemen./ whedir he made nat a p*r*ofete of 22) a scheppard and repleshid ʒoung ydiot*es* w*ith* sprith of profecie / And whed*ir* 23) he chos nat/ rude me*n* and fischer*es* in to apostolys and {....}[16] doughtor*es* /they 24) ar repleschid w*ith* the holy gost Also whedir mary the sust<*er*of> aaron . iudith . 25) and est*er* were geuen the sprith of profecye/

[12] I:12. *et catholicorum*
[13] I:12. *et pedibus conculcetur*
[14] I:13. *matris*
[15] I:15. *et sentimentorum consolacionum*
[16] Lat. has *non doctores*

whedir nat Kinge Iosye. 26) was direct in his ded*es* be . oldam awoma*n* and a .
profetisse / whedir not 27) thinkys and reme*m*bris yat delbora. the p*r*ofetyss
gove*r*nyd the pepil of israel. 28) Also Anne the modir of[17] sampson and odir
wome*n* in y*e* old testament had.[18] **[fol. 248r]** 1) the sprith. of p*r*ofecye Also in
the new testament Anne the dought*er* of fanuel 2) p*r*ofecied Elizabeth . Zacary .
blissid lucy*e* þe v*er*gin as it is red in hir bokis Sibyl 3) tiburtyne and anod*er*
Sibil[19] and many odir of the whech y*o*u schal finde in holy 4) scripture and of
seint*es* And for yat it is p*er*lous on avisid to condempne or to/re 5) preue[20]
sp*irit*ual visiou*n*s/ or the p*er*sonys seing that they haue dyuyn visions/or they
6) be examyned of the q*u*alite of the p*er*sonys And also of ye man*er* of seinge
and of 7) the q*u*alite of the mater of visions. and all may be p*r*euyd be godd*es*
scripture . and 8) of the writing*es* of holy doughttor*es* whedyr yei ar infudid or
mynystred of illusiou*n* 9) or of the sprith. of treuþe. / ffor we see y*a*t pharao be
leuyd not moyses yat he sy 10) god for he was a sympel man. And y*er*fore he
not beleuyng {stodstille}[21] his vision 11) ne*n* his seing*es* and {.} rader the seinge
of god/ but stodstille frouardly in hardnes 12) of {......} <hert and> mysbeleue.
Therfore he was cast wrecchedly in ye red see w*ith* the 13) pepil of egipt. And
also I haue sien ma<n>y moo in my*n* dayes. <the whech> ar mo[v]ed nout 14)
to god counting*e* soche sp*irit*ual p*er*sonys sempil and ydiot*es* and y*er* sp*irit*ual
visiou*n*s -- 15) veyne and feyned and fantasies. ffor the whech thei ar exspert
wrecchidly. 16) the cruel senten*s* of god on them self and on þ*er* sogett*es* be the
p*er*sonys and y*er* 17) visions p*r*enu*n*sid be fore to the*m*./ Be exsampil in
destruccou*n* of the kingedom of 18) cypris / for yat the prince beleuyd not the
visions of blissid brigid to who*m* this 19) p*r*esent booke was shewid . as it is
wretyn in y*e* last heue*n*ly boke xix chapet*er* 20) Also I haue seen and herd odir
yat be levid illusions and fil p*er*lously. The -- 21) exsample of this see in y*e* vi
boke lxviii chapet*er*./ And in ye booke of collacou*n*s 22) of fadris. of John
cassian . collacou*n*[22] the ii chapet*er* w*ith* many like þ*er*fore it is more 23) {wid}
wisdom to discusse w*ith* gret sadnes soche visions and p*er*sonys and yan the*m*
24) wel w*ith* deliberacou*n* and sadnes discussid and discretly iugid
{awdir}<owdir> to preve p*r*euyd 25) or to <be> repreued / The apostil seis
preff whed*er* the sprit*es* be of god / and yan iff[23] 26) it be foundin yat thei be of

---

17 I:25. *Samuelis, Agar et uxor Manue, mater.* The elision of examples here erroneously
   identifies Anna as the mother of Sampson, rather than of Samuel.

18 Catchword: the sprith

19 I:26. *erictea*

20 I:27. *vel approbare*

21 *stodstille* dotted for expunction and deleted. This word occurs on the following line
   about six character spaces to the left, which suggests an eye-slip on the part of the
   scribe. This may indicate that the scribe was copying from an English text, not translating from the Latin.

22 I:34. *collacione II, capitulo 'Et ut hanc eandem'*

23 I:36. *in examine*

god we owe mekely to be leue the*m* and obey 27) them holly. And yf thei be of
the deule as wikkid illusions yan we owe to 28) dispise the*m* and noman*er* of
wyse to geve feith to them // --- // ---

29) The man*er* exsamynacou*n* is put here in theorike of ye qualite of the
*per*sone **[fol. 248v]** 1) seinge visions and the man*er* of hauyng of them and of
the *qua*lite of mat*er* of visions 2) and of reuelacou*n*s // -/ the secunde chaptre
./ 3) holy fadris and doctoris of the chirche seis. yat a *per*sone seinge visions
shuld 4) be exsamynde on this wise. whe[d]i[r] it be a sp{*er*}irit*ua*l p[er]sone[24]
or a wordly and 5) seculer whed*ir* he leuys vnd*er* disciplyn and sp*irit*ual
obediens[25] of any discrete senior[26] 6) or in his owne fre choise and wil . Also
whed*er* he has put anoon his temptacou*n*s 7) and soche odir visions to
examyni*n*g and doom of his sp*irit*ual fadir or odir discret 8) men w*ith* humilite
bredinge to be illudid or alls he had the*m* or has presumyd 9) and <be>
proud of the*m* and di[sp]lisid odir men / Also y*is per*sone shuld be examyned .
seing 10) thos visions whedir he be of obediens humilite and cherite and
tenting pr*ay*our 11) or ded*es* of pride procedis fro him[27] for honouir or dignite .
Also whedir this *per*sone 12) be countyd among sp*irit*ual me*n* feithful and
obedient to ye *pr*elat*es* and gouer*n*our*es* 13) of the chirche / or he be suspect of
the feith or of obediens of *pr*elat*es* of ye chirch . 14) Also whedir he haue
perseuer*y*d <long> in sp*irit*ual liff v*er*tuosly or ell new begynner 15) Also
whedir he haue natural vndirstondinge and sp*irit*ual and veri discret. 16)
doom of resou*n*[28] / or he has but light vndirstondinge or sodeyn and fantastyk.
17) Gregory seis in his dyalogys yat holy me*n* discernys among illusions and .
18) reuelacou*n*s of visions ./ voyces or ymagis w*ith* anInwardly . slombring[29] /
yat 19) they may knowe what y*ei* sshal *per*seyue of agood sprit / or what they
schal 20) suffre of an illusor and whedir this *per*sone was exsamynde <ony>
odyr tyme 21) of the mat*er* and man*er* of visions be lettrid me*n* and sp*irit*ual or
noo / And 22) these ar semyd to be sufficient as to examynacou*n* of the *per*sone
/ As to 23) the man*er* of seing and hering*e* sp*irit*ually visions {and} <or>
reuelacou*n*s / holy fadris 24) and doctoris of the chirch seis / yat it owis to be
examynd. whedir this 25) *per*sone seinge visions and hering the spechis of
the*m* / whedir he se them 26) wakinge or slepinge <or dr[e]myng> or in bodily
vision or ymaginacou*n* and gostly or 27) happili intellectual vision a boue

---

[24] The scribe has crossed the stem of the first p (in spiritual) rather than the second (in
persone).

[25] II:3. *speciali, continua*

[26] II:3. *virtuosi et maturi, catholici et experti patris spiritualis*

[27] II:7. *et iactancie aut superbie seu ostentacionis et elacionis vel appetitus laudis humane aut
negligencia oracionis siue ambicio*

[28] II:10. *et spiritus*

[29] Lat. at this point has *sapore*, 'wisdom, discernment'. It appears that the translator has
mistaken this for *sopore*, 'slumber, drowsiness'.

nature . And whedir in y*at* me*n*tal ravesching³⁰ 28) that is to sey . wha*n* he sees soche thing*es* . he felis su*m* me*n*tal³¹ suetnes . of godd*es* 29) love . or noo / And whedir than he seis and heris ony thing speking to him³² **[fol. 249r]** 1) any misteriis . or sheuyng ony godly douctrinys³³ or noo / And in what {h.} kende the 2) p*er*sone seis soche And whedir he fele than³⁴ ony light of inteligens of manifestacou*n* of godly 3) mat*er* of y*e* visions or noo / Also he³⁵ ought to be exsamyned whedir y*e* visions acordis w*ith* 4) diuyne scripture or discordis³⁶ . And whedir yt indu*ces* ony error³⁷ or no / or ony newe thinge 5) that discordis fro resou*n*³⁸ . Or if these visions be all wey trewe or su*m*tyme fals and lyes.³⁹ 6) And whedir thei speke <of> honour*es* to come or riches or mannys loouyng*es* or humilite 7) in all thing*es* Or mene vs ony thing to obey⁴⁰ . v*er*tuos p*er*sonys⁴¹ / or co*n*trary . And be cause 8) of breffnes finally I sey . to make p*er*fit examinacou*n* in this mater as wel of the q*ua*lite 9) of the p*er*sone seinge this vision / as of the man*er* of seinge and of y*e* q*ua*lite of the mater 10) of visions . to discerne sprit*es* yat scheuys them or mynistris whedir thei be good sprit*es* 11) or ylle . Se moor pleynly . in y*e* heue*n*ly booke of reuelacou*n*s of god . to y*is* holy Brigid . 12) of suecy of the whech is wretyn in y*e* first booke . iiii*te*. chaptre . And in y*e* same booke. liiii*e* 13) chaptre And in y*e* iii*de* booke the {.....} x*o* / *chaptre* And in the iiii*te* booke / xxiii*o capitulo* / and cx*o* {.} *capitulo* 14) And in the vi boke / lii*o capitulo* / and lxvii*o capitulo* / w*ith* many like where the forseyd lady . was 15) infoormyd plenarly of⁴² virgyn mary to discerne sprit*es* and visions⁴³ of this mater 16) But if soche examynacou*n*⁴⁴ goo be fore a perelous errore may happyn to come.⁴⁵ And ʒit 17) soche errour happenys offtyn tymes for defaute of discrete and sad examynacou*n*

18) The qualite of p*er*sone and of v*er*tuys of holi Brigid is conteyned her to

---

³⁰ II:16. *qui exstasis vocatur*
³¹ II:17. *supernaturalem*
³² Catchword: ony misteriis
³³ II:17. *et spirituales*
³⁴ II:18. *illuminacionem seu quandam illustracionem supernaturalis*
³⁵ II:19. *et materia ipsarum visionum*
³⁶ II:20. *et utrum visio illa sit ad humanorum actuum virtuosam direccionem et salutem animarum*
³⁷ II:20. *catholice fidei vel an inducat aliquid monstrum*
³⁸ II:20. *aut a bonis, virtuosis et humilibus moribus nos auertat,*
³⁹ II:21. *scilicet quod illa, que predicunt, aliquando sint vera et aliquando non,*
⁴⁰ II:23. *eciam puris et simplicibus*
⁴¹ II:23. *spiritualibus et prepositis nostris*
⁴² II:24. *a Christo et*
⁴³ II:26. *et mentalia sentimenta*
⁴⁴ II:27. *non (precesserit)*
⁴⁵ II:27–30. This passage deals with the dangers of thinking that a true vision is a false one, and consequently ignoring the will of God.

whom y*is* 19) booke w*ith* in wretyn was schewyd and reuelat /. iii . chaptre. 20)
These thing*es* sen in p*r*actisinge now to the mater of the qualite of the p*er*sone
21) to who*m* this p*re*sent boke was reuelat yt is to be knowin yat y*is* nobil 22)
lady seynt brigid . ye whech sy. and herd .<in sprit> visions of this p*re*sent
booke and also of 23) y*at* gret heue[n]ly boke and many odir thing*es* and wrot
the*m* to gedir . of þe y*e* p*re*cept 24) of god as it is had in y*e* sext heue*n*ly booke /
p*r*imo⁴⁶ *capitulo* / sprongin of the kende of the 25) kinges of gothis / and in the
kingedom of s[ue]cy⁴⁷ . was born . the whech ჳit leuyng 26) in wedloc/
brougth. {to} hir husband to þe p*er*feccou*n* of chas[t]ite . yat yey leuyd 27)
many ჳer*es* wi*th*ought dede of the flesch . And so boye too went on pilgrimage
to Seint Iamys in to galis w*ith* gret laboure and exspensis and w*ith* gret
deuocion . 29) And after ward reternyd hoom to yer owne cuntry of the
kingedom of swecy. **[fol. 249v]** 1) wher as hir husband died. and went to god
Aftir yat sche was kendelid w*ith* the fyre of⁴⁸ cher<i>te 2) she be toke hir self
holly to crist the wheche toke hir benig[n]ly to his spouse . as it is had in ye 3)
first heuenly boke / iio *capitulo* / And frothens forth sche be gan to haue more
clerly. godly visions. the 4) whech anon sche put mekely to ye examynacou*n* of
hir gostly fad*er* an holy ma*n* ye whech 5) was mast*er* in thologie callid mast*er*
Mathie of suecy. acha*n*on of licope*n*us chirch the whech 6) glosid the hol bibil /
as it is wrety*n* in ye vi boke./ lxxixo⁴⁹ *capitulo* / This lady expounyd these 7)
visions mekely to exami*n*acou*n* a*n*d doom of odir prelat*es* and religious
sp*i*r*itu*al me*n* as it 8) is wrety*n* in ye iiii*te* heue*n*ly booke./ lxxviiio *capitulo*⁵⁰
After yat these p*er*fite me*n* in sciens and gostly 9) in lyff p*re*uyd these visions
and reu<e>lacou*n*s shewid to ye seyd lady . and gaff in sentens yat 10) thei
p*r*ocedid fro ye sprith of treuye and not of an yllusor the sprith of falshed. Than
11) she beinge poore folowyd crist poore and to folow his steppis / of all hir
good*es* rese*r*uid no 12) moore but sympil mete and drinke and cloth. And made
distribucou*n* of all hir odir good*es* 13) amonge hir sonys and poore pepil.⁵¹
And be ye p*re*cept of crist went forth⁵² of hir cuntre 14) and knoulache.⁵³ And
so sche come to Rome on pilgremage to ye staciou*n* and to vesite 15) pet*er* and
poule . and odir seint*es* relikis whils y*at* crist bad hir do odyr thinge hauynge
16) eu*er* w*ith* hir ii old men sad and v*er*tuos and v*er*ginis and exp*er*t sp*i*r*itu*al
fadris . the whech 17) folwyd her til sche deyed ./ yt was acording yat the most
chast husband ye wheche 18) co*m*mendid his mood*er* to his discipyl being a
virgin þat he shuld comende his new 19) spowse to v*er*ginys and v*er*tuus fadris

---

⁴⁶ III:2. *CI*

⁴⁷ III:3. *quod est ad aquilonem, . . . Cuius parentes nobiliter et virtuose vixerunt.*

⁴⁸ III:7. *perfecto castitatis amore totam*

⁴⁹ III:8. *lxxxix*

⁵⁰ III:9. *et expressius in prologo Regule Saluatoris ei diuinitus reuelate.*

⁵¹ III:12. *Christi . . . habundantur et a mundi retinaculis se expediens,*

⁵² III:12. *exemplo Abrahe*

⁵³ III:12. *ut patet in legenda vite eius,*

to be gouernyd . Of the whech oon was a monke 20) religious and prior of cistens. a maydin in his flesch and sufficiently le<t>trid And for 21) that seide lady . wrot the revelacouns as it is before seid be the precept of crist in hir 22) gotyk tunge. yerfore the seyd priour be ye commaundement of crist translatid all ye 23) bokis and yis present boke. fro the moodir tunge in to latyn shouyd to ye seid lady .[54] 24) Anodir gostly fadir of this lady was a prest of suecy . a virgin of venerabil[55] liff/ ye 25) wheche gouernyd all the hous of the seid lady . and he taught hir and hir doughter 26) gramer and songe be ye precept of crist[56] The whech fadris she as a meke monke 27) obeyed in all vertuys[57] / in someche yat sche durst nat left vp hir eyin fro ye ground 28) but yf sche had askid him ferst a special licens and grantid . Euery day . sche was 29) shreuyn twis or thryes. And euery sonday sche and hir doughter[58] reseyued with gret deuocoun 30) cristes body.[59] And she was nat only meke owtuardes agenis men but also inwardly. 31) ageyn god countid hir self on worthi sinner[60] as you may clerly see in ye secund 32) heuenly booke ./ capitulo xvo and in the sext boke capitulo liio / And in the secund boke capitulo 33) xviiio / with many moo like / what paciens[61] she had[62] . yow may see in ye iiiite heuenly[63] **[fol. 250r]** 1) boke capitulo cxxiiiio / yat be gynnes thus Agnes spekis to ye spouse {di} seinge[64] .

---

54 III:18. *De quo quidem religioso mencio fit in prologo Libri Celestis in fine.*

55 III:19. *et sanctissime*

56 III:19. *et in viam virtutum paternalibus correcionibus virtuose corrigendo direxit.*

57 III:20–21. *propter quod ipsa in tantam humilitatem et obedienciam et perfectam mortifica-cionem sue proprie voluntatis deuenit, quod, quando ibat per indulgencias et sanctuaria, sociata semper cum predicto presbitero, suo patre spirituali,*

58 III:22. *predicta veneranda . . ., que secum laudabiliter vixit et usque ad mortem in penitencia et castissima viduitate honetissime perseuerauit,*

59 III:23–5. This passage deals with the secret penances Bridget undertook for the glory of God, with the direction of her spiritual directors, and with her immediate submission of her visions to the judgement of these same directors.

60 III:25–6. This passage elaborates on the theme of Bridget's humility before Christ and her professed unworthiness to receive the divine revelations and to write the sacred words which she has been chosen to write.

61 III:27. *et equanimitatem*

62 III:27. *prefata domina, non ego respondere volo, sed pocius respondeat tibi de hoc illa gloriosa virgo, Sancta Agnes,*

63 Catchword: boke

64 At this point, Lat. has *dicens*. The scribe's writing the first two letters of *dicens*, then dotting it for expunction and continuing with *seinge* could indicate that s/he was copying from a text which had Agnes' speech, and perhaps the preamble to it, in Latin in the English translation. This was not unusual; it lent authority and authenticity to the vernacular text. (See I. Johnson, 'Prologue and Practice: The Middle English Lives of Christ', in *The Medieval Translator: The Theory and Practice of Translation in the Middle Ages*, ed. R. Ellis (Cambridge, 1989), p. 82.) However, if this was indeed so, and the scribe decided to translate *all* the Latin, it would suggest that s/he

Come doughte*r* 2) *et cetera*[65] / and what hete of cherite sche had to crist and to virgin mary his moodir ./ see 3) in ye iiii*te* boke /*capitulo* lxiiio / And in ye vi*te* *capitulo* liio / And in the last boke / *capitulo* primo / *and* 4) the xiiio *capitulo*[66] / Sche louyd hir neybours. *with* a modirly compassion[67] . as it scheuys in þe 5) iii*de* boke./*capitulo* xxiiio[68] / On a tyme. whan the kinge of Swecy wold haue greuyd his sogettes 6) *with* gret charges <in> all his regne . yat they shuld pay . as*er*teyne q*u*antite of mony. in the 7) whech he was boundyn . to his borowis ./ yan blissid Bregid seid to ye kinge./ Sere do not 8) so / but take myn too sonys and put the*m* in plegge . wils *yo*u may pay. and offende not 9) god and thin sogettes as it is had moore clerly in hir legend.[69]

10) Here it is sheuyd how many wysis blissid brigid had visions And reuelacouns 11) fferderemore as I seide nowe be fore. and has made opyn to men not knowing*e* 12) su*m*thinge*s* of the q*u*alite of *per*sone and of *ver*tuys of blissid bregid . And for yat now 13) many men ar mervelid and doughtes of this grace of seinge and herynge spi*rit*ual visions 14) geuyn to ye forseid blissid bregid . desiring to be s*er*tified of the mane*r* yat she sy soche 15) thing*es* and herd ./ oftyn tymes thei askid me / yat I shuld telle the*m* be rowe[70] of yat 16) and shuld testifie <the*m*> clerly . of the treuþe . yat be ye infusion of <what> sprith. all <thes> thing*es* ar 17) reuelat*es* . Therfore I to ye honour of god and *ver*gin mary . and of the forseid blissid 18) lady. Shuld shewe first to the*m* to remeue all doughtes of y*er* h*er*tis how and what 19) mane*r* of wise sche sy and herd the visions and reuelacouns and aft*er* wardes I schal 20) p*re*ue be diuyne scripture ./ yat thei procedid fro þe holy sprith . and nout fro ye 21) sprith of illusion./ To ye ferst I sey . yat they may be certified / of yat maner 22) the whech sche sy . ye visions/ not alonly be myn wordis but also be the wordis 23) of hir self blissid Bregid ./ The whech sche hir self notifies clerly . in many chapetris 24) of ye bokis . And namly in ye iiii*te* boke / lxxviio *capitulo* / And in ye vi*te* boke / *capitulo* liio / 25) where sche spekis *with* crist these wordis / O

was literate in Latin, and that s/he was writing for an audience which was not literate enough to cope with even minimal Latin, possibly an audience of lay women.

[65] III:28. *et impone tibi coronam factam ex septem lapidibus preciosis.' Et de hoc vide lacius in legenda vite eiusdem domine, beate Brigide.*

[66] III:29. *in fine cum multis similibus.*

[67] III:30. *pro multis in specie et pro omnibus eciam in genere ad Christum orando, infinitas preces et lacrimas frequenter deuotissime effundebat,*

[68] III:30. *et in multis aliis capitulis Libri Celestis*

[69] III:33–41. This lengthy passage deals with Bridget's divine mission to communicate the substance of her revelations to popes and emperors. lines 40–41 dismiss as ridiculous the idea that such a chaste spouse of Christ should commit adultery with the devil.

[70] Lat. at this point has *seriose* = seriously. It appears that the translator has mistaken this for *series* = in a row, or that s/he has misread an abbreviated form of *seriose*.

most dere god . and bestbelouyd of all 26) men yat *you* has made *with* me yis
meruelous thinge {.} all me*n* heringe . And 27) so foorth.[71] Also I haue seen the
forseid lady . oftyn sethis / god beying <my*n*> witness/ su*m*tyme 28) sittinge
and su*m*tyme to stonde[72] in pr*a*your as sche we*r*e alyenat fro hir self rapt 29) in
hir sprith.[73] nothinge seinge ne*n* hering of yat was doon in *yat* place where as
30) sche was bodyly . The whech whan she was reue*r*tid to hir self she told me
on worthy **[fol. 250v]** 1) thou I were and ye forseid hir ./ii . confessor*es* . the
visions the wheche sche had than 2) and gret secret[74] thing*es* of god. Also the
maner of visions seing is had . clerly I nough 3) in a s*er*teyne vision and secret
reuelacou*n* / send ou*er* be þe seid lady . to lord pope gregory 4) xi*o* wher it is
told how sche beinge inpr*a*your waking was rapt in sprith. And tha*n* 5) all the
strenkthis of hir body . was semyd . as to fayle[75] / neuer the les crist and v*er*gin
6) mary has declarid . to hir seing yat ye mouy*ng* of hir herte was noo*n* illusion.
7) but the gr*a*ce of god And the holy gost op*er*acou*n* as it is had in the secund
boke . xviii*o* c*a*pitulo 8) and in the vit*e* boke./ lxxxviii*o* c*a*pitulo /. Also knowe
yat the seid lady brigid / pr*a*yng wakinge[76] 9) sy in sprith kendis and foormys
ne*n* <yei> were nat declared to hir what they shuld 10) signifie./ but doughte*s*
<sche> remayned and ins*er*teyne of tokenyng*es* of tho visiounys . As 11) it is
had in the iiii*te* boke the secund chapt*re*.[77] And *with* in ye same boke of the
heue*n*ly 12) empr*or*e {of} to ye kinges xxxi*o* c*a*pitulo The whech visiou*n*s was
declarid aftirward*es* 13) of crist as it is had in the seyde chappet*re* xxxi*o* and in
the last chapt*re* of ye 14) iiii*te* booke./ And su*m*tyme no thing was declarid to
{the*m*} hir of þe significacou*n*s of 15) the visions./ but eu*er* she was ins*er*teyn of
the*m*[78] . But thou may spere how may 16) it be yat this blissid lady . vigilant in
preyour might se . as she oftin tyme 17) sy . rapt in sprith./ crist and his mood*er*
and au*n*glis and seint*es* the wheche eu*er* 18) stondis in mutabilly and essenci-
ally . in heuen . And sodeynly . to see soulis to 19) be cruciat and also deulis

---

71 IV:6–10. The prayer continues with Bridget comparing her visionary experiences to
dreams, while being very clear that they arise not out of bodily sleep but out of the
peace of her soul. She continues, using metaphors of hunger and satiety for the effect
of Christ on her soul.

72 IV:10. *prostratem stare*

73 IV:10. *in exstasi spiritus*

74 IV:11. *et archana*

75 IV:13–16. This important passage details how Bridget's mind and spirit were filled
with the love of God, and how then she felt her heart move within her as if it were a
living child in her womb. Initially she feared that this was a diabolical illusion;
however, the movement was visible to her two amazed and admiring confessors.

76 IV:17. *in excessu mentis*

77 IV:19. *cum multis similibus*

78 IV:21–4. This passage explains how Bridget's visions are immediately explained to
her by Christ, the Virgin Mary, an angel or a saint through a process of divinely
inspired understanding.

speking in purgatori and in helle. And also -- 20) personys ʒit leuynge in this word all grese sche sy ordinatly in ye same 21) tyme speking to [g]edir/ and whedir the seyd lady . soule was with in hir body 22) or with out whan sche sy these thinges . To ye whech question . not I but sche 23) merore of all sapiens and {scr} sciens . mary the queen of heuen . schal ansuere 24) the[79] / in ye vite boke liio capitulo[80] / And also soche wise she had the hol boke of questions 24) the whech is the Vte boke in numbyr amonge the bokis[81] Also sumtyme sche 26) sy aunglis[82] with hir bodily eyin[83] And sum tyme oure lord ihesu crist and his 27) modir mary and namly in hir last ende . as it schal showe with Inne[84]

28) here it is examyned be holy scripture vndir what kende of visions 29) the visions of this bo[k]e ar con{tynnyd}<teynid> and odir <thinges> reuelat to blissid bregid . et cetera **[fol. 251r]** 1) Sethin the tyme I certified men doughtynge of the qualite and vertuys of the forseid 2) persone blissid lady brigid . and of diuers manerys {the} and wyse / the wheche the seyd 3) lady sy . herd and felt visions and reuelacons of this present boke and of odir bokis[85] . And for 4) that I haue touchid sufficiently of þe qualite of the mateer of ye seid visions and reue 5) lacouns as it is wretyn in capitulo Also yat thinge And inye chaptre / yerfore o ye {..} emprores[86] 6) ther fore I speke no moore of yat / but now it longis to examyn <and in> declaringe to preue 7) after scripture . and the seinges of holy doughtors/ vnder what kende of visions commounly 8) hir forseid visiouns and reuelacouns ar conteyned./ It is to be knowin ferst / yat Austyn 9) in ye xii boke of genesis to ye lettir And Jerom in his prolog of yapocalips./ iii principal

[79] IV:28. *valde pulchre*

[80] IV:28–30. This passage states that Bridget's revelations are part of the ministry of the Holy Spirit, and are to benefit the entire body of the Church. It continues by describing the format of Book V, in which a monk's questions are answered by various forms of divine illumination.

[81] IV:31. *et Regulam eciam Saluatoris religionis monialium ei reuelatam, ut ibi habetur in fine regule, XXIX capitulo.*

[82] IV:32. *angelum*

[83] IV:32-3. This passage describes the delivery of the *Sermo angelicus*, which provided the daily lessons to be read at matins to the nuns of Bridget's Order. The sermon was written down by her at the same instant that it was spoken to her.

[84] IV:34–40. This passage begins by stating that Bridget told both her daughter and her spiritual fathers of the divine apparitions at her deathbed. The purpose of the revelations is then given – to benefit others, to provide moral direction, stimulate conversion and reveal mysteries. Alfonso then states that sometimes Bridget prophesied, and sometimes she did not; sometimes she could not understand the words in any way. However, sometimes, like St Francis, she could understand once there was a text, although Christ wished her to understand spiritually. Alfonso concludes by saying that Bridget always spoke to him of her visions with sighs and tears.

[85] V:1–2. *ut supra patet, nunc autem restaret videre*

[86] V:3. *et eciam ex preiacente huius libri materia et aliorum librorum suorum patet euidenter,*

10) kendis of visions ar describid ./ that is to sey ./ bodily. gostly. and intellectually./ Abodily 10) vision is whan we see ony thinge *with* oure bodily eyin /
Gostly or ymaginary vision 12) is seid whan we see sleping or waking ymagis
of thing*es* in sprith . be the whech 13) sumodyr thinge is be tokenyd / As
pharao sy eris of corn And moyses sy the buske bren 14) he sleping and his[87]
wakinge. Intellectual vision is whan ama*n* <or ap*er*sone>[88] sees the treuþe of
ye 15) misteryes the holy gost scheuyng*e* *with* the vndirstonding of mynde /
As John sy the thing*es* 16) the whech ar told in the booke of thapocalips. he sy
not only figur*es* in sprith but he 17) vndirstod in mynde the tokenyng*es* of the*m*
. The ferst kende of visions the wheche is 18) corporal or bodyli towchis not
gretly owre mater / Alþow the seyd blissid Brigid su*m* 19) Wylis. sy. the modir
of god and hir sone *with* hir bodily eyin / yat is for to sey whan 20) she was a
maydin / Also sche sy an awter and the modir of god . sitting vp on the 21)
wheche callid hir and set a croun on hir hed . And a nodir tyme wha*n* she was
in perel 22) of childing*e* And the moodir of god come yn to hir / Alle the ladyis
seing*e* yat were 23) ther p*re*sent and sche touchid hir membris And anoon she
was delyuerid./ as it is wretyn 24) in hir le{n}gend. And ageyne wha*n* she sy
feer descende fro heuen on the awter and in 25) the p*re*stes hand se<y>inge
messe and <a> host / and in yat host a lamb . and ye face of a man 26) in the
lomb. and a lombe in ye face / And also {.} sche sy a quyk child in ye{.} host / in
27) the p*re*stes hand . the {.} <whech> blissid the*m* stonding a bought *with* the
signe of the cros seinge .I. 28) blisse yow beleuyng./ I shal be the iuge to the*m*
yat beleue nat //Se this in vi 29) boke lxxxvio *capitulo* And wha*n* sche lay in
extremys / sche sy ageyn bodily . crist comfortinge 30) hir *et cetera.*[89] Soche a
vision is to be beleuyd yat it was scheuyd to ye seid spouse of crist[90] 31) in to
hir comfort/ and not mynistrid of an illusore tho yll sprith./ And yat shewis
clerly [fol. 251v] 1) for ye seyd lord ih*es*u crist told before to hir the day of hir
passinge .v. dayes be foore she 2) deyed bidding hir take the sacrament*es* of the
chirche.[91] The whech. p*re*cept the deule wold 3) not bid hir to take at hir
deynge. Therfore it was preuyd yat that vision was of 4) god. in as moche as at
the last poynt of hir liff sche reseyued the holy comunyng 5) and last
anoyntinge . deuowtly. many personys beinge p*re*sent / the whech reseyued 6)
sche sy crist comfortinge hir *with* hir bodily eyin / comending mekely her

---

87 V:7. *iste*

88 This interlineated phrase does not appear in Lat. The fact that the scribe felt it
necessary to extend *man* specifically to include all persons could suggest that he
knew himself to be writing for a female audience. If the scribe was indeed a woman,
it could be that she resented the implied exclusion of her sex from experiencing intellectual vision. It was a common assumption that women were incapable of the
'higher' intellectual form of vision.

89 V:14. *ut supra dicitur.*

90 V:15. *Spiritus Sancti ministerio*

91 V:16. *et de factis suis et monasterii sui aliqua per eum tunc reuelata disponendo ordinare.*

sprith in to 7) his handis ./ as it schewis in ye last booke. and the last chappetre /[92] In this maner of 8) wyse of seinge visions yat is to sey bodily. I leue now /.[93] Of the secunnd kende of 9) visions yat is to sey. spiritual or gostly . or ymaginary. of sleperis we speke nat ffor 10) thes dremys ar countid be gregory most susspect inn the iiiite boke of dialogis xlviiio capitulo.[94] 11) Alþough sumtyme dremys ar trewe and good and of god./ as it is seid . yer /[95] where 12) thou owis to knowe./ whan soche dremys happenys . And in slepinge soche wise./ yis 13) blissid lady . sy whan she was amaydin / onys sche sy crist as <he was> crucified . a[n]d fro yat 14) oure she was hertily set on his passion. This sompnial vision touchis nat oure 15) mateer / for yat lady s[e]y all hir visions in prayour wakinge and not slepynge.[96] 16) Now to come to ye yis secund kende . of spiritual vision . or ymaginary . of wakinge 17) personys the whech touchis owre mateer / Blissid austyn seis thus in ye xii booke 18) vp on genesis to ye letter whan the intencoun of mynde . is turnyd and takin 19) fro the wittes of the body . yan it is wont to be callid ought of mynde. Than 20) in ony wise what someuyr bodyes ar present and ar non seen with opyn eyin / nen 21) vttirly voyces ar not herd for all the be holdinge of the mynde owdir it is in 22) ymagis of bodyes be spiritual vision or in thinges with ought bodies not figuryd . with 23) ony ymage of a body . be intellectual vision/. Therfore it shewis opinly . yat 24) whan the seid lady . stood in vision sopit with joye and sopoor of suetnes of goddis loue . alienat . fro hir bodily . wittes[97] yat than she stood outh of hir mynde alienat 26) a boue hir self The deule may nat yete in soche swetnes[98] of goddis loue in þe 27) mynde of ony persone As it shal showe with ynforth .{.} for that the deul has nat he 28) may nat geve to odyr men[99] ffor he may nat geue illumynacoun or illustracoun 29) of mynde. in no maner of wise./ to ony persone/ for in intellectual vision / the soule 30) may neuer be

---

[92] V:19. *et in fine legende vite eius.*
[93] V:20. *quia ipsa domina paucis vicibus videbat visiones corporalibus oculis.*
[94] V:22. *Et habetur eciam idem in Libro IIII Celesti, XXXVIII capitulo,*
[95] V:22. *Et ibi in Libro Celesti vide modum,*
[96] V:24. *ut in multis capitulis predicti Libri Celestis hoc patet euidenter.*
[97] V:28. *vt supra ipsa narrat,*
[98] V:29. *et ebrietatem*
[99] V:30–36. This lengthy passage has been excerpted in such a way as to allow the sentence to continue with no apparent loss of continuity. The edited passage describes how God sometimes aroused Bridget's soul, as if from sleep, in order to see or hear celestial matters; when this occurred, her behaviour was just as Augustine describes, rapt and out of her senses. It is in this manner that the entire *Regula Saluatoris* and *Liber Questionum* (Book V) are revealed to her, through an instantaneous illumination of her mind from the words which Christ speaks. Alfonso points out that this experience conforms exactly to all the conventions of intellectual vision.

illudid . of the deul . as it sheuys be Austyn and Thomays de alquino[100] **[fol. 252r]** 1) And all doughtoris acordis on yat /[101] Blissid gregory . seys in ye xxviii boke of morall 2) the secund chapter[102] yat ii maner of wisis the speche of god is vndirstoud / oure lord 3) spekis be him self / or be an aungil creature . wordes ar schapin to vs But whan 4) god spekis be himself alonly . streinkthe of inwardly inspiracoun to vs is openyd. And 5) whan god spekis be him self he spekis of his word with ought wordes and sillablis 6) the hert is taught for his inwardly vertu is knowen be aserteyn lefting vp to ye 7) whech the ful mynd is left vp and voyd mynde as heuyed./[103] thus seys gregory. 8) Soche an ynwardly . godly spekinge this holy lady . was taught and informyd . of 9) these thinges yat ar conteynyd in this celestial boke to spiritual doctrine .[104] as it scheuys 10) be þe hool booke.[105] Also gregory . seis in the chapeter be fore yat sumtyme god spekis 11) to vs be aungelis at a tyme assumpt of the eyer be fore oure bodily eyin. 12) As abraham the whech myght not only see iii men but also to take and 13) reseyue them in his erdly hous./ And seys also / But if sum aungelis telling vs 14) inwardly thinges shuld take {.} bodyes of the eyer at atyme and apere to oure sites 15) thus seis gregory. Soche maner wise god spac oftyn tymes {spac} be his aungil to 16) his forseid spowse.[106] And austyn seis in ye xii boke on genesis/ and thomais de 17) alquino /[107] and odir doughtores

---

100 Catchword: And all doctores
101 V:37–40. This passage states that the purpose of the divine revelations to Bridget is for the use of others, to illuminate the way they should follow. It emphasizes that the faithful should wish to learn from this blessed lady to whom divine mysteries, future events and holy instructions have been revealed through internal speech and intellectual vision.
102 V:40–41. *plene et pulcre nos instruit in hec verba: 'Sciendum' inquit*
103 V:43–6. The quotation from Gregory continues, describing how the soul is elevated by the light of divine intelligence, and how the soul is illuminated without loud conversation, but by that which is heard but which has an unknown sound. It is the spirit of God which inflames the heart of man, not loud and lengthy sermons. The passage concludes by stating that God sends these visions and locutions to illuminate our ignorance.
104 V:47. *imperatorum et regum et summorum pontificum ac prelatorum et omnium gencium et eciam ad conversionem infidelium a sponso suo Christo loquente docebatur et instruebatur,*
105 V:47. *Celestem et per presentem*
106 V:51–4. The passage continues by describing how the angel was sent to Bridget chiefly while she was living in Rome, how this angel dictated the sermon on the excellence of the Virgin Mary, and how Bridget saw this angel daily with her bodily eyes. Alfonso then raises the question of how to interpret the sometimes obscure words of God to the prophet. He cites Christ's command to St Francis, 'Go, and repair my church', as an example of words which ought to be understood spiritually being understood materially and textually.
107 V:55. *in secunda secunde in titulo 'De prophecia'*

That a profete vndirstondis nat alwey right yat ar 18) seid and sheuyd to him in vision / /[108] fforsoye I dar sey boldly. After Thomays of alquny *secunda secundo* q. clxxiii*de* 19) and after oder doctores yat yis gre of profecy was geuyn to this blissid lady . godly . amonge 20) odir greis of profecy and is iugid hier whan aprophete sees not only the tokenys 21) of wordis or of dedes but also he sees wakynge su*m* bo[d]ly spekinge to him ar su*m*what /hit/ 22) scheuynge And namly yf yat spekis or scheuys./ be in the kende of god. ffor 23) they sey . yat be yat thinge the prophet drauys ner moore to the cause sheuynge 24) than yf he yat spekis or sheuys / shuld sheue him in ye kende of a man or in ye 25) kende of an aungil. After the seying' of ysay ./ *vio capitulo* / I sy god sittyng / etc[109] ffor nycholas 26) de lyra in ye prolog on the sawter and odir doughters seis the same. That ye 27) degre of profecie is moor excellent wher to odir like the vndirstondinge is clerer

28) her it is preuyd be go[d]ly scripture . that the visions and reuelacouns of this 29) boke and of odir of blissid bregid has procedid of the holy. sprith. and not of ye 30) illusion of the deule and yat is prevyd be vii tokenys or vii resounys conteyned her[110] **[fol. 252v]** 1) Therfore now we shal see after the seinges of holy men . whedir the visions and 2) reuelacouns has ben mynstrid of the holy spright of treuþe of {of} the illusore þe 3) sprith of falshed . Therfore I sey that yer ar many diffrens[es] in ye whech . clerly . reuelacoun 4) or vision may be discernyd of agood sprith or an yll . as wel in ye qualite of the 5) persone seinge soche thinges as in sencibil inwardly thinges of yat sowle . as in maner 6) of leuynge /[111] here folowys vii signis tokenys or resounys with in wretyn be ye whech 7) the vision of agod . sprith is discernyd fro ye deulys illusion./ The

---

108 V:56–61. This passage continues to discuss the question of the prophet's interpretation of the word of God, claiming that sometimes Bridget understands the words of her visions corporeally and literally, and at other times she understands them spiritually and figuratively. Alfonso claims that one of the gifts of a prophet is the ability to understand the Divine word, and to communicate the matter of her revelations, irrespective of the form in which she receives them. He then cites Augustine, *Super Genesi ad Litteram* XII, on imaginary and intellectual vision.

109 V:66. *et maxime ex eo quod inter omnes scripturas omnium prophetarum clariori modo intelligendi a Deo scriptura ista prefate domine, quam alie scripture aliis prophetis, fuerit reuelata,*

110 Rubric: *Capitulum VI.* VI:1. *Sane quia iam supra proximo ostensum est subtiliter intuenti, sub quo genere visionum contineantur iste presens liber et alii, reuelati prefate beatissime domine Brigide*

111 VI:3–14. This lengthy and important passage testifies to Bridget's gift for *discretio*, which has been augmented by the Virgin Mary's teaching her seven differences between the visions of a good spirit and those of an evil one. Alfonso also cites numerous and lengthy examinations of Bridget and her visions by theologians and ecclesiastical officials, all of which satisfied the authorities and effectively silenced all doubters and detractors.

ferst most serteyn 8) sygne . is yat ye vision is of god . whan yat persone seing visions is really meke 9) and levis undir obediens of sum spiritual fadir vertuos and expert in spiritual lyff And 10) the persone yat s[e]is presumys not on him self nen is not left vp with pride[112] nen 11) desires no mannys praysinges nen hydis not the visions . but leuys with verry humilite 12) And anoone tellis his visiouns and temptacouns And expounys it mekely to ye examynacoun 13) and iugement of his spiritual fadir and odir old spiritual fadris . And takis it approbat 14) that he or they preuys / I sey that soche asoule may nat be illudid./ As the cler text 15) of this is in ye boke of collacouns of fadris in ye collacoun of John cassian capitulo iio[113] 16) the whech spekis of a monke deludid of adeul vndir the kende of an aungel of light 17) And in ye same collacoun Than moyses . et cetera where ye seid abbot moyses spekis on yis 18) these wordes In no maner of wise aman schal be desseyued . the wheche leuys not 19) only in his owne doom but be ye exsampil of his better /[114] Therfore whan the forseid 20) lady brigid leuyd alwey . vndir special obediens and doctrine of spiritual old fadris 21) and vertuos / et cetera.[115] yerfore clerli it is concludid of the forseid determynacoun of yat holy 22) fadir moyses and odir holy fadris / yat al thinges þat <was> reuelat to them in bokis was 23) of the holy gost and not of the deul / illusor/[116] The secund signe of godly visiouns is 24) in ye whech a soule may not be disceyuyd whan the soule in ye tyme yat it sees ye 25) vision felis him self yan holly to be repleschid[117] and inflamyd with the fyre of infusioun 26) of godly cherite and savor[118] of goddis love /[119] the whech the deule has not in ony wise[120] 27) And yerfore it is concludid yat he yat werkys soch thinges {god is} in his soule is god[121] 28) The iiide signe is in the

---

[112] VI:17. *nec se iactat*

[113] VI:20. *collacione secunda, capitulo 'Et vt hanc eandem',*

[114] VI:21–5. The quotation from Cassian continues, warning of the necessity for submitting to the discernment of older, wise men in order to escape the deceitful machinations of the devil. Cassian says that if such discernment had been exercised earlier, the serpent would have been condemned to the subterranean depths. As it is, he continues to insinuate offensive thoughts into our minds which are kept secret in our hearts.

[115] VI:26–7. This passage recounts how Bridget always submitted herself, her visions, and her temptations with the utmost humility to the judgement of her spiritual fathers.

[116] VI:29. *et hoc est clarum et manifestum signum apud omnes vere spirituales et doctrina generalis omnium ad euadendum temptaciones et dyabolicas suggestiones et illusiones.*

[117] VI:30. *et quodammodo dulciter inebriari*

[118] VI:30. *interne dulcedinis*

[119] VI:31. *Dico enim, quod istam internam caritatem et dulcedinem amoris diuini,*

[120] VI:31. *potest eam infundere in anima alicuius, quia nullus dat quod non habet,*

[121] VI:33–43. The passage continues by stating that a further sign that the visionary is divinely illuminated is if her faith, obedience and reverence to the Catholic faith and Holy Mother Church are strengthened, as Bridget's were. Alfonso then cites Hugh

wheche godly vision is knowyn[122] whan the soule beinge 29) in vision bodily
or ymaginary and sp*iritu*al felis an intellectual sup*er*natural of[123] **[fol. 253r]**
1)[124] light of treuþe and than takis trew tokenys of yo thing*es* seen and word*es*
and the vnd*er* 2) stonding of it than clerly is openyd . and the treuþe of yat
mat*er* is mad opin*n* . this[125] may 3) not be infudid of the deule / in a soule but
only of god As thomas seys in s[e]c*un*da s[e]c[un]de ca*pitulo* dep*ro*phecia 4)
q.clxxiii*d* where he seis thus. Deulis makis opyn to me*n* ye ying*es* yat they
knowe 5) not be yllumyni*n*ge of vndirstondinge . but be su*m* vision ymaginyd .
or ell sensibill in 6) speking but not yllumynyn*g* his vndirstondinge[126] Therfore
clerly it is concludid yat 7) whan ye forseid lady Brigid . shuld take the flood of
intellectual light and sup*er*natural 8) in hir visions . yer eu*er* {..} body
expougny*n*g as crist or his moodir or an aungil or 9) su*m* seynt of the whech the
si*m*litudis was declarid and expoun*n*yd to hir the v*er*ry tokenys 10) of the
visions . as it sheuys in hir bokis. Therfore it folwis yat all hir reuelacou*n*s 11)
and scripture of these bokis . was mynistrid of god . the wheche is mighty to
werke soche 12) thing*es* and not of the deul illusor to hom it is inpossibil to do
soche thing*es*./ as it scheuys 13) be Austyn and Thomais[127] . and all holy fadris
and dought[r]is The iiii*te* signe is . in 14) what thing the vision or reuelacou*n* of
the good . sprith {fro} differis fro ye illusion of the 15) deul whan yat p*ro*fete or
the seer tellis be fore eu*er* trewe thing*es*. And spekis holy misteris 16) and
teching*es* and scheuys honest and v*er*tuos man*er*ys And these ar signes yat
they ar of god 17) ffor the deule seis su*m* while . trewe[128] in his illusions and

---

of St Victor, *De arrha animae*, the *Vita beati Antonii abbatis*, and Gregory's *Moralia*,
Book XXVIII, ch. II. All of these authorities conclude that the sense of internal
sweetness and illumination is an unmistakable sign that a vision is inspired by the
Holy Ghost, and not by a demon, since the devil is incapable of such sweetness, and
so cannot inspire it in others. References to the occasions when Bridget experienced
this internal sweetness are given, and the conclusion drawn that her visions were
truly of God.

[122] VI:44. *seu discernitur (visio diuina) ab illusione dyabolica,*

[123] Catchword: intelligibil

[124] Catchword not repeated.

[125] VI:47. *enim influxus intellectualis, supernaturalis luminis seu visionis, siue precedat visio corporalis aut ymaginaria siue non,*

[126] VI:49–60. This passage deals with the fallibility of corporeal vision as opposed to the infallibility of intellectual vision, citing Augustine, *De Genesi ad litteram* Book XII. Alfonso then discusses the difference between imaginary vision, which is a creation of the human mind, and divine revelation to the intellect. He cites Aquinas, *Summa theologiae, 2a2ae, qu. CLXXIII: II*, and concludes that imaginary vision is stimulated by divine illumination flooding the soul, and therefore cannot be diabolically inspired.

[127] VI:64. *quia in hoc differt visio illusoria a visione diuina,*

[128] VI:66. *vt decipiat,*

su*m*tyme fals . But the trew sprith 18) tellis eu*er* trewe and neu*er* fals.[129] And y*er*fore whan this holy lady brigid . told eu*er* trewe thing*es* 19) and thei be wel vndirstondin / nen {neu*er*} sche seyd <neu*er*> ony. thing*e* fals or lesing' or inhonest 20) but all was trew[y]*at* sche told.[130] Therfore it is clerly concludid yat all these thing*es* 21) were infudid and scheuyd to hir be goddis gr*a*ce and not be the deulis illusiou*n* The v*te* 22) signe in ye whech visions ar discernyd . mynistred of a good sprith or <of> ylle is the frute 23) and the werkis yat pr*o*cedis fro yo visions or reuelacou*ns*. ffor aftir the gospel . an 24) ylle tre may nat make good frute . *et cetera* / Ye shal know the*m* be yer frute.[131] Therfore it 25) is concludid yat all thes flood*es* has pr*o*cedid fro ye mos[t] pure[132] welle of ye holy gost[133] 26) The v*ite* signe is . yat yes thing*es* be of god and not of the yll sprith . and y*ou* see ye 27) deth or the ende laudabil and v*er*tuos of yat p*er*sone . seinge visions./ ffor it is to wet 28) yat sum p*er*sonys has ben disseyued . of visions but radire callid illusions vndir the 29) kende of light / the deule shuld deseyue them . sheuynge <to> the*m* many trew thing*es* and **[fol. 253v]** 1) and[sic] in ye ende shuld deseyue them in oon fals po[yn]t /[134] The vi*ite* signe of agood sprith is 2) clarifieng of meraclis aft*er* the {desh} deth . of the personys seing visions . ffor he yat is illudid 3) be visiou*ns* of the deul on tyl his deth . it is

---

129 VI:67–73. This passage cites Aquinas, Chrysostom on Matthew, Deuteronomy XVIII and Augustine, *De Genesi ad litteram*, Book XII, on the fact that the devil sometimes gives false visions and prophecies, whereas the revelations of the Holy Spirit are always true.

130 VI:75. *et confirmancia fidem catholicam ac dampnancia hereticos et semper virtutes indicauerit, vt patet in isto libro et aliis libris ei reuelatis*

131 VI:79–89. The very perfunctory treatment of the fifth sign in the translation is considerably fuller in the Latin. Alfonso states that the purpose of prophecy is to lead the people in the ways of God; he cites Aquinas and Proverbs XXIX: 'Cum defecerit prophecia, dissipabitur populus.' When, as a result of such visions, the people are turned from vice, sin and hatred to humility, peace and a religious life, then it is a sign that the revelation was from God, since it is impossible that good should proceed from the devil. The *Liber celestis* demonstrates that Bridget's visions, which were of God, had a salutary effect on the lives of many people, in many places.

132 VI:90. *et limpidissimo*

133 VI:90–92. The passage continues by extending the metaphor and stating that these visions did not originate in that shadowy pool from which the dark rivers of illusion flow. In these latter days of cloudy darkness, by following the sacred teaching in these books, people can escape terrible and impersonal divine justice and rest in the bosom of God.

134 VI:95–107. Like the fifth sign, the sixth is radically abridged in the translation. The passage continues with a comparison of the death of a visionary who has been deceived with that of one who has not. The true visionary will know the hour of her or his death, which will be a celestial marriage of the soul with Christ. This happens to Bridget, and is described in the *Liber celestis* and in her *vita*.

not worthy . yat he be clarified *with* godly 4) meraclis aftyr his deth. And for yat this worthi spowse of crist was not illudid {with} 5) of the deule in hir visiouns in hir liff Therfore af*ter* hir deth she schinyd of crist *with* 6) many meruelous meraculys. yat is to sey be resussitacou*n* of many ded bodyes illumynacou*n* 7) of blinde men And hel*þe* of deffmen*n* and be innum*e*rabil meruelous kewris of diuers 8) infirmyteis of seke bodyes./ yat <the whech he> {she} made cler in liff / aftyr hir deth. he scheuyd to vs 9) more cler The whech all thing*es* ar so opyn and knowin . shewyd and p*r*euyd be awte*n*tyk 10) docume*n*tes As wel in the kingedom of Swecy as in Rome. and in the kingedom of cecyll[*e*] 11) and in many odir p*er*tes of the word. where as in ye memory and reuerens of trew 12) cristen pepil an ymage of hir is depictid in many chirchis yat nedis noo*n* odir p*r*obacou*n* 13) ne*n* may not be lauyd in ony thinge.[135] Thes heue*n*ly word*es* of these bokis techis vs to 14) drede god aright / to loue him mekely and desire celestial thing*es* sapiently. Therfore ye 15) yat redis p*r*eue these forseid thing*es* And if 3e finde ony thing odirwise . sey ageyns 16) it boldly.[136] Therfore geue we thankinge*s* to ye fadir of m*er*cyes And to god of al co*m*fort 17) and consolacou*n* / ye wheche metys wrecchis *with* as many m*er*cyes as ar mis*er*iis in ye 18) word . yat thei fall nat into ye pres[ou]n of desparacou*n*

19) This is the recapitulacou*n* of all the forseyd./ vii chap*ter* 20) In recapi-tulinge the forseid man*er* wise of examinacou*n* {.} doynge or making 21) in p*er*sonys the whech sees visiou*n*s and reuelacou*n*s / I sey breffly . yat ye p*er*sone 22) the whech is foundin very meke in examynacou*n* And namly. if he leue vndir obediens co*n*tinua[l] 23) of a sp*irit*ual fadir to hos discrecou*n* he cast*es* all thing*es* vndir And {.} his mynde is rapt in 24) pr*a*your and felis asingler suetnes of goddis loue / and tha*n* he thus being*e* in ymaginary 25) vision or only intellectual[l] simpilly . felis aflood of a supe*r*natural light and intellectual 26) of god[*des*] treu*þe* and yan the treu[*þ*]e . of yat mateer may . be made opyn to him And 27) tellis eu*er* trew thing*es* in his visions . ffro ye whech visou*n*s frute of edifyeng and amending of him self and of his neybouris . alwey p*r*ocedis / I sey yat soche apersone 29) is not illudid of the deul ne*n* his visions ar not illusory . ne*n* to be disspisid . fforso*þe*[137] **[fol. 254r]** 1) alholly ar godly . and mekely[138] to be reseyued and beleyued and alman*er* of wise to be

---

135 VI:112–14. This passage urges belief in the visions and miracles granted to Bridget, and a renewed faith in the mercy and justice of Christ. It ends by stating that this message is the same as that clearly given in the books of other prophets.

136 VI:116–18. This passage urges the reader to let go of suspicious and foolish judge-ments and recognize the grace and glory of God, which seem incredible to those of little faith and great ignorance.

137 Catchword: alholly

138 VII:6. *tamquam de manu Dei*

obeyed 2) and folowyd. As it schewis breffly In/all thing*es* before seid and of the seying*es* of al doctours 3) and holy fadris vp on this mateer diffusly and manyfold wise spekinge /.-// -//

BIBLIOGRAPHY

Primary sources

Manuscripts
The Book of Margery Kempe, London, British Library, MS Additional 61823.
The Revelation of Sainct Bridgitte, London, British Library, MS Cotton Claudius Bi.
The Revelations of S. Bridget, London, British Library, MS Cotton Julius Fii.
Sancta Birgitta Revelationes, London, British Library, MS Harley 612.

Printed editions
Angela of Foligno: Complete Works, trans. and ed. P. Lachance OFM (New York, 1993).

Aquinas, Thomas, *Summa theologiae, 2a2ae, qu. 171–8* XLV, ed. and trans. R. Potter OP (London, 1970).

Athanasius, *The Life of St Anthony*, trans. R. Meyer (Westminster, Md, 1950).

Aristotle, *The Works of Aristotle*, ed. W. D. Ross (Oxford, 1931).

Audelay, John, *The Poems of John Audelay*, ed. E. K. Whiting, EETS (Oxford, 1971).

Augustine, *De Genesi ad Litteram: Liber Duodecimus, PL* XXXIV, 453–86, ed. J.-P. Migne (Paris, 1844–64).

Augustine, *The Literal Meaning of Genesis: Books 7–12*, trans. J. H. Taylor, vol. XLII of Ancient Christian Writers: The Works of the Fathers in Translation (New York, 1982).

Bazire, J. and E. Colledge, ed., *The Chastising of God's Children and the Treatise of Perfection of the Sons of God* (Oxford, 1957).

Bernard of Clairvaux, *De Diversis, PL* CLXXXIII, 537–747, ed. J.-P. Migne (Paris, 1854).

———, *On the Song of Songs*, trans. K. Walsh OCSO, 4 vols. (Kalamazoo, Cistercian, 1979–83).

Biblia Sacra cum glossis Nicolai Lyrani postilla et moralitatibus, Burgensis additionibus et Thoringi replicis. Lugduni: Gaspanis Trechsel, 1545. 6 tom.

Bignami-Odier, J., 'Les Visions de Robert D'Uzès OP (+ 1296)', *Archivum Fratrum Praedicatorum* 24 (1954), 258–309.

Blamires, A. and C. W. Marx, 'Woman Not to Preach: A Disputation in British Library MS Harley 31', *The Journal of Medieval Latin* 3 (1993), 34–63.

Blunt, J. H., ed., *The Myroure of Oure Ladye*, EETS (London, 1981).

Boland, P., *The Concept of Discretio Spirituum in John Gerson's De Probatione Spirituum and De Distinctione Verarum Visionum a Falsis* (Washington, DC, 1959).

Bridget of Sweden, *The Liber Celestis of Bridget of Sweden: The Middle English Version in British Library MS Claudius Bi.*, ed. R. Ellis, EETS (Oxford, 1987).

———, *Revelaciones: Book I*, ed. C.-G. Undhagen, SSFS, ser. 2. Lat. skrifter 7:1 (Uppsala, 1978).

————, *Revelaciones: Book V, Liber questionum*, ed. B. Bergh, SSFS, ser. 2, Lat. skrifter 7:5 (Uppsala, 1971).

————, *Revelaciones: Book VII*, ed. B. Bergh, SSFS, ser. 2, Lat. skrifter 7:7 (Uppsala, 1967).

————, *The Revelations of Saint Birgitta: Edited from the Fifteenth-Century MS in the Garrett Collection in the Library of Princeton University*, ed. W. P. Cumming, EETS (London, 1929).

————, *Reuelaciones Extrauagantes*, ed. L. Hollman, SSFS, ser. 2, Lat. skrifter 5 (Uppsala, 1956).

————, *Sancta Birgitta Revelationes*, Bartholomaeus Ghotan (Lübeck, 1492).

Brown, B. D., ed., *The Southern Passion*, EETS (London, 1971).

Cassian, John, *Conferences, A Select Library of Nicene and Post-Nicene Fathers*, XI, ed. P. Schaf and H. Wace (Grand Rapids, reprinted 1978).

Catherine of Siena, *The Dialogue*, trans. and ed. S. Noffke OP (New York, 1980).

Colledge, E. and N. Chadwick, ' "Remedies Against Temptation": The Third English Version of William of Flete', *Archivo italiano per la storia della pietà* 5 (1968), 199–240.

Colledge, E. and R. Guarnieri, 'The Glosses by "M.N." and Richard Methley to *The Mirror of Simple Souls*', *Archivo italiano per la storia della pietà* 5 (1968), 357–82.

Collijn, I., ed., *Acta et Processus Canonizacionis Beate Birgitte*, SSFS, ser. 2, Lat. skrifter 1 (Uppsala, 1924–31).

Cowper, J. M., ed., *Meditations on the Supper of Our Lord, and the Hours of the Passion*, EETS (London, 1897).

Crapillet, Pierre, *Le Cur Deus Homo d'Anselme de Canterbury et le De Arrha Animae d'Hugues de Saint-Victor*, ed. R. Bultot and G. Hasenohr (Louvain-la-Neuve, 1984).

Dupré-Theseider, E., ed., *Epistolario di Santa Caterina da Siena*, 2 vols. (Rome, 1940).

Garrett, R. M., '*De Arte Lacrimandi*', *Anglia Zeitschrift* 32 (1909), 269–94.

Gerson, Jean, *Oeuvres Complètes*, 10 vols., ed. P. Glorieux (Paris, 1960–73).

Gertrude the Great, *The Herald of God's Loving Kindness: Books One and Two*, trans. and ed. A. Barratt (Kalamazoo, 1991).

Gertrude the Great, *Revelationes Gertrudianae ac Mechtildianae*, 2 vols., ed. Benedictines of Solesmes (Paris, 1875).

Gregorsson, Birger, *Birgerus Gregorii Legenda S. Birgitte*, ed. I. Collijn, SSFS, ser. 2 (Uppsala, 1946).

Gregorsson, Birger and Thomas Gascoigne, *The Life of Saint Birgitta*, trans. J. B. Holloway (Toronto, 1991).

Gregory the Great, *Dialogues*, trans. O. J. Zimmerman OSB (New York, 1959).

————, *Moralia in Iob: Libri XXIII–XXXV*, ed. M. Adriaen, CC vol. 143B (Turnhout, 1966–).

Guarneri, R., ed., 'Il "Miroir des simples ames" di Margherita Porete', *Archivo italiano per la storia della pietà* 4 (1965), 501–635.

Harley, M. P., *A Revelation of Purgatory by an Unknown, Fifteenth Century Woman Visionary: Introduction, Critical Text and Translation* (Lewiston, 1985).

Harris, M. T., ed., *Birgitta of Sweden: Life and Selected Revelations* (New York, 1990).

Henry of Ghent, *Summa Questionum Ordinariarum: Facsimile reprint of the 1520 edition* (St Bonaventure, New York, 1953).

Hildegard of Bingen, *Hildegardis Scivias*, ed. A. Fuhrkotter OSB and A. Carlevaris OSB, 2 vols. CC vols. 43 and 44 (Turnhout, 1966–   ).

———, *Scivias*, trans. C. Hart and J. Bishop (New York, 1990).

Hilton, Walter, *The Scale of Perfection*, trans. J. P. H. Clark and R. Dorward (New York, 1991).

Hodgson, P., ed., *Deonise Hid Diuinite and Other Treatises on Contemplative Prayer Related to The Cloud of Unknowing*, EETS (Oxford, reprinted 1990).

———, ed., *The Cloud of Unknowing and The Book of Privy Counselling*, EETS (Oxford, 1944).

Horstman, C., ed., *Yorkshire Writers: Richard Rolle of Hampole, an English Father of the Church, and His Followers* (London, 1895).

Jacques de Vitry, *The Life of Marie d'Oignies*, trans. and ed. M. H. King (Toronto, 1989).

Jönsson, A., *Alfonso of Jaén: His Life and Works with Critical Editions of the Epistola solitarii, the Informaciones and the Epistola serui Christi* (Lund, 1989).

Julian of Norwich, *A Book of Showings to the Anchoress Julian of Norwich*, ed. E. Colledge and J. Walsh, 2 vols. (Toronto, 1978).

Julian of Norwich, *A Revelation of Love*, ed. M. Glasscoe (Exeter, 1986).

Lemay, H. R., *A Translation of Pseudo-Albertus Magnus's De Secretis Mulierum with Commentaries* (Albany, 1992).

Margery Kempe, *The Book of Margery Kempe*, ed. S. B. Meech and H. E. Allen, EETS (Oxford, 1940).

Marguerite Porete, 'The Mirror of Simple Souls: A Middle English Translation', ed. M. Doiron, *Archivo italiano per la storia della pietà* 5 (1968), 243–355.

Matarasso, P. M., trans., *The Quest of the Holy Grail* (Harmondsworth, 1969).

McNeill, J. T. and H. M. Gamer, ed., *Medieval Handbooks of Penance: A Translation of the Principal libri poenitentiales and Selections from Related Documents* (New York, 1990).

Mechthild von Magdeburg, *Flowing Light of the Divinity*, trans. C. M. Galvani, ed. S. Clark (New York, 1991).

Mechtild of Hackeborn, *The Booke of Gostlye Grace of Mechtild of Hackeborn*, ed. T. A. Halligan (Toronto, 1979).

Millett, B. and J. Wogan-Browne, ed., *Medieval English Prose for Women: Selections from the Katherine Group and Ancrene Wisse* (Oxford, 1992).

Netter, Thomas, *Doctrinale antiquitatem fidei catholicae ecclesiae*, ed. F. B. Blanciotti, 3 vols. (Venice, 1757–9).

Petroff, E. A., ed., *Medieval Women's Visionary Literature* (Oxford, 1986).

Philo, *On the Creation*, trans. F. H. Coulson and G. H. Whitaker (London, 1956).

———, *Questions and Answers on Genesis*, trans. R. Marcus (London, 1953).

Pickering, F. P., ed., *Christi Leiden in Einer Vision Geschaut (A German Mystic Text of the Fourteenth Century)* (Manchester, 1952).

Ragusa, I. and R. Green, ed. and trans., *Meditations on the Life of Christ: An Illustrated Manuscript of the Fourteenth Century* (Princeton, 1961).

Richard of Saint-Victor, *Selected Writings on Contemplation*, trans. C. Kirchberger (London, 1957).

Robert of Basevorn, *The Form of Preaching (Forma Praedicandi)*, trans. L. Krul OSB, in *Three Medieval Rhetorical Arts*, ed. J. J. Murphy (Berkeley, 1971), pp. 109–215.

Salu, M. B., trans., *The Ancrene Riwle* (Notre Dame, 1955).

Sargent, M., 'Self-Verification of Visionary Phenomena: Richard Methley's *Experimentum Veritatis*', *Analecta Cartusiana* 55:2 (1981), 121–37.

Schmidtke, J. A., 'Adam Easton's Defense of St Birgitta from Bodleian MS Hamilton 7, Oxford University' (unpublished Ph.D. dissertation, Duke, 1972).

Swanson, J., *John of Wales: A Study of the Works and Ideas of a Thirteenth-Century Friar* (Cambridge, 1989).

Tertullian, *Tertullian, A Select Library of the Ante-Nicene Fathers of the Christian Church*, ed. A. Roberts and J. Donaldson, vol. 4 (Grand Rapids, 1951).

Tolkien, J. R. R., ed., *Ancrene Wisse*, EETS (Oxford, 1962).

Torrell, J.-P., OP, *Théorie de la prophétie et philosophie de la connaissance aux environs de 1230: la contribution d'Hugues de Saint-Cher* (Louvain, 1977).

Voaden, R., 'The Middle English *Epistola solitarii ad reges* of Alfonso of Jaén: An Edition of the Text in British Library Ms Cotton Julius Fii', in *Studies in St Birgitta and the Brigittine Order*, ed. J. Hogg, 2 vols. (New York, 1993), I, 142–79.

Wakefield, W. L. and A. P. Evans, trans. and ed., *Heresies of the High Middle Ages* (New York, 1969).

Secondary Sources

Aers, D., *Community, Gender, and Individual Identity: English Writing 1360–1430* (London, 1988).

Aili, H., 'St Birgitta and the Text of the *Revelationes*. A Survey of Some Influences Traceable to Translators and Editors', in *The Editing of Theological and Philosophical Texts from the Middle Ages*, ed. M. Asztalos (Stockholm, 1986), pp. 75–91.

Allen, J. B., *The Ethical Poetic of the Later Middle Ages: A Decorum of Convenient Distinction* (Toronto, 1982).

Allen, P., *The Concept of Woman: The Aristotelian Revolution 750 BC – AD 1250* (Montreal, 1985).

———, 'Hildegard of Bingen's Philosophy of Sex Identity', *Thought: Fordham University Quarterly* 64 (1989), 231–41.

Andersson, A., *St Bridget of Sweden* (London, 1980).

Anderson, B. S. and J. P. Zinsser, ed., *A History of Their Own: Women in Europe from Prehistory to the Present*, 2 vols. (Harmondsworth, 1988).

Ardener, S., ed., *Defining Females: The Nature of Women in Society* (London, 1978).

Aston, M., *Lollards and Reformers: Images and Literacy in Late Medieval Religion* (London, 1984).

Asztalos, M., ed., *The Editing of Theological and Philosophical Texts from the Middle Ages* (Stockholm, 1986).

Atkinson, C. W., *Mystic and Pilgrim: The Book and the World of Margery Kempe* (Ithaca, 1983).

———, *The Oldest Vocation: Christian Motherhood in the Middle Ages* (Ithaca, 1991).

Barratt, A., 'Margery Kempe and the King's Daughter of Hungary', in *Margery Kempe: A Book of Essays*, ed. S. J. McEntire (New York, 1992), pp. 189–201.

———, ed., *Women's Writing in Middle English* (London, 1992).

———, 'Works of Religious Instruction', in *Middle English Prose: A Critical Guide to*

Major Authors and Genres, ed. A. S. G. Edwards (New Brunswick, 1984), pp. 413–32.

Beadle, R., 'A Handlist of Later Middle English Manuscripts Copied by Norfolk Scribes', in *Regionalism in Late Medieval Manuscripts and Texts: Essays Celebrating the Publication of A Linguistic Atlas of Late Mediaeval English*, ed. F. Riddy (Cambridge, 1991), pp. 102–8.

Beckwith, S., *Christ's Body: Identity, Culture and Society in Late Medieval Writings* (London, 1993).

———, 'Problems of Authority in Late Medieval English Mysticism: Language, Agency and Authority in *The Book of Margery Kempe*', *Exemplaria* 4:1 (1992), 171–99.

———, 'A Very Material Mysticism: The Medieval Mysticism of Margery Kempe', in *Medieval Literature: Criticism, Ideology, History*, ed. D. Aers (Brighton, 1986), pp. 34–57.

Bell, R. M., *Holy Anorexia* (Chicago, 1985).

———, 'Telling Her Sins: Male Confessors and Female Penitents in Catholic Reformation Italy', in *That Gentle Strength: Historical Perspectives on Women in Christianity*, ed. L. L. Coon, K. Haldane and E. Sommer (Charlottesville, Va, 1990), pp. 118–33.

Benton, J. F., 'Trotula, Women's Problems, and the Professionalization of Medicine in the Late Middle Ages', in *Culture, Power and Personality in Medieval France*, ed. T. Bisson (London, 1991), pp. 363–86.

Beonio-Brocchieri, M. F., 'The Feminine Mind in Medieval Mysticism', in *Creative Women in Medieval and Early Modern Italy: A Religious and Artistic Renaissance*, ed. E. A. Matter and J. Coakley (Philadelphia, 1994), pp. 19–33.

Bergh, B., 'A Saint in the Making: St Bridget's Life in Sweden (1303–1349)', in *Papers of the Liverpool Latin Seminar* III, ed. F. Cairns, ARCA Classical and Medieval Texts, Papers and Monographs 7 (1981), pp. 371–84.

Bériou, N., 'Femmes et Prédicateurs: La transmission de la foi aux XIIe et XIIIe siècles', in *La religion de ma mère: Le rôle des femmes dans la transmission de la foi*, ed. J. Delumeau (Paris, 1992), pp. 51–70.

Bestul, T., 'Devotional Writing in England between Anselm and Richard Rolle', in *Mysticism, Medieval and Modern*, ed. V. Lagorio (Salzburg, 1986), pp. 12–28.

Blamires, A., *Woman Defamed and Woman Defended: An Anthology of Medieval Texts* (Oxford, 1992).

Blumenfeld-Kosinski, R. and T. Szell, ed., *Images of Sainthood in Medieval Europe* (Ithaca, 1991).

Boffey, Julia, 'Women Authors and Women's Literacy in Fourteenth- and Fifteenth-Century England', in *Women and Literature in Britain, 1150–1500*, ed. C. M. Meale (Cambridge, 1993), pp. 159–82.

Bolton, B., 'Daughters of Rome: All One In Christ Jesus!', in *Women in the Church*, ed. W. J. Shiels and D. Wood (Oxford, 1990), pp. 101–15.

———, 'Mulieres Sanctae', in *Women in Medieval Society*, ed. S. M. Stuard (Philadelphia, 1976), pp. 141–58.

Børreson, K. E., *Subordination and Equivalence: The Nature and Role of Women in Augustine and Thomas Aquinas*, trans. C. Talbot (Washington, DC, 1981).

Bosse, R. B., 'Margery Kempe's Tarnished Reputation: A Reassessment', *Fourteenth-Century English Mystics Newsletter* 5:1 (1979), 9–19.

Bradley, R., 'Mysticism in the Motherhood Similitude of Julian of Norwich', *Studia Mystica* 8 (1985), 4–13.

Bremner, E., 'Margery Kempe and the Critics: Disempowerment and Deconstruction', in *Margery Kempe: A Book of Essays*, ed. S. J. McEntire (New York, 1992), pp. 117–35.

Brooten, B. J., 'Paul's Views on the Nature of Women and Female Homoeroticism', in *Immaculate and Powerful: The Female in Sacred Image and Social Reality*, ed. C. W. Atkinson, C. H. Buchanan and M. R. Miles (Boston, 1985), pp. 61–87.

Brown, D. C., *Pastor and Laity in the Theology of Jean Gerson* (Cambridge, 1987).

Brown, J. C., *Immodest Acts: The Life of a Lesbian Nun in Renaissance Italy* (Oxford, 1986).

Brown, P., *The Body and Society: Men, Women and Sexual Renunciation in Early Christianity* (London, 1988).

Brownlee, K. and W. Stephens, ed., *Discourses of Authority in Medieval and Renaissance Literature* (Hanover, NH, 1989).

Bullough, V., 'Medieval Medical and Scientific Views of Women', *Viator* 4 (1973), 485–501.

———, *The Subordinate Sex: A History of Attitudes toward Women* (Chicago, 1973).

Burr, D., 'Olivi, Apocalyptic Expectation, and Visionary Experience', *Traditio* 41 (1985), 273–88.

Burrow, J. A., 'Autobiographical Poetry in the Middle Ages: The Case of Thomas Hoccleve', in *Middle English Literature: British Academy Gollancz Lectures*, ed. J. A. Burrow (Oxford, 1989), pp. 223–46.

Butler, C., *Western Mysticism: The Teaching of SS. Augustine, Gregory and Bernard on Contemplation and the Contemplative Life* (London, 1926).

Bynum, C. W., ' "... And Woman His Humanity": Female Imagery in the Religious Writing of the Later Middle Ages', in *Gender and Religion: On the Complexity of Symbols*, ed. C. Bynum, S. Harrell and P. Richman (Boston, 1986), pp. 257–88.

———, *Fragmentation and Redemption: Essays on Gender and the Human Body in Medieval Religion* (New York, 1991).

———, *Holy Feast and Holy Fast: The Religious Significance of Food to Medieval Women* (Berkeley, 1987).

———, *Jesus as Mother: Studies in the Spirituality of the High Middle Ages* (Berkeley, 1982).

———, 'Religious Women in the Later Middle Ages', in *Christian Spirituality: High Middle Ages and Reformation*, ed. J. Raitt (New York, 1988), pp. 121–39.

———, 'Women Mystics and Eucharistic Devotion in the Thirteenth Century', *Women's Studies* 11 (1984), 179–214.

Cadden, J., *Meanings of Sex Difference in the Middle Ages: Medicine, Science and Culture* (Cambridge, 1993).

Callaway, H., ' "The Most Essentially Female Function of All": Giving Birth', in *Defining Females: The Nature of Women in Society*, ed. S. Ardener (London, 1978).

Cardman, F., 'The Medieval Question of Women and Orders', *The Thomist* 42 (1978), 582–99.

Carruthers, M. J., *The Book of Memory: A Study of Memory in Medieval Culture* (Cambridge, 1990).

Cazelles, B., *The Lady as Saint: A Collection of French Hagiographic Romances of the Thirteenth Century* (Philadelphia, 1991).

Chidester, D., *Word and Light: Seeing, Hearing and Religious Discourse* (Urbana, Ill., 1992).

Christian, W. A., Jr, *Apparitions in Late Medieval and Renaissance Spain* (Princeton, 1981).

Clanchy, M. T., *From Memory to Written Record: England 1066–1307* (London, 1979).

Clark, A. L., *Elisabeth of Schönau: A Twelfth-Century Visionary* (Philadelphia, 1992).

Clark, D. L. 'Optics for Preachers: The *De oculo morali* by Peter of Limoges', *Michigan Academician* 9 (1977), 329–43

Clark, E. A., *Jerome, Chrysostom and Friends: Essays and Translations* (New York, 1979).

———, *Women in the Early Church* (Wilmington, 1983).

——— and H. Richardson, ed., *Women and Religion: A Feminist Sourcebook of Christian Thought* (New York, 1977).

Cleve, G., 'Margery Kempe: A Scandinavian Influence in Medieval England?', in *The Medieval Mystical Tradition in England V*, ed. M. Glasscoe (Cambridge, 1992), pp. 163–78.

———, 'Semantic Dimensions in Margery Kempe's "Whyght Clothys" ', *Mystics Quarterly* 12:4 (1986), 162–70.

Coakley, J., 'Friars as Confidants of Holy Women in Medieval Dominican Hagiography', in *Images of Sainthood in Medieval Europe*, ed. R. Blumenfeld-Kosinski and T. Szell (Ithaca, 1991), pp. 222–46.

———, 'Gender and the Authority of Friars: The Significance of Holy Women for Thirteenth-Century Franciscans and Dominicans', *Church History* 60:4 (1991), 445–60.

Coleman, J., *Medieval Readers and Writers 1350–1400* (London, 1981).

Colledge, E., '*Epistola solitarii ad reges*: Alphonse of Pecha as Organizer of Birgittine and Urbanist Propaganda', *Mediaeval Studies* 43 (1956), 19–49.

———, 'The Treatise of Perfection of the Sons of God: A Fifteenth-Century English Ruysbroek Translation', *English Studies* 33 (1952), 49–66.

Constable, G., 'The Popularity of Twelfth-Century Spiritual Writers in the Late Middle Ages', in *Renaissance Studies in Honor of Hans Baron*, ed. A. Molho and J. A. Tedeschi (Dekalb, Ill., 1971).

Copley, S., *Literature and the Social Order in Eighteenth-Century England* (London, 1984).

Costello, M. S., 'Women's Mysticism and Reform: The Adaptation of Biblical Prophetic Conventions in Fourteenth-Century Hagiographic and Visionary Literature' (unpublished Ph.D. dissertation, Northwestern, 1989).

Courtenay, W. J., *Schools and Scholars in Fourteenth-Century England* (Princeton, 1987).

Cross, C., ' "Great Reasoners in Scripture": The Activities of Women Lollards 1380–1530', in *Medieval Women*, ed. D. Baker (Oxford, 1978), pp. 359–80.

Curtius, E. R., *European Literature and the Latin Middle Ages*, trans. W. R. Trask (London, 1953).

Daly, M., *The Church and the Second Sex* (New York, 1975).

Davis, N. Z., 'Women on Top', in *Society and Culture in Early Modern France* (Stanford, 1975), pp. 124–151.

Dean, R., 'Elizabeth of Schönau and Roger of Ford', *Modern Philology* XLI:4 (1944), 209–20.

de Certeau, M., *Heterologies: Discourse on the Other*, trans. B. Massumi (Manchester, 1986).

Despres, D., 'Franciscan Spirituality: Margery Kempe and Visual Meditation', *Mystics Quarterly* 11:1 (1984), 12–18.

———, *Ghostly Sights: Visual Meditation in Late-Medieval Literature* (Norman, Okla., 1989).

———, 'The Meditative Art of Scriptural Interpolation in *The Book of Margery Kempe*', *The Downside Review* 106 no. 365 (1988), 253–63.

Dickman, S., 'Margery Kempe and the English Devotional Tradition', in *The Medieval Mystical Tradition in England I*, ed. M. Glasscoe (Exeter, 1980), pp. 156–72.

Dinzelbacher, P., 'The Beginnings of Mysticism Experienced in Twelfth-Century England', in *The Medieval Mystical Tradition in England IV*, ed. M. Glasscoe (Cambridge, 1987), pp. 111–31.

———, 'La littérature des révélations au Moyen Age: un document historique', *Revue historique* 275:2 (1986), 289–305.

———, *Vision und Visionliteratur im Mittelalter* (Stuttgart, 1981).

———, and D. R. Bauer, ed., *Frauenmystik im Mittelalter* (Ostfildern bei Stuttgart, 1985).

Douglas, M., *Purity and Danger: An Analysis of the Concepts of Pollution and Taboo* (London, 1966).

Dubois, D. J., 'Thomas Netter of Walden OC (*c.* 1372–1430)' (unpublished B.Lit. dissertation, Oxford, 1978).

Duffy, E., *The Stripping of the Altars: Traditional Religion in England, 1400–1580* (New Haven, 1992).

Dutton, M., 'Christ Our Mother: Aelred's Iconography for Contemplative Union', in *Goad and Nail*, Studies in Medieval Cistercian History 10, ed. E. R. Elder (Kalamazoo, 1985), pp. 21–45.

———, 'The Cistercian Source: Aelred, Bonaventure and Ignatius', in *Goad and Nail*, Studies in Medieval Cistercian History 10, ed. E. R. Elder (Kalamazoo, 1985), pp. 151–78.

Edwards, A. S. G., ed., *Middle English Prose: A Critical Guide to Major Authors and Genres* (New Brunswick, 1984).

Egres, O., OC, 'Mechthild von Magdeburg: Exile in a Foreign Land', in *Goad and Nail*, Studies in Medieval Cistercian History 10, ed. E. R. Elder (Kalamazoo, 1985), pp. 133–47.

———, 'Mechthild von Magdeburg: *The Flowing Light of God*', in *Cistercians in the Late Middle Ages*, Studies in Medieval History 6, ed. E. R. Elder (Kalamazoo, 1981), pp. 19–37.

Elkins, S. K., *Holy Women of Twelfth-Century England* (Chapel Hill, 1988).

Elliott, D., *Spiritual Marriage: Sexual Abstinence in Medieval Wedlock* (Princeton, 1993).

——, 'The Physiology of Rapture and Female Spirituality', in *Medieval Theology and the Natural Body*, ed. P. Biller and A. J. Minnis (York, 1997), pp. 141–74.

Ellis, R., 'The Choices of the Translator in the Late Middle English Period', in *The Medieval Mystical Tradition in England II*, ed. M. Glasscoe (Exeter, 1982), pp. 19–46.

——, 'The Divine Message and Its Human Agents: St Birgitta and Her Editors', in *Studies in St Birgitta and the Brigittine Order*, ed. J. Hogg, 2 vols. (New York, 1993), I, 209–33.

——, '*Flores ad fabricandam . . . coronam*: An Investigation into the Uses of the Revelations of St Bridget of Sweden in Fifteenth-Century England', *Medium Aevum* 52 (1983), 163–186.

——, 'Margery Kempe's Scribe and the Miraculous Books', in *Langland, the Mystics and the Medieval English Religious Tradition*, ed. H. Phillips (Cambridge, 1990), pp. 161–75.

——, 'The Swedish Woman, the Widow, the Pilgrim and the Prophetess: Images of St Bridget in the Canonization Sermon of Pope Boniface IX', in *Santa Brigida: Profeta dei Tempi Nuovi. Proceedings of the International Study Meeting. Rome, October 3–7, 1991*, no ed. (Rome, 1993), pp. 93–119.

——, *Viderunt Eam Filie Syon: The Spirituality of the English House of a Medieval Contemplative Order from its Beginnings to the Present Day* (Salzburg, 1984).

——, 'The Visionary Universe of St Bridget of Sweden: A Revelation and its Editors: The *Epistola Solitarii* of Alphonse of Jaén, and Book VI, Chapter 52, of the *Liber Celestis* of St Bridget of Sweden', in *Interdisciplinary Research on Imagery and Sight (I.R.I.S.): Vision et Perception Fondamentales. Actes du Colloque* (Lyon, 1981), pp. 77–96.

Erskine, J. A., 'Margery Kempe and her Models: The Role of the Authorial Voice', *Mystics Quarterly* 15:2 (1989), 75–85.

Ferrante, J. M., *To the Glory of her Sex: Women's Role in the Composition of Medieval Texts* (Bloomington, 1997).

Fienberg, N., 'Thematics of Value in *The Book of Margery Kempe*', *Modern Philology* 87:2 (1989), 132–41.

Finke, L. A., 'Mystical Bodies and the Dialogics of Vision', in *Maps of Flesh and Light: The Religious Experience of Medieval Women Mystics*, ed. U. Wiethaus (Syracuse, 1993), pp. 28–44.

Finnegan, M. J., OP, *The Women of Helfta: Scholars and Mystics* (Athens, Ga, rev. edn 1991).

Flanagan, S., *Hildegard of Bingen, 1098–1179: A Visionary Life* (London, 1990).

Foucault, M., *The Archaeology of Knowledge*, trans. A. M. S. Smith (London, 1972).

——, 'The Order of Discourse', trans. I. McLeod, in *Untying the Text: A Post-Structuralist Reader*, ed. R. Young (London, 1981), pp. 48–77.

George, K. and C. George, 'Roman Catholic Sainthood and Social Status: A Statistical and Analytical Study', *The Journal of Religion* 35 (1955), 85–98.

Georgianna, L., *The Solitary Self: Individuality in the Ancrene Wisse* (Cambridge, Mass., 1981).

Gilchrist, R., *Women and Material Culture* (London, 1994).

Gilkaer, H. T., 'New Perspectives on the *Liber Celestis Imperatoris ad Reges* (Book VIII of the Revelations)', in *Santa Brigida: Profeta dei Tempi Nuovi. Proceedings of the*

International Study Meeting, Rome, October 3–7, 1991, no ed. (Rome, 1993), pp. 846–52.

Gillespie, V., 'Lukynge in haly bukes': *lectio* in some Late Medieval Spiritual Miscellanies', *Analecta Cartusiana* 106:2 (1984), 1–27.

Gilligan, C., *In a Different Voice: Psychological Theory and Women's Development* (Cambridge, Mass., 1982).

Gilmore, L., *Autobiographics: A Feminist Theory of Women's Self-Representation* (Ithaca, 1994).

Glasscoe, M., *English Medieval Mystics: Games of Faith* (London, 1993).

Goodich, M., '*Ancilla Dei*: The Servant as Saint in the Late Middle Ages', in *Women of the Medieval World: Essays in Honor of John H. Mundy,* ed. J. Kirshner and S. F. Wemple (Oxford, 1985), pp. 119–32.

———, 'The Politics of Canonization in the Thirteenth Century: Lay and Mendicant Saints', in *Saints and their Cults: Studies in Religious Sociology, Folklore and History,* ed. S. Wilson (Cambridge, 1983), pp. 169–87.

———, *Vita Perfecta: The Ideal of Sainthood in the Thirteenth Century* (Stuttgart, 1982).

Goodman, A., 'The Piety of John Brunham's Daughter of Lynn', in *Medieval Women,* ed. D. Baker (Oxford, 1978), pp. 351–3.

Greenblatt, S., *Renaissance Self-Fashioning: From More to Shakespeare* (Chicago, 1980).

Griffiths, J., ed. *The Cell of Self-Knowledge* (Dublin, 1981).

Grundman, H., *Religious Movements in the Middle Ages,* trans. S. Rowan (Notre Dame, 1995).

Hagen, S. K., *Allegorical Remembrance: A Study of The Pilgrimage of the Life of Man as a Medieval Treatise on Seeing and Remembering* (Athens, Ga, 1990).

Hale, R., '*Imitatio Mariae*: Motherhood Motifs in Devotional Memoirs', in *Medieval German Literature: Proceedings from the 23rd International Congress on Medieval Studies. Kalamazoo, Michigan, May 5–8, 1988* (Göppingen, 1989), pp. 129–45.

Hamburger, J., 'The Visual and the Visionary: The Image in Late Medieval Monastic Devotions', *Viator* 20 (1989), 161–82.

Hathaway, R. T., *Hierarchy and the Definition of Order in the Letters of Pseudo-Dionysius* (The Hague, 1969).

Hauptmann, J., 'Images of Women in the Talmud', in *Religion and Sexism: Images of Woman in the Jewish and Christian Traditions* ed. R. R. Ruether (New York, 1974), pp. 184–212.

Hill, T. D., 'Half-Waking, Half-Sleeping: A Tropological Motif in a Middle English Lyric and its European Context', *Review of English Studies* 29 (1978), 50–6.

Hirsh, J. C., 'Author and Scribe in *The Book of Margery Kempe*', *Medium Aevum* 44 (1975), 145–50.

———, 'Margery Kempe', in *Middle English Prose: A Critical Guide to Major Authors and Genres,* ed. A. S. G. Edwards (New Brunswick, 1984), pp. 109–20.

———, *The Revelations of Margery Kempe: Paramystical Practices in Late Medieval England* (Leiden, 1989).

Hodgson, P., *Three Fourteenth Century English Mystics* (London, 1967).

———, '*The Orcherd of Syon* and the English Mystical Tradition', in *Middle English Literature: British Academy Gollancz Lectures,* ed. J. A. Burrow (Oxford, 1989), pp. 71–91.

Hogg, J., 'The Contribution of the Brigittine Order to Late Medieval English Spirituality', *Analecta Cartusiana* 35:3 (1983), 153–74.

———, 'Mount Grace Charterhouse and Late Medieval English Spirituality', *Analecta Cartusiana* 82:3 (1980), 1–43.

———, 'A Mystical Diary: The *Refectorium Salutatis* of Richard Methley of Mount Grace Charterhouse', *Analecta Cartusiana* 55:1 (1981), 208–38.

———, 'Richard Methley: To Hew Heremyte, A Pystyl of Solytary Lyfe Nowadayes', *Analecta Cartusiana* 31 (1977), 91–119.

———, 'St Birgitta's *Revelationes* Reduced to a Book of Pious Instruction', in *Vox Mystica: Essays on Medieval Mysticism in Honor of Professor Valerie Lagorio*, ed. A. C. Bartlett et al. (Cambridge, 1995), pp. 201–30.

———, ed., *Studies in St Birgitta and the Brigittine Order*, 2 vols. (New York, 1993).

Holbrook, S. E., ' "About Her": Margery Kempe's Book of Feeling and Working', in *The Idea of Medieval Literature: New Essays on Chaucer and Medieval Culture in Honor of Donald R. Howard*, ed. J. M. Dean and C. K. Zacher (Newark, 1992), pp. 265–84.

———, 'Margery Kempe and Wynken de Worde', in *The Medieval Mystical Tradition in England IV*, ed. M. Glasscoe (Cambridge, 1987), pp. 27–46.

———, 'Order and Coherence in *The Book of Margery Kempe*', in *The Worlds of Medieval Women: Creativity, Influence, Imagination*, ed. C. Berman, C. Connell and J. R. Rothschild (Morgantown, 1985), pp. 97–110.

Homan, R. L., 'Old and New Evidence of the Career of William Melton', *Franciscan Studies* 49 (1989), 25–33.

Horsfield, R. A., '*The Pomander of Prayer*: Aspects of Late Medieval English Carthusian Spirituality and its Lay Audience', in *De Cella in Seculum: Religious and Secular Life and Devotion in Late Medieval England*, ed. M. G. Sargent (Cambridge, 1989), pp. 205–13.

Holdsworth, C., 'Visions and Visionaries in the Middle Ages', *History: Journal of the Historical Association* 48 no. 163 (1963), 141–53.

Howard, D. R., *Writers and Pilgrims: Medieval Pilgrimage Narratives and their Posterity* (Berkeley, 1980).

Hudson, A., *The Premature Reformation: Wycliffite Texts and Lollard History* (Oxford, 1988).

Huizinga, J., *The Waning of the Middle Ages* (New York, 1954).

Hunicker, R., 'Studien über Heinrich von Halle', *Thüringisch-sächsiche Zeitschrift für Geschichte und Kunst* 23 (1935), 102–17.

Hussey, S. S., 'The Audience for the Middle English Mystics', in *De Cella in Seculum: Religious and Secular Life and Devotion in Late Medieval England*, ed. M. G. Sargent (Cambridge, 1989), pp. 109–22.

Hutchison, A. M., 'Devotional Reading in the Monastery and in the Late Medieval Household', in *De Cella in Seculum: Religious and Secular Life and Devotion in Late Medieval England*, ed. M. G. Sargent (Cambridge, 1989), pp. 215–27.

Irigaray, L., 'La Mystérique', in *Speculum of the Other Woman*, trans. G. Gill (Ithaca, 1974), pp. 191–202.

Jacobus, M. 'The Difference of View', in *Reading Women: Essays in Feminist Criticism*, ed. M. Jacobus (London, 1986), pp. 27–40.

Jacquart, D. and C. Thomasset, *Sexuality and Medicine in the Middle Ages*, trans. M. Adamson (Oxford, 1988).

Jantzen, G., ' "Cry out and write": Mysticism and the Struggle for Authority', in *Women, the Book, and the Godly*, ed. L. Smith and J. Taylor (Cambridge, 1994), pp. 67–76.

Jeffrey, D. L., *The Early English Lyric and Franciscan Spirituality* (Lincoln, Neb., 1975).

Jelinek, E. C., *The Tradition of Women's Autobiography: From Antiquity to the Present* (Boston, 1986).

Johnson, I., 'Prologue and Practice: The Middle English Lives of Christ', in *The Medieval Translator: The Theory and Practice of Translation in the Middle Ages*, ed. R. Ellis (Cambridge, 1989), pp. 69–85.

Johnson, L. S., 'The Trope of the Scribe: The Question of Literary Authority in the Works of Julian of Norwich and Margery Kempe', *Speculum* 66 (1991), 820–38.

Johnson, P. D., *Equal in Monastic Profession: Religious Women in Medieval France* (Chicago, 1991).

———, '*Mulier et Monialis*: The Medieval Nun's Self-Image', *Thought* 64 no. 284 (1989), 242–53.

Jorgensen, J., *Saint Bridget of Sweden*, trans. I. Lund, 2 vols. (London, 1954).

Keiser, G. R., 'The Mystics and the Early English Printers: The Economics of Devotionalism', in *The Medieval Mysticai Tradition in England IV*, ed. M. Glasscoe (Cambridge, 1987), pp. 9–26.

———, 'St Jerome and the Brigittines: Visions of the Afterlife in Fifteenth-Century England', in *England in the Fifteenth Century*, ed. D. Williams (Woodbridge, 1987), pp. 143–52.

Kerby-Fulton, K., *Reformist Apocalypticism and Piers Plowman* (Cambridge, 1990).

———, ' "Who Has Written this Book?": Visionary Autobiography in Langland's C-Text', in *The Medieval Mystical Tradition in England V*, ed. M. Glasscoe (Cambridge, 1992), pp. 101–16.

———, and D. Elliott, 'Self-Image and the Visionary Role in Two Letters from the Correspondence of Elizabeth of Schönau and Hildegard of Bingen', *Vox Benedictina* 2:3 (1985), 204–23.

Kieckhefer, R., *Magic in the Middle Ages* (Cambridge, 1989).

———, 'Mysticism and Social Consciousness in the Fourteenth Century', *University of Ottawa Quarterly* 48 (1978), 179–86.

———, *Unquiet Souls: Fourteenth-Century Saints and their Religious Milieu* (Chicago, 1984).

Knowles, D., *The English Mystical Tradition* (London, 1961).

———, *What is Mysticism?* (London, 1967).

Klaniczay, G., *The Uses of Supernatural Power: The Transformation of Popular Religion in Medieval and Early-Modern Europe*, trans. S. Singerman, ed. K. Margolis (Princeton, 1990).

Kleinberg, A. M., *Prophets in their Own Country: Living Saints and the Making of Sainthood in the Later Middle Ages* (Chicago, 1992).

———, 'Proving Sanctity: Selection and Authentication of Saints in the Later Middle Ages', *Viator* 20 (1989), 182–205.

Kruger, S. F., *Dreaming in the Middle Ages* (Cambridge, 1992).

Labarge, M. W., *Women in Medieval Life: A Small Sound of the Trumpet* (London, 1986).

Lagorio, V., 'The Continental Women Mystics of the Middle Ages: An Assessment', in *The Roots of the Modern Christian Tradition*, ed. E. R. Elder (Kalamazoo, 1984), pp. 71–90.

———, 'Problems in Middle English Mystical Prose', in *Middle English Prose: Essays on Bibliographical Problems*, ed. A. S. G. Edwards and D. Pearsall (New York, 1981), pp. 129–48.

———, 'Social Responsibility and the Medieval Women Mystics on the Continent', *Analecta Cartusiana* 35 (1983), 95–104.

———, 'Variations on the Theme of God's Motherhood in Medieval English Mystical and Devotional Writings', *Studia Mystica* 8 (1985), 15–37.

———, 'The Medieval Continental Women Mystics', in *An Introduction to the Medieval Mystics of Europe*, ed. P. Szarmach (Albany, 1984), pp. 161–93.

Laqueur, T., *Making Sex: Body and Gender from the Greeks to Freud* (Cambridge, Mass., 1990).

Lawrence, C. H., *The Friars: The Impact of the Early Mendicant Movement on Western Society* (London, 1994).

———, *Medieval Monasticism: Forms of Religious Life in Western Europe in the Middle Ages* (London, 1989).

Lawton, D., 'Voice, Authority and Blasphemy in *The Book of Margery Kempe*', in *Margery Kempe: A Book of Essays*, ed. S. J. McEntire (New York, 1992), pp. 93–115.

Leclercq, J., OSB, 'Le Sacré-Coeur dans la Tradition Bénédictine au Moyen Age', in *Cor Jesu: Commentationes in Litteras Encyclicas PII PP. XII 'Haurietis Aquas'*, ed. A. Bea SJ et al., 2 vols. (Rome, 1959), II, 3–28.

———, *The Love of Learning and the Desire for God: A Study of Monastic Culture*, trans. C. Misrahi (New York, 1982).

———, *Women and St Bernard of Clairvaux*, trans. M. Saïd (Kalamazoo, 1989).

Lejeune, P., *On Autobiography*, trans. K. Leary, ed. P. J. Eakin (Minneapolis, 1989).

Lerner, R. E., 'The Black Death and Western European Eschatological Mentalities', *American Historical Review* 86 (1981), 533–52.

———, 'Ecstatic Dissent', *Speculum* 67 (1992), 33–57.

———, *The Heresy of the Free Spirit in the Later Middle Ages* (Notre Dame, 1972).

———, 'Literacy and Learning', in *One Thousand Years: Western Europe in the Middle Ages*, ed. R. DeMolen (Boston, 1974), pp. 165–233.

———, 'Medieval Prophecy and Religious Dissent', *Past and Present* 72 (1976), 3–24.

———, *The Powers of Prophecy: The Cedar of Lebanon Vision from the Mongol Onslaught to the Dawn of the Enlightenment* (Berkeley, 1983).

Lewis, I. M., *Ecstatic Religion: A Study of Shamanism and Spirit Possession* (London, 1989).

Leyser, H. *Medieval Women: A Social History of Women in England, 450–1500* (London, 1995).

Lloyd, G., *The Man of Reason: 'Male' and 'Female' in Western Philosophy* (London, 1984).

Lochrie, K., '*The Book of Margery Kempe*: The Marginal Woman's Quest for Literary Authority', *Journal of Medieval and Renaissance Studies* 16 (1986), 34–55.

———, 'The Language of Transgression: Body, Flesh and Word in Mystical

Discourse', in *Speaking Two Languages: Traditional Disciplines and Contemporary Theory in Medieval Studies*, ed. A. J. Frantzen (Albany, 1991), pp. 115–40.

————, *Margery Kempe and Translations of the Flesh* (Philadelphia, 1991).

Lomperis, L. and S. Stanbury, ed., *Feminist Approaches to the Body in Medieval Literature* (Philadelphia, 1993).

Louth, A., *Denys the Areopagite* (London, 1989).

————, *The Origins of the Christian Mystical Tradition* (Oxford, 1981).

Lovatt, R., 'The "Imitation of Christ" in Late Medieval England', *Transactions of the Royal Historical Society* 18 (1968), 97–121.

Lowe, K. J. P., 'Female Strategies for Success in a Male-Ordered World: The Benedictine Convent of Le Murate in Florence in the Fifteenth and Early Sixteenth Centuries', in *Women in the Church*, ed. W. J. Shiels and D. Wood (Oxford, 1990), pp. 209–21.

Macdonell, D., *Theories of Discourse: An Introduction* (Oxford, 1986).

Mack, P., *Visionary Women: Ecstatic Prophecy in Seventeenth-Century England* (Berkeley, 1992).

Martin, C. A., 'Middle English Manuals of Religious Instruction', in *'So meny people longages and tonges': philological essays in Scots and mediaeval English presented to Angus McIntosh*, ed. M. Benskin and M. L. Samuels (Edinburgh, 1981), pp. 283–98.

McDonnell, E. W., *The Beguines and Beghards in Medieval Culture: with special emphasis on the Belgian scene* (New Brunswick, 1954).

McGann, J. J., 'The Monks and the Giants: Textual and Bibliographical Studies and the Interpretation of Literary Works', in *The Beauty of Inflections: Literary Investigations in Historical Method and Theory* (Oxford, 1985), pp. 69–89.

McGinn, B., '*Teste David cum Sibylla*: The Significance of the Sibylline Tradition in the Middle Ages', in *Women of the Medieval World: Essays in Honor of John H. Mundy*, ed. J. Kirshner and S. F. Wemple (Oxford, 1985), pp. 7–35.

————, *Visions of the End: Apocalyptic Traditions in the Middle Ages* (New York, 1979).

McGuire, B. P., 'Holy Women and Monks in the Thirteenth Century: Friendship or Exploitation?', *Vox Benedictina* 6:4 (1989), 343–73.

McLaughlin, E. C., 'Equality of Souls, Inequality of Sexes: Woman in Medieval Theology', in *Religion and Sexism: Images of Woman in the Jewish and Christian Traditions*, ed. R. R. Ruether (New York, 1974), pp. 213–66.

McNamara, J. and S. F. Wemple, 'Sanctity and Power: The Dual Pursuit of Medieval Women', in *Becoming Visible: Women in European History*, ed. R. Bridenthal and C. Koonz (Boston, 1977), pp. 92–118.

McSheffrey, S., 'Literacy and the Gender Gap in the Late Middle Ages: Women and Reading in Lollard Communities', in *Women, the Book, and the Godly*, ed. L. Smith and J. Taylor (Cambridge, 1994), pp. 157–70.

Meale, C. M., ed., *Women and Literature in Britain, 1150–1500* (Cambridge, 1993).

Medcalf, S., ed., *The Later Middle Ages* (London, 1981).

Meier, H. H., 'Middle English Styles in Translation: The Case of Chaucer and Charles', in *'So meny people longages and tonges': philological essays in Scots and mediaeval English presented to Angus McIntosh*, ed. M. Benskin and M. L. Samuels (Edinburgh, 1981), pp. 367–76.

Minnis, A. J., 'The *Accessus* Extended: Henry of Ghent on the Transmission and

Reception of Theology', in *Ad litteram: Authoritative Texts and their Medieval Readers*, ed. M. D. Jordan and K. Emery Jr (Notre Dame, 1992), pp. 275–326.

————, 'Affection and Imagination in *The Cloud of Unknowing* and Hilton's *Scale of Perfection*', *Traditio* 39 (1983), 323–66.

————, *Chaucer and Pagan Antiquity* (Cambridge, 1982).

————, 'Chaucer's Pardoner and the "Office of Preacher"', in *Intellectuals and Writers in Fourteenth-Century Europe*, ed. P. Boitani and A. Torti (Cambridge, 1986), pp. 88–119.

————, '*De impedimento sexus*: Women's Bodies and Medieval Impediments to Ordination', in *Medieval Theology and the Natural Body*, ed. P. Biller and A. J. Minnis (York, 1997), pp. 109–40.

————, '*De Vulgari Auctoritate*: Chaucer, Gower and the Men of Great Authority', in *Chaucer and Gower: Difference, Mutuality, Exchange*, ed. R. F. Yeager (Victoria, B.C, 1991), pp. 36–74.

————, 'Langland's Ymaginatif and Late-Medieval Theories of Imagination', *Comparative Criticism* 3 (1981), 71–103.

————, *Medieval Theory of Authorship: Scholastic Literary Attitudes in the Later Middle Ages* (Philadelphia, 2nd rev. edn, 1988).

————, with A. B. Scott and D. Wallace, *Medieval Literary Theory and Criticism* (Oxford, 1988).

Monter, E. W., 'The Pedestal and the Stake: Courtly Love and Witchcraft', in *Becoming Visible: Women in European History*, ed. R. Bridenthal and C. Koonz (Boston, 1977), pp. 119–36.

Mooney, C. M., 'Women's Visions, Men's Words: The Portrayal of Holy Women and Men in Fourteenth-Century Italian Hagiography' (unpublished Ph.D. dissertation, Yale, 1991).

————, 'The Authorial Role of Brother A. in the Composition of Angela of Foligno's Revelations', in *Creative Women in Medieval and Early Modern Italy: A Religious and Artistic Renaissance*, ed. E. A. Matter and J. Coakley (Philadelphia, 1994), pp. 34–63.

Morris, B., 'Labyrinths of the Urtext', in *Heliga Birgitta – budskapet och förbilden. Proceedings of the Symposium at Vadstena 3–7 October, 1991*, ed. A. Härdelin and M. Lindgren (Västervik, 1993), pp. 23–33.

————, 'The Monk-on-the-Ladder in Book V of St Birgitta's *Revelaciones*', *Kyrkohistorisk Arsskrift* (1982), 95–107.

————, 'Swedish Foreign Policy of the 1340s in the Balance: An Interpretation of Book IV Chapter 2 of St Bridget's *Revelations*', in *Studies in St Birgitta and the Brigittine Order*, ed. J. Hogg, 2 vols. (New York, 1993), I, 180–91.

Mueller, J. M., 'Autobiography of a New "Creatur": Female Spirituality, Selfhood and Authorship in *The Book of Margery Kempe*', in *Women in the Middle Ages and the Renaissance: Literary and Historical Perspectives*, ed. M. B. Rose (Syracuse, 1986), pp. 155–71.

Murray, A., *Reason and Society in the Middle Ages* (Oxford, 1978).

Neaman, J. S., 'Sight and Insight: Vision and the Mystics', *Fourteenth-Century English Mystics Newsletter* 5:3 (1979), 27–43.

Nelson, J. L., 'Women and the Word in the Earlier Middle Ages', in *Women in the Church*, ed. W. J. Shiels and D. Wood (Oxford, 1990), pp. 53–78.

Newman, B., *From Virile Woman to WomanChrist: Studies in Medieval Religion and Literature* (Philadelphia, 1995).

———, *Sister of Wisdom: St Hildegard's Theology of the Feminine* (Berkeley, 1987).

Nieva, C. S., *This Transcending God: The Teaching of the Author of The Cloud of Unknowing* (London, 1971).

Nolan, E. P., *Cry Out and Write: A Feminine Poetics of Revelation* (New York, 1994).

Nyberg, T., 'Birgitta von Schweden – die Aktive Gottesschau', in *Frauenmystik im Mittelalter*, ed. P. Dinzelbacher and D. R. Bauer (Ostfildern bei Stuttgart, 1985), pp. 275–89.

Oakley, F., *The Western Church in the Later Middle Ages* (Ithaca, 1979).

Ober, W., 'Margery Kempe: Hysteria and Mysticism Reconciled', *Literature and Medicine* 4 (1985), pp. 24–40.

Oberman, H. A., *The Harvest of Medieval Theology: Gabriel Biel and Late Medieval Nominalism* (Cambridge, Mass., 1963).

Ong, W. J., 'Orality, Literacy and Medieval Textualization', *New Literary History* 16 (1984), 1–11.

Ozment, S., *Homo Spiritualis: A Comparative Study of the Anthropology of Johannes Tauler, Jean Gerson and Martin Luther (1509–16) in the Context of their Theological Thought* (Leiden, 1969).

———, *Mysticism and Dissent: Religious Ideology and Social Protest in the Sixteenth Century* (New Haven, 1973).

———, 'Mysticism, Nominalism and Dissent', in *The Pursuit of Holiness in Late Medieval and Renaissance Religion*, ed. C. Trinkhaus and H. Oberman (Leiden, 1974).

Pagels, E., *Adam, Eve, and the Serpent* (New York, 1988).

———, 'Paul and Women: A Response to Recent Discussion', *Journal of the American Academy of Religion* 42 (1974), 538–49.

Partner, N., ' "And Most of All for Inordinate Love": Desire and Denial in *The Book of Margery Kempe*', *Thought* 64 (1989), 254–67.

———, 'No Sex, No Gender', in *Studying Medieval Women*, ed. N. Partner (Cambridge, Mass., 1993), pp. 117–41.

Petroff, E., *Body and Soul: Essays on Medieval Women and Mysticism* (Oxford, 1994).

———, *Consolation of the Blessed* (New York, 1979).

Pezzini, D., 'Brigittine Tracts of Spiritual Guidance in Fifteenth-Century England', in *The Medieval Translator II*, ed. R. Ellis (London, 1991), pp. 174–207.

Raitt, J., ed., *Christian Spirituality: High Middle Ages and Reformation* (New York, 1988).

Ranke-Heineman, U., *Eunuchs for the Kingdom of Heaven: Women, Sexuality and the Catholic Church*, trans. P. Heinegg (New York, 1990).

Reeves, M., *The Influence of Prophecy in the Later Middle Ages: A Study in Joachimism* (Oxford, new edn, 1993).

Riddy, F., ' "Women talking about the things of God": a Late Medieval Sub-culture', in *Women and Literature in Britain, 1150–1500*, ed. C. M. Meale (Cambridge, 1993), pp. 104–27.

Riehle, W., *The Middle English Mystics*, trans. B. Standring (London, 1981).

Rimmon-Kenan, S., *Narrative Fiction: Contemporary Poetics* (London, 1983).

Rosen, G., *Madness in Society: Chapters in the Historical Sociology of Mental Illness* (New York, 1968).

Rosenthal, J. T., ed., *Medieval Women and the Sources of Medieval History* (Athens, Ga, 1990).

Rubin, M., *Corpus Christi: The Eucharist in Late Medieval Culture* (Cambridge, 1991).

Ruether, R. R., 'Misogynism and Virginal Feminism in the Fathers of the Church', in *Religion and Sexism: Images of Woman in the Jewish and Christian Traditions*, ed. R. R. Ruether (New York, 1974), pp. 150–83.

——, 'The Persecution of Witches: A Case of Sexism and Ageism?', *Christianity in Crisis* 34 (1974), 291–5.

Russell, J. B., *Dissent and Order in the Middle Ages: The Search for Legitimate Authority* (New York, 1992).

——, *A History of Medieval Christianity: Prophecy and Order* (Arlington Heights, Ill., 1968).

Saenger, P., 'Silent Reading: Its Impact on Late Medieval Script and Society', *Viator* 13 (1982), 367–414.

Sahlin, C. L., ' "A Marvellous and Great Exultation of the Heart": Mystical Pregnancy and Marian Devotion in Bridget of Sweden's *Revelations*', in *Studies in St Birgitta and the Brigittine Order*, ed. J. Hogg, 2 vols. (New York, 1993), I, 108–28.

Sallmann, J., 'La sainteté mystique féminine à Naples au tournant des XVIe et XVIIe siècles', in *Culto dei santi, istituzioni e classi social in età preindustriale*, ed. S. B. Gajano and L. Sebastiani (Rome, 1984), pp. 683–702.

Salisbury, J., *Church Fathers, Independent Virgins* (London, 1991).

Sargent, M., 'Contemporary Criticism of Richard Rolle', *Analecta Cartusiana* 35:1 (1981), 160–87.

——, 'Minor Devotional Writings', in *Middle English Prose: A Critical Guide to Major Authors and Genres*, ed. A. S. G. Edwards (New Brunswick, 1984), pp. 147–75.

——, 'The Transmission by the English Carthusians of Some Late Medieval Spiritual Writings', *Journal of Ecclesiastical History* 27 (1976), 225–40.

Scarry, E., *The Body in Pain: The Making and Unmaking of the World* (Oxford, 1985).

Schmidt, M., '*Discretio* bei Hildegard von Bingen als Bildungselement', *Analecta Cartusiana* 35 (1983), 73–93.

Schmidtke, J. A., ' "Saving" by Faint Praise: St Birgitta of Sweden, Adam Easton and Medieval Antifeminism', *American Benedictine Review* 33 (1982), 149–61.

Scholem, G., *On the Kabbalah and its Symbolism*, trans. R. Mannheim (New York, 1969).

Scholtz, B., 'Hildegard von Bingen on the Nature of Woman', *American Benedictine Review* 31 (1980), 361–83.

Schulenberg, J. T., 'Female Sanctity: Public and Private Roles, ca. 500–1100', in *Women and Power in the Middle Ages*, ed. M. Erler and M. Kowaleski (Athens, Ga, 1988), pp. 102–25.

Seidlmayer, M., 'Ein Gehilfe der hl. Birgitta von Schweden: Alfons von Jaen', *Historisches Jahrbuch* 50 (1930), 1–18.

Shahar, S., *The Fourth Estate: A History of Women in the Middle Ages*, trans. C. Galai (London, 1983).

Smalley, B., *The Study of the Bible in the Middle Ages* (Oxford, 1952).

Smith, S., *A Poetics of Women's Autobiography: Marginality and the Fictions of Self-Representation* (Bloomington, 1987).

Southern, R. W., *Western Society and the Church in the Middle Ages* (Harmondsworth, 1970).

Spencer, H. L., *English Preaching in the Late Middle Ages* (Oxford, 1993).

Spitzer, L., 'Note on the Poetic and Empirical "I" in Medieval Authors', *Traditio* 4 (1946), 414–22.

Staley, L., *Margery Kempe's Dissenting Fictions* (Pennsylvania, 1994).

Stargardt, U., 'The Influence of Dorothea von Montau on the Mysticism of Margery Kempe' (unpublished Ph.D. dissertation, University of Tennessee, 1981).

Stock, B., *The Implications of Literacy: Written Language and Models of Interpretation in the Eleventh and Twelfth Centuries* (Princeton, 1983).

Stone, R. K., *Middle English Prose Style: Margery Kempe and Julian of Norwich* (The Hague, 1970).

Strohm, P., *Hochon's Arrow: The Social Imagination of Fourteenth-Century Texts* (Princeton, 1992).

Surtz, R. E., *The Guitar of God: Gender, Power and Authority in the Visionary World of Mother Juana de la Cruz (1481–1534)* (Philadelphia, 1990).

Switek, G., SJ, '*Discretio spirituum*: Ein Beitrag zur Geschichte der Spiritualität', *Theologie und Philosophie* 47 (1972), 36–76.

Szarmach, P., ed., *An Introduction to the Medieval Mystics of Europe* (Albany, 1984).

Szell, T. K., 'From Woe to Weal and Weal to Woe: Notes on the Structure of *The Book of Margery Kempe*', in *Margery Kempe: A Book of Essays*, ed. S. J. McEntire (New York, 1992), pp. 73–91.

Tanner, N. P., *The Church in Late Medieval Norwich 1370–1532* (Toronto, 1984).

Tentler, T. N., *Sin and Confession on the Eve of the Reformation* (Princeton, 1977).

Thomas, K., *Religion and the Decline of Magic: Studies in Popular Beliefs in Sixteenth-and Seventeenth-Century England* (London, 1988).

Tobin, F., 'Medieval Thought on Visions and its Resonance in Mechtild von Magdeburg's *Flowing Light of the Godhead*', in *Vox Mystica: Essays on Medieval Mysticism in Honor of Professor Valerie Lagorio*, ed. A. C. Bartlett et al. (Cambridge, 1995), pp. 41–56.

Turner, V. and E. Turner, *Image and Pilgrimage in Christian Culture: Anthropological Perspectives* (New York, 1978).

Underhill, E., *Mysticism: A Study in the Nature and Development of Man's Spiritual Consciousness* (Oxford, 1993).

Undhagen, C., 'Une source du prologue (chap. 1) aux *Révélations de Sainte Brigitte* par le cardinal Jean de Turrecremata', *Eranos: Acta Philologica Suecana* 58 (1960), 214–26.

Vagaggini, C., OSB, 'La Dévotion au Sacré Coeur Chez Sainte Mechtilde et Sainte Gertrude', in *Cor Jesu: Commentationes in Litteras Encyclicas PII PP. XII 'Haurietis Aquas'*, ed. A. Bea SJ et al., 2 vols. (Rome, 1959), II, 31–48.

Vauchez, A., *Faire Croire: Modalités de la diffusion et de la reception des messages religieux du XIIe au XVe siècle* (Rome, 1981).

———, 'La diffusion des *Révélations* de sainte Brigitte dans l'espace français à la fin du Moyen Age', in *Santa Brigida: Profeta dei Tempi Nuovi. Proceedings of the International Study Meeting, Rome, October 3–7, 1991*, no ed. (Rome, 1993), pp. 151–63.

———, *The Laity in the Middle Ages: Religious Beliefs and Devotional Practices*, ed. D. Bornstein, trans. M. J. Schneider (Notre Dame, 1993).

———, *La sainteté en Occident aux derniers siècles du moyen âge* (Rome, 1981).

Veith, I., *Hysteria: The History of a Disease* (Chicago, 1970).

Voaden, R., 'God's Almighty Hand: Women Co-Writing the Book', in *Women, the Book, and the Godly*, ed. L. Smith and J. Taylor (Cambridge, 1994), pp. 55–66.

———, 'Beholding Men's Members: The Sexualizing of Transgression in *The Book of Margery Kempe*', in *Medieval Theology and the Natural Body*, ed. P. Biller and A. J. Minnis (York, 1997), pp. 175–90.

———, 'Rewriting the Letter: Variations in the Middle English Translation of the *epistola solitarii ad reges* of Alfonso of Jaén', in *The Translation of St Birgitta of Sweden's Works into the European Vernaculars*, ed. B. Morris and V. O'Mara (Turnhout, forthcoming).

———, 'Words of Flame and Moving Cloud: The Articulation Debate in the Revelations of Medieval Women Visionaries', in *The Medieval Translator VI*, ed. R. Ellis and R. Tixier (Turnhout, 1998), pp. 159–74.

Wallace, D., 'Mystics and Followers in Siena and East Anglia: A Study in Taxonomy, Class and Cultural Mediation', in *The Medieval Mystical Tradition in England V*, ed. M. Glasscoe (Cambridge, 1985), pp. 169–91.

Ward, B., 'Saints and Sybils: Hildegard of Bingen to Teresa of Avila', in *After Eve: Women, Theology and the Christian Tradition*, ed. J. M. Soskice (London, 1990).

Warner, M., *Alone Of All Her Sex: The Myth and Cult of the Virgin Mary* (London, 1985).

———, *Joan of Arc: The Image of Female Heroism* (London, 1991).

Watson, N., 'The Composition of Julian of Norwich's *Revelation of Love*', *Speculum* 68:3 (1993), 637–83.

———, *Richard Rolle and the Invention of Authority* (Cambridge, 1991).

Weber, A., *Teresa of Avila and the Rhetoric of Femininity* (Princeton, 1990).

Weinstein, D. and R. M. Bell, *Saints and Society: The Two Worlds of Western Christendom, 1000–1700* (Chicago, 1982).

Weissman, H. P., 'Margery Kempe in Jerusalem: *Hysterica Compassio* in the Late Middle Ages', in *Acts of Interpretation: The Text and its Contexts 700–1600* (Norman, Okla., 1982), pp. 201–17.

Wiethaus, U., ed., *Maps of Flesh and Light: The Religious Experience of Medieval Women Mystics* (Syracuse, 1993).

———, 'Sexuality, Gender, and the Body in Late Medieval Women's Spirituality: Cases from Germany and the Netherlands', *Journal of Feminist Studies in Religion* 7 (1991), 35–52.

Wilson, S., ed., *Saints and their Cults: Studies in Religious Sociology, Folklore and History* (Cambridge, 1983).

Wolfson, E. R., *Through a Speculum that Shines: Vision and Imagination in Medieval Jewish Mysticism* (Princeton, 1994).

Woodward, K. L., *Making Saints: How the Catholic Church Determines Who Becomes a Saint, Who Doesn't, and Why* (New York, 1990).

Woolf, R., *Art and Doctrine: Essays on Medieval Literature*, ed. H. O'Donoghue (London, 1986).

Zaleski, C., *Otherworld Journeys: Accounts of Near-Death Experience in Medieval and Modern Times* (Oxford, 1987).

INDEX